Success with Languages

Learning a new language is exciting but can be a daunting prospect. You may not have studied for some time, lack confidence, or simply wish for some practical guidance on making the most of your language study. *Success with Languages* is designed to help you to develop the skills you need to become an effective language learner.

Written by experienced teachers of languages at the Open University, this book offers practical advice and support in such key areas as:

- choosing your language and study programme
- becoming an effective learner
- setting personal goals for language learning
- monitoring your progress
- using ICT to support your language learning.

Each of the ten chapters contains a number of activities which give you the opportunity to try out different ideas and suggestions for improving your learning and language skills.

While designed primarily for students in adult, further and higher education studying a language or a course that includes a language component, this study guide is relevant to anyone learning a language in any situation. Whatever your motivation and goals, this book will help you to realize your potential and gain access to new cultures, peoples and their heritage.

Stella Hurd is a Senior Lecturer and **Linda Murphy** is a Staff Tutor in the Department of Languages at the Open University, UK.

The Open University offers language courses in French, German and Spanish from beginner to degree level. Its specially designed materials and unique method of study enable you to learn in your own time with the support of a personal tutor and optional face-to-face or online tutorials. Our courses are designed to develop language skills for the real world as well as encouraging an understanding of the cultures, history and other aspects of life in the countries whose language you are learning. For more details visit our website at http://www.open.ac.uk/courses

Success with Languages

Edited by
Stella Hurd and Linda Murphy

Routledge
Taylor & Francis Group

LONDON AND NEW YORK

The Open
University

First published 2005 by Routledge
2 Park Square, Milton Park, Abingdon, Oxon OX14 4RN

Simultaneously published in the USA and Canada
by Routledge
270 Madison Ave, New York, NY 10016

Reprinted 2006

Routledge is an imprint of the Taylor & Francis Group

© 2005 The Open University

Typeset in Goudy by Keystroke, Jacaranda Lodge, Wolverhampton
Printed and bound in Great Britain by
MPG Books Ltd, Bodmin

British Library Cataloguing in Publication Data
A catalogue record for this book is available from the British Library

Library of Congress Cataloging in Publication Data
A catalog record for this book has been requested

ISBN 0–415–36836–7 (hbk)
ISBN 0–415–36837–5 (pbk)

All website addresses contained herein are correct at time
of publication.

Contents

Contents

Contents   vii

Contents

6 **Developing competence in the language (2): writing and
speaking skills** **110**
*Lina Adinolfi, Christine Pleines, Felicity Harper, Tita Beaven,
Pete Smith, Xavière Hassan, Helga Adams and Margaret Nicolson*

Preface

Whether you are studying a language independently, attending classes or a mixture of both, *Success with Languages* provides an ideal support for all aspects of your language learning. The book is divided into ten chapters, each of which covers a specific area of importance for adult language learners. There are also practical tasks throughout the book which are designed to help you think about the way you learn and how you might improve it.

Chapter 1 considers what learning a language as an adult involves, and helps you find out what type of learner you are, which learning style suits you best and why this self-knowledge is important. Chapter 2 gives practical suggestions for setting up your study area and organizing your resources so that you can access them easily. It also contains sections on keeping effective records, establishing your priorities and managing your time. Chapter 3 offers ideas to help you learn effectively, including guidance in making notes for different purposes, using mind maps, flow charts and dictionaries. It also gives suggestions for strategies to improve your learning, including developing an independent approach and taking responsibility. In Chapter 4 you can find out how to become more aware of the language and of yourself as a language learner, and also how to assess your strengths and weaknesses, monitor your progress, set and review your own goals. Chapters 5 and 6 discuss ways of developing competence in reading, listening, speaking and writing in the foreign language and suggest strategies for developing these skills. Chapter 7 shows you what real-life resources are available to you, and how you can use them to build your confidence and improve your language proficiency. In Chapter 8 you learn about the role information and communications technology can play in supporting your language learning. Chapter 9 deals with issues to do with course work and exams and the important role of feedback. 'Making the most of support' is the title of Chapter 10, the final chapter, which invites you to consider the variety of sources of support available to you as a language learner.

How much of the book is relevant to you, and when you should use it, will depend on your own particular circumstances and personal goals. You may decide to work systematically through each chapter or dip in as you see fit. You can use it in whatever way suits you best.

You will find a glossary of terms used throughout the book before the index.

Acknowledgements

We would like to thank the following people for their invaluable critical comments which have had a significant influence on the development and shaping of this book: Kate Beeching (University of the West of England); Ruth Pilkington (University of Central Lancashire); Bob Powell (University of Warwick); and our OU colleagues: Jean Adams, Lina Adinolfi, Inma Álvarez, Carolyn Batstone, Uwe Baumann, Tita Beaven, Graham Bishop, Neil Broadbent, Jim Coleman, Valérie Demouy, Matilde Gallardo, Cecilia Garrido, Regine Hampel, Felicity Harper, Barbara Heins, Sarah Heiser, Tim Lewis, Margaret Nicolson, Christine Pleines, Margaret Southgate, Mike Truman. A special thanks also to those who kindly contributed examples in different languages to add to those of our authors and to Lucy Byrne for her excellent secretarial assistance.

1

Language learning and language learners

Tim Lewis, Christine Pleines and Stella Hurd

Welcome to the world of language learning! This book is intended for people studying a new language. It is aimed at learners in adult, further and higher education, but is also relevant to anyone learning a language in any situation. Whether you are completely new to language learning or have been learning for a while, you will obviously want to make a success of it. You may be following a course leading to a qualification, or learning entirely on your own with the help of audio-visual materials. Alternatively, you may be living abroad and looking for ways to get the most out of your environment in order to help you learn the language. Whatever your reason for learning and your chosen method, this book should help you to achieve your goals. Learning a new language as an adult is an exciting prospect which opens windows on other cultures, their people and how they live and think, the history of these countries, their literature, music and heritage. This book aims to keep alive that sense of excitement while giving you practical help and guidance in all aspects of language learning.

You will find the terms 'L2' (second language) and 'target language' throughout the book. Both these terms refer to the language you are studying as opposed to your mother tongue which is often referred to as 'L1' (first language).

WHY LEARN A LANGUAGE AS AN ADULT?

To start with, take a little time to think about your reasons for learning another language and what you hope to achieve.

Task 1.1 Learning a new language: why, what and how

Note down some ideas in answer to the following questions:

> Why do I want to learn another language?
> What do I want to be able to do in my new language?
> How do I want to learn?

Comment

It is important to take time to consider these questions, not just now, but also from time to time in the course of your study, because the reasons you have for learning a language will determine the kind of tasks you want to be able to carry out in your chosen language. These in turn will shape what and how you learn, the skills you want to develop, the strategies you use and so on. There is a link, in other words, between:

- ■ your reasons for studying a language;
- ■ what you want to be able to do with the language;
- ■ what and how you learn.

The clearer you are about these three things and the connection between them, the more likely it is that you will stay motivated, be an effective and successful learner and fulfil the aspirations you had when you started learning.

Your reasons for learning a language may be largely **practical**:

- You want to be able to book hotels or concert tickets, order meals and buy things in shops and markets in a country you visit. This might include checking whether a hotel abroad charges extra for single-room occupancy or whether a concert hall has wheelchair access.
- Your work may involve dealing with speakers of another language.
- Proficiency in another language may help you advance your career, or gain promotion.
- You may live abroad or be planning to move abroad, and need to deal with estate agents, lawyers, tradespeople and the authorities.

Or they may be more **personal** or prompted by **interest in the world** around you:

- You may not have had the opportunity to learn a language at school and wish to make up for that now.

- You may have had a difficult time learning languages at school and be determined to 'have another go'.
- You may want to be able to communicate with people from other countries for a variety of reasons, e.g. if you have a disability, you may wish to keep in touch with people across the world who have the same disability as yourself.
- You may want to learn (or relearn) the language of your parents if the language you mainly use differs from theirs.
- You may want to learn a language for pleasure or intellectual stimulation: for example to be able to read literature, or watch films in your chosen language.
- You may want to understand the language of the country (or countries) you visit during holidays abroad.
- You may feel that learning a language will enable you to understand better the countries and cultures in which it is used.

All of these are sound reasons for learning a language. They often overlap with and reinforce one another, and you may well find in the course of your learning that you develop new reasons for learning and ways of keeping yourself motivated that you hadn't thought of originally.

Which language to choose?

If your motivation for studying a language is not based purely on academic grounds, such as enabling you to read a text in the original version, you will need to consider which language to choose. Do you opt for the language you have studied unsuccessfully at school or for a language you have no notion of at all, in order to gain insight into a culture you are unfamiliar with? Some people are attracted to the music and rhythm of a particular language. Others feel frustrated at not being able to pronounce certain sounds which are unfamiliar to them in their mother tongue. Each language has its own characteristics, some of which will attract you more than others.

Success in language learning and all that comes with it can differ from person to person, but research suggests that you are more likely to be a successful learner: (a) if you have a genuine interest in the country or community whose language you are learning, and (b) if you feel you are making progress in learning the language. These are both associated with the idea of self-awareness, in other words beginning to get to know more about yourself as a learner, what it is you are hoping to achieve and what you need to concentrate on in particular in order to reach your personal goals.

You may be learning for pleasure, or for more vocational purposes, or it may be a mixture of both. Task 1.2 asks you to focus in more detail on all your reasons for taking up the language, and which are the most important.

Task 1.2 Refining your reasons

You may now wish to reconsider and fine-tune the first question in Task 1.1: Why am I learning *this particular* language? and maybe add to your previous answer.

If you have a number of reasons, try to rank them in order of importance. This will help you concentrate on what is important to you.

WHAT DOES LEARNING A LANGUAGE INVOLVE?

Within the broad field of Second Language Acquisition theory, some scholars stress the key role of internal factors in learning a language, such as the innate capacity human beings appear to have for grasping the structure of language. Others stress the importance of our interaction with the world of language around us. Second Language Acquisition theory also draws on other disciplines, such as linguistics, psychology and increasingly information-processing, to explain what is involved in language learning. This all makes for a fascinatingly rich mix of ideas, insight and argument, but, as yet, no one has a complete explanation of what takes place when you learn a language.

Nonetheless, learning a foreign language does appear to differ from the study of other subjects, in that it involves not just learning something new, but also using that knowledge to communicate. This entails both conscious learning of language forms and spontaneous and natural use of the language.

The basic unit for conveying meaning in a language is the word. Among the questions you should ask yourself as a learner are which words you need to learn and how they are best learned. It may help to know that the 1,000 or so most frequently occurring words in a language will meet roughly three-quarters of your communicative needs. There are several effective ways in which you can expand the number of words you are able to use in the target language. One common technique is to memorize new vocabulary by jotting down new words and their translations. Once you have been learning for a while, reading can also help you to acquire vocabulary, provided that the texts tackled are not too difficult. Some other techniques are also thought to be particularly useful in vocabulary development. One is inferring or guessing the meaning of a word from its context. Another is using a dictionary in order to (1) identify or confirm the meaning of an unfamiliar word and (2) explore the meaning of the various terms that are related to it. Words come in families, and understanding the family relationship can be of great help in expanding both your comprehension and your ability to express yourself.

Grammar is the name given to the patterns followed by the smaller units of language (e.g. words) as they combine to form larger units (e.g. sentences). These patterns are often described in terms of 'rules', but such rules are actually based on descriptions of the way in which a language is used by most of those who have grown up using it. Grammar distributes words into categories (e.g. nouns, verbs, adjectives). It also distinguishes between the role they play, in relation to one another, within a sentence (e.g. subject, verb, object). Grammar also charts the systematic ways in which words change their form when combined with other words to form larger units. The way in which grammar structures the language also has an impact on meaning. Consider the two sentences:

The man bites the dog.
The dog bites the man.

Both use exactly the same words. But the grammatical relationship between them is different. So too is the meaning of the two sentences. Learning grammar is therefore clearly important and not merely for structural reasons. It is probably best tackled by using the language as much as you can, for communicating and carrying out practical tasks, while at the same time paying attention to the structures you are meeting and using. Chapter 6, 'Accuracy and fluency', gives ideas for improving both grammatical accuracy and fluency. There are also books available which explain grammatical terms in English for English learners of other languages (see the series *English Grammar for Students of . . .* Hodder Education).

In addition to gathering and processing information, learning to use another language involves acquiring and practising four main skills: reading, listening, writing and speaking. The last two of these often strike learners as more difficult to master, because they involve putting into practice knowledge you may only recently have acquired. Your reasons for learning a language will determine which of these skills are of most value to you. If, for example, your main aim is to undertake work-based correspondence on behalf of an employer, you will put the emphasis on reading and writing. If, however, you just want to be able to converse with people you meet on holiday, your interest will lie in understanding and using the spoken language. However, all four skills are interconnected and developing one of them often results in greater proficiency in using another. Chapters 5 and 6 deal with developing competence in the four language skills.

However, learning a language goes beyond the acquisition of the four skills. It also implies gaining a genuine understanding of the culture(s) of the people who speak it. Speakers of the target language often easily 'forgive' linguistic inaccuracies; lack of cultural awareness could be more difficult to accept. Becoming competent in engaging with other cultures requires taking a genuine interest in discovering the customs and other various manifestations of the culture, including what interests and worries its members. It also involves reflecting on the other culture as well as on your own, and being aware of the attitudes and preconceptions you may have.

Task 1.3 Developing language skills

Take a little time to think about and answer this question:

> Which skill(s) do I want to develop and for what purpose?

If you want to develop more than one skill, try to rank them in order of their importance to you.

Comment

Thinking about the different skills and their particular importance to you as a language learner will keep you focused in your learning and also help you to work out the areas you need to work on in particular.

As an adult, you will be used to expressing quite complex ideas and concepts. When you are learning a foreign language, there is a mismatch between the complexity of the ideas you want to express and the language you have available to do so. This can be quite frustrating. So try to be aware of this difference and say things in a simpler way. Many complex concepts can be expressed in simple words. Don't be embarrassed when you make mistakes. When people speak in their first language they also make mistakes and speak ungrammatically. Making mistakes is part of the learning process and research into language learning increasingly suggests that being aware that you are making them is a healthy sign. It indicates that you are developing your own understanding of the grammar of the foreign language.

Learning a language as an adult has a number of positive aspects, compared with learning as a child. You will have a vastly superior knowledge of your mother tongue in terms of the vocabulary you have already acquired and will probably also know a lot more about how languages work. This will help you to make short cuts and learn more effectively. You will be able to work out for yourself which of several approaches to memorizing vocabulary and structures and learning grammatical rules works best for you, and consciously select the most useful strategy for different situations. You are intellectually mature, know more about the world and have almost certainly developed sound analytical, problem-solving and organizational skills in other contexts. It is no surprise, therefore, that many adult learners become highly successful communicators in a new language.

A key to learning a foreign language is the amount of exposure you have to it. Using the language on a daily basis will enable you to make more rapid progress towards mastering it in the specific contexts in which you wish to use it. You should do what you can to maximize your exposure to the target language, by reading newspapers, surfing websites, listening to the radio and watching films and television (see Chapter 7). But above all, it is interaction with native, or competent speakers, which is likely to stimulate both the development of your language skills and your awareness of how members of the L2 culture think. How easy such contact is to achieve will depend on your situation. Seeking out native speakers to converse with means overcoming shyness or lack of confidence. But the benefits are beyond dispute. And you may well find that they too are very keen to exchange conversation with you and find out a little more about you and your culture.

HOW FAR DO YOU WANT TO TAKE IT?

How far you wish to take your language learning depends entirely on you and of course any personal constraints you may have, particularly relating to the time you have available, but also the degree of access you have to resources and facilities. You may wish to master just the basics of the language, in order to be able to communicate in straightforward, everyday situations, and leave it at that. On the other hand, you may want to aim for high levels of language competence. In short, you can achieve a great deal if you are prepared to put in the time and practice. Keep in mind that even a short period of learning can produce striking gains in your ability to communicate, while a lifetime's familiarity with a second language and its culture will still leave you with more to learn. There are many examples of adult learners who have started with modest aspirations but, having achieved their original goals, have decided to set their sights higher. This is often because they find they are really enjoying learning a language, but also because they find themselves becoming much more confident about their own abilities.

Often as learners we set out with unrealistic assumptions, some of which may be fostered by the advertising employed by some providers of language learning, along the lines of 'Learn a language in three weeks!'. It is important to be realistic about what you can achieve in the time that you have, in order to keep focused and stay motivated when the going gets tough. Motivation is one of the keys to successful language learning and you will need to think about what keeps you personally on track. Do you tend to take setbacks in your stride or are you easily discouraged?

Don't be overambitious at the outset. Try splitting your overall aim into achievable next steps. Review your achievements and consider what your future goals are.

Task 1.4 Keeping motivated: steps towards reaching your goals

Think about the following questions:

What are my main learning goals? (E.g. (a) very specific: *I want to be able to get a French qualification for working abroad*; (b) more general: *I want to be able to understand and talk to my grandchildren who only speak Russian, but I've no time to attend a class*; or (c) concentrating on a particular aspect: *I'm OK on the grammar, but I want to improve my accent in German.*)

What steps do I need to achieve on the way to reaching them?

What is likely to help keep me motivated?

Comment

You may have found this task easy if you have been clear from the outset about what you want to achieve. On the other hand, it may have taken you some time to work out how to break down your general goals into shorter manageable ones. If you can do this you will have a much greater chance of reaching the larger goals. In relation to the examples in the first question, you might consider the following:

a   Join the French conversation class at work and find out about the qualifications available; aim to spend an hour a day on my studies.

b   Look for a course that doesn't require class attendance; learn 10 new words each week; say hello to my grandchildren in Russian on the phone or in an email as soon as I have enough words.

c   Listen to German radio on the Internet for 15 minutes three times a week; choose 10 words that I frequently hear and try to imitate the sounds.

Small achievements can really help to keep you motivated and it is important to think regularly about how you feel you are getting on, and if necessary review what you can realistically achieve. Chapter 4 deals with this in much more detail. You will have your own ideas as to what works for you personally in addition to our suggestions. Making the most of any opportunities to hear or use the language will help maintain your interest and enjoyment, e.g. TV and radio programmes, films, meeting with other speakers of the language, local language groups, etc.

If you are particularly motivated by the prospect of gaining a qualification, you should check what qualification, if any, your preferred course leads to, before committing yourself to enrolling. If you have a disability, you may also want to check if there are any special arrangements for assessment. For all-round learners seeking what is essentially an academic qualification, a course preparing for a GCSE, Standard Grade or Intermediate Certificate (or A level/Higher/Leaving Certificate) is probably the most suitable. Those wishing to gain accreditation for professional language skills may find qualifications from the following awarding bodies fit their needs:

- The Oxford, Cambridge and RSA examinations (OCR) offers a Certificate in Business Language Competence in French, German, Italian and Spanish, at three levels, which correspond to NVQ1, NVQ2 and NVQ3. The same qualification is offered in Russian and Japanese at Level 1 only.
  http://www.ocr.org.uk/OCR/WebSite/docroot/index.jsp
- The London Chamber of Commerce and Industry Examinations Board (LCCIEB) offers French, German and Spanish for Business at three levels, plus a preliminary level.
  http://www.churchillhouse.com/en-lcci.html
- The Institute of Linguists
  http://www.iol.org.uk/qualifications/exams.asp
- The French Institute offers accreditation through the Paris Chamber of Commerce. The *Diplôme de français des affaires* (DFA1 and DFA2) is also available in a number of UK centres.
  http://www.fiaf.org/school/exams.htm
  http://www.france-langue.fr/en_11_paris.php

WHAT DO YOU HOPE TO GET OUT OF YOUR LANGUAGE LEARNING?

Learning a new language can bring some very rapid benefits. For a start, it can dispel the sense of isolation and helplessness associated with an environment where every one else is using a language you simply do not understand. Even the ability to understand a few words of the language will help you make sense of notices, menus, short newspaper articles and other simple everyday texts and help you feel more at ease. You may just want to be able to chat with a neighbour who comes from another country in their own language. On the other hand, you may have always wanted to be able to understand Wagner operas or French *chansons*, or read García Lorca in the original. The willingness to use another language at whatever level often makes its native speakers better disposed towards you, and having some competence in another language will almost certainly give you an insight into the way the speakers of that language think. As well as giving you privileged access to another set of cultural attitudes, you may find there are other, more personal, benefits, for example, the capacity to think more flexibly, by offering you alternative ways of viewing the world and thinking about life.

Task 1.5   Other benefits of language learning

See if you can list a few outcomes you would like from your language learning in addition to the general goal of achieving a specific level of competence and/or gaining a qualification.

Even a small amount of success in communicating in a foreign language is likely to raise your levels of confidence and your self-esteem. Language learners who have attained a reasonable level of fluency often report that when speaking the foreign language, they assume a different, more worldly, persona than in their native tongue. Becoming fluent in another language may help you to grow, in a number of ways, but above all as a person. That is not perhaps the main reason why most people start learning, but it is a benefit that language learners often report as a welcome, if unexpected, outcome.

WHAT SORT OF A LEARNER ARE YOU?

Individual differences

Learners differ in many ways. Their expectations of language learning, for example, are influenced by past experience. Task 1.6 offers some statements which reflect some of the many different starting points for learning a language. Whichever comments reflect the way you feel, this book offers you some guidance on how to proceed and helps you find ways of learning which meet your expectations and requirements.

Task 1.6   Different types of learner

Consider which of the following statements apply to you:

■ I've never learned a foreign language before and am not sure what to expect.

- I learned another language at school, but never used it much. I'm now not sure how to start again.
- I'm good at language learning and want to achieve a higher level than I have at the moment.
- I enjoy language learning and want to find the most effective ways of making progress.
- I used to enjoy language learning but have forgotten almost everything.
- I find learning a foreign language quite hard because of my disability, but I need it (for example because of my job or because of family living abroad).
- I really would like to speak another language but find it difficult.
- I enjoy using the foreign language when abroad and now want to learn it 'properly'.

Differences between individual learners are, of course, not limited to their expectations and the kinds of 'baggage' they bring along, but, to put it very simply, different people learn in different ways. Consider, for example, the following quotation from a biography of the German politician Willy Brandt. His wife writes about their visits abroad:

W [Willy Brandt] mocked my way of learning languages – armed with dictionary and grammar book. He was a bit of a parrot. He disliked the written word; listening was enough for him.

Brandt and his wife clearly represent opposite ends of the spectrum of language learning: some learners prefer to acquire languages naturally, while others need to rely on explanations and explicit knowledge of rules. Most learners will fall somewhere in between. Indeed, adults often learn best when they have access to both exposure to 'real' language and the kinds of explanations and reinforcement provided in language classrooms and textbooks.

Self-awareness

Awareness of yourself as a learner and of the differences between learners are important when setting out to study a language. Your tutor (if you have one) may also be aware of and, quite possibly, cater for different learner types. Nevertheless it is better to be well informed yourself rather than assume that someone else will take care of your individual needs.

Knowing how you learn will help you to get the most out of language study and is invaluable for organizing your learning. Research conducted with distance learners (i.e. learners who are enrolled at an institution, but do most of their studying at home without attending face-to-face tuition) has produced some interesting results. Those new to learning outside the classroom attach relatively little importance to 'knowing how you learn' whereas more experienced learners recognize it as one of the most important factors, second only to 'motivation'. Other studies have concentrated on the characteristics of successful language learners and, again, having insight into your own learning styles and preferences and taking an active approach to the learning task feature prominently.

Task 1.7 will start you off on the process of thinking about how you learn best.

Task 1.7 Learning preferences

Read through the sentences below and decide the extent to which they apply to you.

	Definitely applies	Sometimes applies	Does not apply
1 I like to see the language written down.			
2 I need to hear the language spoken.			
3 I find it helpful to see pictures that illustrate what I'm learning.			
4 I learn best when I can actually handle the objects I'm learning about.			
5 I like to make a note of everything I think is important.			
6 I often copy out my initial notes in order to organize them in a different way.			
7 I like to read texts out loud.			
8 I make lists of words and phrases.			
9 I invent situations in which I would use the language.			

Task 1.7 continued

	Definitely applies	Sometimes applies	Does not apply
10 I make tables in which I organize the grammar I'm trying to learn.			
11 I need to understand the rules of the language.			
12 I repeat phrases many times in order to learn them.			
13 I like to immerse myself in the foreign language.			
14 I learn best when talking to people.			
15 In a classroom, I enjoy moving about and working on different tasks with different people, e.g. role-plays.			

Some of the sentences are about your preferred way of processing information, which may be:

- *visual*: you prefer to see everything written down or look at pictures (1, 3, 5, 6);
- *auditory*: you need to hear the language spoken (2, 7, 12, 13, 14); or
- *tactile*: you prefer hands-on learning (4);
- *kinaesthetic*: you like learning that involves physical responses (15).

Other sentences describe either:

- a more *analytical* learner, who likes to analyse the different elements of the language (6, 8, 10, 11); or
- a more *holistic* learner, who likes to hear and use or practise the language in context (9, 13, 14, 15).

It is useful to know which works best for you; very often, a combination of several methods will lead to better learning. Your preference for particular ways of processing information and structuring your learning may change, and it is worth reassessing these from time to time. The idea of distinguishing between 'learner types' is not to put you in a category once and for all.

Learner independence

Whatever type of learner you are, the most important thing is that you are the one who controls what and how you are learning. For example, if you like grammar tables, it is more helpful to create your own than simply to rely on the ones presented in books. If you like to learn through repetition, it is better for you to choose the phrases that are important to you rather than let someone else choose for you.

You will also find that it is not enough to 'accumulate' phrases or structures (for example by writing them down or repeating them after listening to a recording). You have to make active use of them, even if it is just by having conversations in your head. Otherwise you may find that you very quickly forget the language you have learned. Chapter 6 contains information on activating your vocabulary and using your language in speaking and writing.

Throughout this book you will come across many different techniques and strategies for enhancing your language learning. Trying them out will help you find out more about what kind of a learner you are and enable you to select a learning style that suits you.

MODES OF STUDY

Languages can be learned in many different ways. What sort of a learner you are and what you want from a language course will influence your decision on what kind of programme to follow. Two distinct approaches to study are independent and classroom-based learning. There are, of course, many subdivisions within the two approaches, and often learning will involve more than one mode: for example classroom-based study is normally supplemented by more independent learning at home. It is not enough to rely solely on the time you spend listening to and practising language in a classroom. Successful progress in classroom-based study should be complemented by periods of independent study between classes and therefore provide you with good learning habits once the course comes to an end.

Task 1.8 Choosing the kind of tuition that suits you

Here are some considerations you may want to take into account when deciding how you want to learn. Read through the list and check which questions are important for you:

- Is there any flexibility over where and when you study?
- What provision is made for people with disabilities?
- Is there a choice of learning materials and content?
- What is the language of instruction? (Is most or all teaching done through the target language or will your mother tongue be used?)
- Are there any examinations or in-course assessments?
- Does the course lead to a qualification?
- Does the course follow a particular syllabus?
- Can the course be tailored to your own individual needs?
- Will you be taught in a classroom with other students? How many?
- How much time will you spend working independently?
- Will you be supported by a tutor during that time?
- What use is made of technology?
- What and how do you learn about the target culture?

When you have found answers to the questions in Task 1.8, you may also wish to consider the:

- *Teaching method* Most courses use what is known as a 'communicative approach' which has the development of communication as its main aim. Some courses use a more specific methodology to serve the same purpose. If your course comes labelled, for example, as 'Superlearning' or 'Michel Thomas course', find out what exactly is involved.
- *Main focus of the course* Most courses focus on communicative skills which include listening, speaking, reading and writing and are often based on materials which will help you understand the people and culture of the country. Others have a more specific focus, for example, conversation classes, or courses concentrating on reading skills, or literature-based courses.

Opportunities and providers

A wide spectrum of language learning opportunities is available, ranging from totally independent language learning to directed, classroom-based study. Self-access centres are at one end of the spectrum: they are resource libraries with access to books, tapes, videos and CD-ROMs. Self-access centres offer very high flexibility in terms of time and learning content but support for learners varies. They are normally more suitable for highly motivated experienced learners who have specific needs and know exactly what they want. At the other end of the spectrum are classroom-based courses with prescribed learning content. Many learners appreciate the practice opportunities and the support from the other students and the teacher they get in such classes. In between, you can find institutions such as the Open University, offering learning that is more flexible in terms of time and place of study but with prescribed learning content and support from a tutor. Self-study materials, which you can buy in most bookshops, give you total freedom to decide when to study, but also require a lot of determination.

Here is a summary of some of the main providers:

Adult Education Centres offer language classes at various levels, sometimes, but not necessarily leading to a qualification (for example a GCSE or Intermediate Certificate or Higher, an *Alliance Française* certificate, or Open College Network (OCN) credits); many also offer tailor-made courses for businesses.

Further Education Colleges offer language classes at various levels, often leading to a qualification; many also offer tailor-made courses for businesses.

Schools may have continuing education programmes available in the daytime or in the evening. Some community schools also welcome the integration of adults into their timetabled programmes.

Universities usually have an Institution-wide language programme (IWLP) located in a Language Centre or within a Languages Department, which is open to students of all faculties and sometimes members of the general public. Some University Language Centres also provide business language training.

The Open University runs language courses in French, German and Spanish, which lead to a Certificate, Diploma or Degree, and combine self-study of specially designed materials with tutorial provision.
http://www.open.ac.uk/

The National Extension College offers study packs combined with tutor support leading to qualifications in French, German, Spanish or Italian at various levels.
http://www.nec.ac.uk/courses/

The Goethe-Institut, Alliance Française, Instituto Cervantes and *the Italian Institute* are cultural institutions sponsored by their respective governments. They run language classes at all levels and offer their own, well-regarded qualifications.
http://www.goethe.de/gr/man/deindex.htm
http://www.alliancefrancaise.org.uk/
http://www.cervantes.org.uk/new_index.html
http://www.italcultur.org.uk/institute.htm

The BBC publishes self-learning materials supported by audio-visual aids. These are likely to be entirely web-based in the future.
http://www.bbc.co.uk/languages/

Private language schools offer language classes at various levels, often leading to a qualification. Some will follow a particular approach, for example, 'total immersion', which means that the learners are steeped in the target language and no use will be made of their mother tongue.

Institutions that are part of the TANDEM network will arrange conversation exchange between speakers of different languages, and may offer classes which mix, for example, English-speaking students who want to learn Spanish with Spanish-speaking students who want to learn English. TANDEM learning requires some previous knowledge of the language. http://www.slf.rub.de

Private tutors teach individuals, groups or businesses and may offer tailor-made provision.

Providers abroad may offer both long-term tuition (for those who live there) and intensive courses for those who want to combine a holiday abroad with language study.

Many institutions will have a self-access centre offering courses you can register for and some will provide resources and even tuition online. Online language courses from beginners to more advanced are also offered by Learndirect, and include a 'language diagnostic'. http://catalogue.learndirect.co.uk/browse/languages/

The availability of different types of programme does, of course, depend quite considerably on the language you wish to study. If you are intending to study a commonly taught language you may find that there is quite a lot of choice, especially if you live near a major town or city. If you want to study a less commonly taught language, fewer choices will be available. You should be able to get initial advice and testing from all good providers of language tuition. It is very important that the course you choose is right for you in terms of type of course, language level and value for money.

HOW TO USE THIS BOOK

This book is unlikely to cover everything you need. Nevertheless, it should support you in developing certain important skills in language learning and sufficient skill and confidence to be able to use other resources.

Success with Languages aims to:

• give practical guidance on how to go about starting to learn a language or taking up a language after a break;

continued

- encourage you to identify how you learn;
- provide useful ideas and insights into the process of language learning, as well as drawing on the experiences of language learners;
- help you to develop effective study techniques and manage your own time in order to achieve your goals;
- help you gain proficiency through using different learner strategies that suit your needs;
- help you to develop a more reflective approach to language learning;
- give guidance on self-evaluation of progress and study technique while studying a language;
- give information and guidance on available resources such as books, CDs, videos, CD-ROMs or web-based learning materials;
- give information about how to access and use these resources;
- help you to make the most of support from others.

Task 1.9 Finding what you need in this book

Read through the contents page and check where you can find information on:

- how to choose a dictionary;
- how to set realistic goals;
- what use you can make of computers in language learning;
- how best to tackle a text in the target language (for example a letter, a report, or a brochure);
- how to evaluate your own progress.

Which questions or topics are foremost in your mind when thinking about your language studies? Where (in this book or elsewhere) might you turn to get some answers?

Decide which chapters you are most interested in and mark the sections which you:

- want to read in detail;
- want to read through quickly to see whether you are familiar with the content;
- want to come back to later.

You can use this book to prepare for your language learning and to support you while you are studying. It is not meant to be read from start to finish, although you can, of course, read it in that way if you want to. You may, however, prefer to read those sections that seem important to you at the moment and then refer to other sections as and when they become relevant.

You will find that while it is useful to think about the ideas in this book at an early stage of your learning, some parts are most useful if you read them while you are involved in the kind of activity they deal with. For example, you may well want to read about assessment at the beginning of your studies to get a general idea of what it may involve, but the chapter will appear to you in a different light while you are actually doing an assignment or preparing for an examination. Equally, you will find it useful to get a general idea of some of the principles and techniques for learning vocabulary before you start, and then return to them at various points of the course.

As you make progress in your learning, you will find different parts of this book interest you for different reasons. You may also initially just latch on to one or two ideas contained in a chapter, but revisit it as a more experienced learner at a later stage. The book is meant to be read 'actively', which is why it contains small tasks for you to complete and questions for reflection. Most of all, the book is meant to encourage you to try out some of the ideas and suggestions contained in it, so that you can find out what is most useful for you.

Summary of key points

- Being clear about why and how you want to learn a new language is a great asset to language study.

- Being realistic about what you can achieve is an important first step.

- Motivation is a very important part of language learning.

- Breaking down your goals into smaller 'steps' can help motivation.

- Learning a language involves acquiring a range of skills.

- There are additional benefits from learning a language, such as getting access to other societies and cultures, and being able to communicate and interact across cultural boundaries.

- Knowing what sort of a learner you are and how you feel you learn best can give you more control over your learning and make you a more effective learner.

continued

- There is a range of different teaching methods and learning opportunities to choose from.

- This book covers a wide range of topics and you can use it in whatever way suits you best.

2

Getting started

Annie Eardley, Helga Adams and Margaret Nicolson

This chapter looks at how to prepare yourself for studying a language as an adult learner. Learning a language means more than acquiring vocabulary, mastering grammar and doing exercises. It involves being well prepared and well organized from the start. This means thinking carefully about your needs, working out which level is appropriate for you and using this knowledge to help you choose a course that matches your requirements. It also involves organization (1) of your resources so that you can access them easily and (2) of your study area so that you have the optimum conditions for learning. Getting organized also means keeping effective records and thinking about what works well for you.

Good time management is one of the keys to successful study and is particularly important when learning a language, as you need to build in regular practice, rather than rely on long stretches of study at infrequent intervals. Establishing priorities, making selections and reviewing your progress on an ongoing basis will ensure that you remain in control of your learning and make the best use of your time. It is also important to remember that there are many ways to practise a language outside your scheduled study sessions.

CHOOSING THE RIGHT COURSE

Importance of past experience

There may be many reasons why people speak only their mother tongue and have no mastery of another language. An inability to speak another language does not necessarily stem from laziness or unwillingness. It could be due to lack of opportunity or bad past learning experiences. Language learning may be associated with long lists of words to be learned by heart, endless grammar exercises and lots of repetition. Attempts at speaking the language may have been mocked or ridiculed. Such negative experiences can cause feelings of inadequacy. On the other hand, you may have been doing well at another language at school, but had to give up for a variety of reasons: moving schools, lack of space on your timetable, no encouragement from family, etc.

Task 2.1 Thinking back

Think about your previous experience of studying a language formally. Which aspects did you enjoy and which discouraged you? Why did you stop?

Comment
Many factors can have a negative influence in the early years and these will shape your opinion of a particular subject. For example, the teaching approach may not have been the right one for you, or you might have been discouraged by too much criticism. Thinking back on what was good or bad about your previous experiences can help you focus better on what, when and how you want to learn a language now as an adult.

Matching your requirements with what the course offers

Chapter 1 gives information on learning opportunities and providers. It also emphasizes the importance of thinking about the kind of learner you are and your reasons for studying the language. It is worth taking time to consider all these factors, so that you can make sure that the course matches your requirements as far as possible. If you are learning in an institution which provides a learning adviser, he or she will be able to discuss your personal circumstances with you and guide you in your choice of courses. You could also consult websites such as:
http://www.cilt.org.uk/careers/courses/index.htm

All educational institutions make provision for those with a disability. If you are learning with the Open University, you will find information on the services available, including course materials offered in alternative formats at: http://www3.open.ac.uk/learners-guide/disability/

Choosing your starting level

This is not always straightforward. You may feel that the time you spent in what you perceived as the rather tedious language lessons as a teenager have left little or no trace in your memory and decide to start from scratch again as a 'false beginner'. This may be the right decision for you, but remember that you will be with real beginners who may be struggling to acquire the basics of the language, and this could prove frustrating. You will probably be surprised at how much you have actually retained and how quickly you reach the level you had previously. On the other hand, be careful not to overestimate your level or the demands of the course. For example, you may feel that spending holidays year after year on a campsite in France surrounded by local holidaymakers has given you a flying start. If you then enrol in a course that requires you to write and have some knowledge of grammar, you could find yourself disillusioned as you struggle with the more formal aspects of the language.

The various course levels set out in an institution's programme will provide you with the basic information you need, and help you understand what the expectations are with regard to terms such as 'intermediate' or 'advanced'. Many providers match their course levels to national or European standards which can be accessed, for example, from: http://www.cilt.org.uk/qualifications/cef.htm

Amount of contact with the language

Another factor to consider is whether during the course of your studies, you will have contact with a country where it is spoken or with speakers of the language. For instance, if you travel frequently to Sweden on business, you will have many opportunities to practise your Swedish in real situations. You may also have a friend who is fluent in the language you are studying and is prepared to spend some time practising with you. Naturally, this will require some effort on your part, but the key to successful language learning is maximum exposure to the language. If you have the opportunity to practise in a real-life situation, you will soon feel more confident.

Placement and diagnostic tests

You may find it helpful to look at tests that are specially designed to 'diagnose' what you can and cannot do in the language and then 'place' you at the right level. The Open University currently offers self-assessment tests to prospective students of French, German and Spanish to guide them to the right course. These tests are paper-based and available in all OU regional centres: http://www3.open.ac.uk/contact

The OU also offers the *Tour de France*, an online activity designed to test your level of French so that you can decide which course is best for you: http://www.open.ac.uk/tour-de-france/

There are other tests not linked to any particular course or institution which may help you, for example the Dialang online diagnostic tests, developed with the support of the European Commission: http://www.dialang.org

Task 2.2 Choosing your level

Tick the statements that best describe your previous experience of learning the language you intend to study:

- ■ I have no knowledge of it
- ■ I studied it at school for up to 3 years
- ■ I studied it for a qualification but failed
- ■ I studied it for a qualification and passed
- ■ I studied it more than 10 years ago
- ■ I have not had any opportunity to practise it since I finished studying
- ■ I never studied it formally but have had many opportunities to speak it
- ■ I studied it formally but never had any opportunity to speak it.

Comment
Taking time to consider these questions before embarking on your studies will help you to place yourself at the appropriate level and prevent the frustration that can arise when you find you have made the wrong choice.

Choosing the right course

- What past experience of studying a language do I have?
- How much do I remember?
- What sort of course am I looking for?
- How much time do I have available for my studies?
- How much contact with the country or with speakers of the language do I have?
- Do I really need to go back to the beginning?
- What tests are available for me to check my level?
- Can I take a look at the course materials?
- Are there descriptors of the levels or prior knowledge expected of the student?
- Have I checked all available information from websites and other sources?

CHOOSING AND ORGANIZING YOUR LEARNING
RESOURCES

Dictionaries, grammar books

Once you have decided on your course, consider what additional resources you need to help you in your studies. You may be able to use books you already own but if they are dated, you will need to buy books that have been published more recently. A pocket dictionary or phrase book can be a real help during a trip abroad but is unlikely to be adequate if you decide to engage in more serious study of the language. You will also need a grammar book which explains the new structures you will come across in more detail. The choice here is much more complicated as there are many such books on the market, varying in clarity and complexity. The advice from your tutor and other learners will be invaluable. Some institutions, such as the Open University, will provide you with the title of specific (set) books that you are required to purchase and use during the course. Chapter 3 deals in more detail with dictionaries.

VCR and DVD players

Chapter 7 explains how you can best use videos for language learning. However, in a busy household, this may create problems, for example, competing for the equipment. Some courses include video resources with their course material and you will need to organize your study sessions to ensure access to the required equipment when you need it. DVDs can be viewed on computers equipped with a DVD drive. Many students use long business trips as an opportunity for studying. If this applies to you, you may need to rely on transcripts or a personal DVD player.

CD players and cassette recorders

As discussed earlier, exposure to the language needs to be frequent. One way of ensuring this is by using cassettes and CDs. You can listen to them while travelling, for example. Language cassettes and CDs are often interactive and ask you to respond to prompts. Although they are a little artificial, it is nevertheless a good way to practise structures and expressions. You will see in Chapter 6 that an excellent way to improve your intonation and pronunciation is to record yourself, so make sure your machine has this facility.

Computers

Computers, although not strictly necessary to study a language effectively, are a useful tool. You may decide to invest in one in order to access material on the Internet, talk to people in other countries or enhance the presentation of your written work. What you want to do with your computer will influence the quality of the equipment and software you buy. Check that your computer can run any software necessary for your course but beware of buying too sophisticated a piece of equipment which may prove frustrating rather than helpful.

Choosing and organizing your learning resources

- What type of dictionary do I have?

- Do I need to buy a new one? What type?

- Do I need to buy a grammar book or to check online resources?

- How am I going to work with videos and DVDs?

- What equipment do I need in order to record myself?

- Will I need to upgrade my computer, for example, to be able to use video files or interactive software?

ORGANIZING YOUR PHYSICAL RESOURCES

Where to study

As well as deciding on the equipment to use, you will also need to organize your study area. Efficient studying requires concentration, often best achieved in a quiet and organized place. If possible, find yourself somewhere in your home, a spare room if you have one, or a corner that you can make your own and which will be solely used for your language studies. This is particularly important if you live with other people. They will know not to disturb you when you are settled in your study area. Make sure the place you have chosen is adequately lit and warm enough and that you have enough space for your needs. If you have a disability you will find the following OU website useful: http://www3.open.ac.uk/learners-guide/disability/study_needs/study_needs.htm

It is not always possible to find a suitable place in a home you share and if this is the case for you, you may need to adopt other strategies. For instance, some students have found it useful to:

- store study materials in boxes, crates or bags so they can be used in different places at different times;
- ask their employer if their place of work can be used before or after work;

- study in the kitchen late at night or very early in the morning;
- work at the local library or at a friendly neighbour's house;
- share child-minding with other parents, to create some time for study;
- get headphones to be able to isolate external sound and study audio, video or Internet-based material.

If you plan to study on the move, find a suitable bag for the things you will need to take with you; personal CD player and spare batteries, pen and paper, a small dictionary, for instance. Alternatively, you could draw up a checklist of resources to consult when planning each study week to ensure that you do not forget anything.

Study environment

The environment you create in your study area will of course be personal to you and will depend on the type of learner you are (see Chapter 1, 'What sort of learner are you?'). However, you can add some local colour by displaying pictures of a country where the language you are studying is spoken. You could also have a board to display expressions and structures you are studying if you retain information better when you see what you want to acquire.

If playing music while you study helps you to learn, select some songs in the language you are studying, for example, and put them in your study area. One language teaching method known as *Suggestopedia* actually encourages the use of background music in order to stimulate learning of new structures and vocabulary in the L2.

Storage and filing

You will save time and reduce frustration if you can access information easily, for example:

- work plans and timetables;
- exercises;
- assessment material;
- course material;
- course documentation;
- cassettes and CDs.

The way you organize your material is up to you. A basic filing system can be set up in a box but a dedicated shelf will ensure that you can access material more easily. You could also use ring binders and dividers, punched plastic pockets, etc. You may like to set up an electronic filing system for storing some aspects of your work, e.g. useful vocabulary and phrases. The most important thing is not to waste time searching for material.

Organizing your physical resources

- Where is the best place for me to study?

- Can I find a space in my home that will be dedicated to my studies?

- If not, what other arrangements can I make?

- How am I going to arrange my study space to make it comfortable to work in?

- How will I organize the various material and documents that I will need for my studies?

WORKING WITH AND AROUND FRIENDS AND FAMILY

Committing yourself to a programme of study will have an impact on your friends and family. They may support you or hinder your progress; sometimes they do both. To enjoy your studies as fully as possible, you will need to let people know what you are doing and most importantly why you are doing it. Whether learning a language enhances your career prospects or simply makes trips abroad more enjoyable, your family will benefit. If they know about your course and the level of commitment it requires, they will be in a better position to support you by giving you time and space for your studies. In return, you also need to be aware that their routine may be disrupted. It is all too easy to want to share your new experience but try not to become a 'study bore'!

Among your friends and relatives, there may be people who already speak the language you are studying and are willing to help you by giving you tips or spending some time speaking with you in that language. Other friends could become study partners or 'buddies' if they enrol in the same course as you. You will thus be able to support one another and share experiences and study tips (see Chapter 3, 'Studying independently', for more information on study buddies).

MANAGING YOUR TIME

Juggling your studies with other commitments can sometimes be difficult. You will undoubtedly need to make room in your life, as studying a language successfully will require more than an hour now and again, if you want to make progress. You may feel you do not have as much time as you need, or that things take longer than expected. What can you do? Try considering the 3 Ds: Defer, Delegate and Delete. Look at tasks you are planning and decide on their urgency. Can whatever it is wait or not? Consider delegating some of the responsibilities you have to somebody else, at least temporarily. Remember that nobody is indispensable and if you can be freed of certain tasks, you will be able to devote more quality time to your studies. Think of other changes you could make to your life that would free up time, for example missing your favourite soap or cutting out one of your less essential social activities. Effective time management will help you increase time for study.

Task 2.3 Managing your time

Take some time to think about a typical week and fill in your weekly schedule below showing:

- approximately how much time you spend on the *important* and *regular* activities in your week;
- where you will find the hours you need.

	Mon	Tues	Wed	Thurs	Fri	Sat	Sun
early morning							
9 a.m.– 12 p.m.							
12–2 p.m. 2–5 p.m.							
5–7 p.m.							
7–10 p.m.							
after 10 p.m.							

When you have finished, ask yourself the following:

- Have I found some free 'slots' in my week?
- If not, is there something I can give up, put off or delegate?
- Whose help will I need to make this work for me?
- If all my language learning is going to be late in the evening, is this realistic or sensible for me? Am I at my best at the end of the day or would I be better getting up early in the morning?

> **Comment**
>
> Plan for what suits you and your lifestyle and remember that subjects like
> languages need regular practice, so little and often will be more effective than
> long stretches of study. Research shows that concentration lapses after 20
> minutes so remember to vary the tasks. Retention is affected after 90 minutes,
> so if you are planning longer study sessions, make sure you plan a break.

Making the best use of your time

Common wisdom regarding language learning usually indicates that
short sharp bursts are best, but don't worry if your work and home life do
not allow for this. Do what you can in the time you have. If you do have
to study for longer periods then try to vary activities so you do not get
bored. Learn to stop an activity if you are getting nowhere with it and come
back to it later. Break longer activities up into manageable chunks, and
make sure you allow enough time overall for what you are required to do.
You will need to match up the time you have with what you are required
to do. If your course provides a study calendar, then consult this and check
deadlines. Try to develop your own timetable, but incorporate some flexibility, so that you do not become discouraged if unexpected circumstances
disrupt your schedule. Ensure that you build in time for checking over any
assignments you are required to submit, and also for revision. If you do not
have much time available, work out what sections of the course material
you really need to do and the sections you can risk spending less time on.

Low and high concentration times

You soon begin to work out which times of the day or night are best for
you to study, and you may find that there are times when you are more tired
or less able to concentrate. If you have no choice and have to study during
these low concentration times, try to undertake tasks that are less
demanding. Below are some examples:

- listen to recorded material for intonation and pronunciation;
- revise a text or exercise you have worked on before and know well;
- go over some notes you have already worked on;
- tidy up and do a final check on any written work you are about to
  submit;
- do something you find easy.

All of these have the added benefit of reinforcing what you have learned
previously and building your confidence.

During high concentration times, i.e. times when you know you study
well, try the following:

- do tasks which require you to write or speak in the language;
- listen to or read materials you have never studied before;
- make notes on new language points;
- tackle something that you find difficult;
- work on new items of grammar.

Establishing priorities and making selections

Prioritizing your learning needs is important. If there are a lot of materials and/or activities you want or feel you ought to work on, it will to a certain extent be up to you to select the ones that you consider most important at any given point in your study. If you are studying in a distance or open learning environment it is unlikely that you will have regular face-to-face tutor contact, so learning decisions will be mainly in your hands. Learning to select is important. The course you are studying may be designed for a wide variety of abilities and backgrounds, so you may need to skip some aspects or spend more time on others. This may be necessary when:

- you lack time to do some activities, particularly if your study involves assignment deadlines;
- you already know an area well;
- you want to improve on a particular aspect of the language;
- you are having difficulty with a particular aspect of the language.

Think about your own strengths and weaknesses to help you decide where to focus your efforts (see Chapter 4, 'Assessing your strengths and weaknesses: setting goals'). When learning vocabulary, for example, you might want to differentiate between words and phrases you simply want to recognize and ones you will actively use. You will need to spend more time and effort on the latter. In some circumstances, if you are really short of time, you may have no option but to plan your work around assessment.

Take the same approach to tutorial or classroom sessions and ask your tutor to give you details in advance of what s/he is planning to cover. If you are following a distance learning course, it would be a pity if you missed out on valuable practice because you had not been able to cover all the material up to that point.

In the early stages of language learning it is important to define your priorities even more closely. Much of what you learn by way of basic vocabulary, grammar and sentence structures will be essential for any meaningful communication. However, the quantity of vocabulary presented in the early stages of a course may be overwhelming. You will therefore need to select what is useful to you or what is best linked to the topics and/or assessments in the course. It is also a good idea to go through the course materials to find language you can use for very specific purposes. For example, before going on holiday, see if your course can help you with booking a hotel room, ordering a meal, buying souvenirs and so on. This helps to make your course materials more relevant to real life.

Opportunities for study

Learning does not just take place in your study area. Make the most of all the other opportunities for learning that might be available to you, for example:

- while driving to work, relaxing in the bath or going for a walk: listen to a cassette or CD;
- while travelling on the train or bus: learn or revise vocabulary and grammar;
- when on your own: talk to yourself about a topic of interest, or ask yourself lots of questions. Talking out loud may not always be possible but articulating the words through whispering will be more beneficial than just talking in your head.

- Keep a small notebook handy and use 'dead time' to jot down words or phrases you have learned recently. Then write short sentences using them in different contexts.

- Write words or phrases you find difficult to remember on Post-it™ labels and stick them up around the house (perhaps on a pin board or on your fridge door) or at work if possible.

- Make vocabulary cards with the target language word or phrase on one side and your own language on the other. Test yourself and put the ones you know into a separate pile. Use the cards for revision at a later date.

Task 2.4 Identifying where and when to set up opportunities for study

Think about your own circumstances and add some more ideas for when or where you might be able to set up opportunities for studying.

However organized you are, there will undoubtedly be times when you feel 'stuck' or that you are not coping very well. Try the following:

- take a break;
- change to a different task or skill;
- concentrate for a while on things you find easy;
- speak to your tutor or a learning adviser, if you have one;
- talk to another student.

KEEPING RECORDS

As well as planning your learning sessions, you will find it helpful to keep a record of your progress. This will involve reflecting on what works well and not so well for you and may include a consideration of:

- the timing and frequency of your study periods;
- the way you store new information, for example vocabulary and language points;
- the type of learner you are.

Chapter 4 talks about learner diaries and learning logs and how to use checklists to monitor your progress. However you choose to do this, take time too at regular intervals to make brief notes on the progress you think you have made and compare this with notes you have made on previous occasions. Record yourself speaking at regular intervals, for practice but also to see if you notice any improvements in pronunciation and intonation, and get a sense of where you need to direct your efforts. Go back to the beginning of your course from time to time and see how much more you can do now and how recordings in the course materials that seemed impenetrable at first are now much easier to understand.

You should also keep a note of useful resources, such as those described in Chapters 7 and 8. Spend some time getting to know the structure of your course material so that you can easily locate grammar points, the index and the assessment schedule. Try to organize your notes logically so that you can access what you need quickly and easily. This is particularly important as you are likely to refer many times to the same page of your notes, your course material or your dictionary. Finally, make a note of your tutor contact details or office hours so that you can find them easily, for example on a pinboard in your study area or in your electronic address book.

Keeping records

- What has worked well for me so far?

- What study skills and strategies am I finding useful?

- Have I made a note of useful resources including websites?

- What progress have I made this week/since I started?

- Where can I get help if I am stuck?

Summary of key points

- Assess your requirements to help you choose the right course for you.

- Think carefully about the resources you will need.

- Organize your study area to suit you.

- Consider the amount of time you have available and how best to use it.

- Identify where and when to set up opportunities for study.

- Keep records of your progress and of useful resources.

3

Becoming an effective learner

*Margaret Nicolson, Helga Adams,
Concha Furnborough, Lina Adinolfi and
Mike Truman*

This chapter provides some ideas to help you develop your approaches to learning and studying a language so that you make the best progress possible. Becoming an effective language learner depends both on how you approach your learning and on the knowledge you acquire. Whatever your mode of study, the strategies you adopt are crucial in helping you to progress. The kinds of strategies you choose will also need to reflect what you want to get out of your study. You may be learning a language in order to talk with other speakers of the language or you may wish to improve your ability to read texts in that language.

Chapter 1 explains how people learn in different ways. Part of the challenge is recognizing what works for you and being able to build on this. This chapter offers a variety of strategies for you to try out before adopting, adapting or indeed rejecting them according to your needs. On occasion it is good to challenge old ways of doing things. In language learning, new approaches to study can open up greater opportunities and encourage you to overcome challenges that previously seemed difficult. All this brings with it a feeling of success which assists progress.

LEARNING ON YOUR OWN

Learning is a highly individual process. However, a distinction is usually made between studying independently and studying with a tutor and other learners. Learning a language on your own may take various forms, including mastering a few expressions from a phrase book, working through a teach-yourself course or using the resources of a self-access centre. It is, of course, possible to alternate between studying independently and studying with others. You may choose to study alone in the early stages of your language learning and join a group when you are more advanced.

Alternatively, you may prefer to learn with others for an initial period and switch to studying independently as you become more proficient.

Task 3.1 Advantages and disadvantages of learning on your own

Before you read on, try to think of some of the positive and less positive aspects of studying on your own.

Comment

You may have considered some of these advantages:

- being able to choose study times that suit you;
- having more choice as to where you study;
- being able to progress at your own pace;
- being able to choose your own learning materials.

. . . and some of these disadvantages:

- difficulty in maintaining motivation;
- feeling isolated;
- not having a prescribed course structure;
- absence of immediate feedback or correction.

It is helpful to be aware of these aspects, so that you can make the most of the advantages of learning on your own. Being aware of some of the less positive aspects will make you better prepared and in a position to take action where necessary, e.g. setting manageable goals to aid motivation; finding others to learn with to reduce isolation; developing good time and organization skills to help structure your work; using the feedback with answer keys and model answers provided by many courses, and opportunities for reinforcing what you have learned by using the language in different contexts.

LEARNING WITH OTHERS

You may be attending a language class with other students, studying a language in a self-access centre or following a distance course through independent learning. Wanting to communicate with others is often a key reason for learning a language and this can take place in a variety of contexts, for example, email exchanges, notes and letters. Communication in the wider sense also includes understanding, for example street signs, and reading newspapers and other informative material. But it is speaking that involves others in the most direct and spontaneous way.

Task 3.2 Using the language you are learning

Think about situations in real life where you might need to *use* the language you are learning.

Comment

The situations you noted may have involved either talking to one person or having a conversation in a group in a variety of contexts. You may have been stating facts or giving opinions, or reporting to a wider audience, either orally or in writing.

Learning with others in a language classroom

Classroom activities are likely to reflect different types of real-life contact.

Pair work with another learner
This may include:
- tasks where you need to get and/or give information, prompted by instructions from your tutor, on a topic such as leisure activities or holidays;
- tasks where you and your partner play different roles in a situation (with varying degrees of tutor guidance, depending on the topic, situation and your language level);
- games, such as building up a story together (perhaps based on pictures), or using an outline to create the rest of the story;
- reading the same text, but with different tasks, for example telling the story from the point of view of different characters; agreeing or disagreeing with a point of view expressed in the text, as you might in a discussion or if you needed to report an event.

Small-group work
This may involve each learner taking part in a discussion, or taking a different role which has been assigned beforehand. One speaker may also be chosen to report on conclusions reached to the other groups.

Whole-group activities
Depending on the level of the learners, these may include a question/answer session and discussion based on presentations given by the tutor or other students, or general discussion of a selected topic, possibly as follow-up to work already carried out in smaller groups.

Learning a language with others has benefits. One is that it gives you practice in the language and also develops the interpersonal skills you need in real-life situations. It is not just a question of using the appropriate vocabulary and grammar or the correct pronunciation and intonation. Equally important is the need to understand what others are saying and doing in a particular situation, to take account of this and interact with them appropriately. This might involve discussing a contentious topic or reacting sympathetically. When you take part in such activities in a class, you find out how much you can do already and what you still need to revise or practise, since you are getting immediate reactions from both fellow learners and tutor. This can also be a source of great satisfaction, demon-strating that you have succeeded in communicating, and encouraging you to progress further.

Studying independently

If you are studying on your own, either on a distance-learning course or in a self-access centre, finding others to learn with may seem much more difficult, so it is important to take active steps to get in touch with other learners or speakers of the language. This can include 'meetings' in a virtual environment using conferencing tools via the Web (see Chapter 8, 'Using CMC in your studies'). Contact with other people will increase your understanding of other cultures and make you more able to question and compare different ways of life and beliefs and attitudes. All of this may well contribute to a greater enjoyment of language learning.

One useful tactic is to establish a learning partnership. A learning partner may be someone studying the same course or not involved with it at all. In TANDEM learning, for example, speakers of different languages exchange their language skills and cultural knowledge with each other (see the information on the TANDEM network in Chapter 1, 'Opportunities and providers'). If you like this idea but don't know anyone suitable, try putting an advert in a local centre or library, or finding an e-TANDEM partner (see also Chapter 10, 'Making the most of support from other speakers of the language'). Once you have found your partner or 'study buddy', you can plan how to work together for mutual benefit.

Task 3.3 Learning with a study buddy

Draw up a list of language activities you could usefully do with a study buddy.

Comment
Your course materials will contain activities that you could easily adapt to use with a partner, e.g. talking about pictures, adverts, photos or paintings, describing the people in them, giving your opinions about them, saying what

---

they are doing, guessing what they might be talking about, making up dialogues between the people, continuing the story beyond the picture, speculating about their future or what happens next. Also consider the types of classroom activity in the previous section which are appropriate to real-life situations, e.g. gathering information about someone you don't know well or about a place you would like to visit. You might then go on to talk about simple personal matters, e.g. what you did last weekend; what types of food you like; which parts of, for example, Italy, China, Russia you know, what they are like, and so on.

- Look out for opportunities which may be less obvious in order to learn something or to put your language knowledge to good use. For example you may observe a breakdown of communication between people who do not speak the same language. You might consider stepping in to assist.

- Try to make comparisons between your own and other cultures. Be aware of cultural practices which differ from your own, e.g. at mealtimes, in social behaviour, religious practice, dress, conventions for greeting and taking leave.

- Be sensitive to any stereotypes which exist with regard to the other cultures or peoples.

- Be aware that cultural differences also link to aspects of communication. For example the gestures and facial expressions people use can mean different things in different cultures.

BUILDING ON PREVIOUS EXPERIENCE

Chapter 2 considers the impact of past bad experiences of learning a language and how these can shape your attitudes. It is important, however, to build on the positive. If you attend classes as part of your learning you may feel that your experience of studying is not as great as that of other people in your group, but remember that life experience is in itself a transferable skill. Use your experience to try to overcome any negative views you may have; your expectations and approach will be key factors in successful learning. Your tutor will be happy for you to ask questions or to suggest that you do something differently, particularly if you are learning in an open or distance setting. It is important to free yourself of other people's agendas if you are going to be a successful learner. Be ready to question the way an activity is structured, for example. Doing it a different way may enable you to get more out of it. Also, be prepared to challenge your own views, as the way you have always done something may not be the best. Listen to advice from those who have done it before.

MAKING USE OF PRIOR KNOWLEDGE

Learning a new language does not necessarily mean starting from a blank canvas. You will probably be surprised at how much you already know, for example about cultural aspects of the country or countries where the language is spoken. You may even know a few simple words in the language and be acquainted with other languages and cultures. The combination of this and your knowledge of your own language will provide you with a strong foundation on which to build your skills. Table 3.1 summarizes some of the types of knowledge you may have and how this can help you in your learning.

Initially you will be building a lot on the similarities between your mother tongue and other languages you know and the language you are learning. Words that may be the same in your language and the language you are learning are known as **cognates**. As you make progress you will also become more aware of the differences between languages, which will help you avoid potential pitfalls. Look at the differences in the tenses below:

I have been living in Cardiff for two years (Eng: perfect continuous)

But note the use of the present tense in the following languages:

J'habite à Cardiff depuis deux ans (Fr); *Ich wohne seit zwei Jahren in Cardiff* (Ger); *Vivo en Cardiff desde hace dos años* (Sp); *Abito a Cardiff da due anni* (It)

Note too the different uses of the indefinite article in the following examples, i.e. you do not use *a* when talking about professions, except in the English example:

I am a teacher (Eng)
Je suis professeur (Fr)
Sono professoressa (It)
Soy profesora (Sp)
Ich bin Lehrerin (Ger)

You will also find that there are so-called 'false friends' in every language. These are words which look alike in two languages but have different meanings. Compare for instance *sensible* (Fr and Sp); *sensibel* (Ger) and *sensibile* (It) which all mean *sensitive* and not *sensible* as in English. You will

Table 3.1 Using prior knowledge to help you learn

Type of knowledge	This can help you to:	Examples
Knowledge of your own and other cultures	interpret what you see, hear or read; raise your awareness of differences and similarities	If you have travelled to other countries or other regions within your own country, you may have noticed that daily routines differ, people have different attitudes or express their feelings in different ways. Awareness of such areas of potential difference will help your understanding of the target language and culture.
Knowledge of topics	understand what you hear or read	If you know about sports, you will find it easier to make sense of a sports commentary in the target language.
Familiarity with different formats of spoken and written communications	anticipate the meaning of what you are going to hear or read	If you are a regular reader of newspapers in your own language, you know about the kind of information that is conveyed in the headings, subheadings, first paragraphs etc. of newspaper articles.
Knowledge of your own and other languages	understand vocabulary and phrases that are similar	(1) Vocabulary *finish/end/terminate* (Eng); *finir/ terminer* (Fr); *enden/beenden* (Ger); *terminar* (Sp); *finire/terminare* (It); *taxi* (Eng/Fr/Sp); *tassì* (It); такси (*taksi*) (Rus); ταξί (Greek); *tagsaidh* (Gaelic); شارع (Arabic) (2) Idiomatic phrases *I have lost the thread* (Eng); *Ich habe den Faden verloren* (Ger); *J'ai perdu le fil* (Fr); *He perdido el hilo* (Sp); *Ho perduto il filo* (It)
Knowledge of how language works at a structural and practical level	understand grammar, anticipate what comes next	(1) Past tenses: *I have eaten* (Eng); *j'ai mangé* (Fr); *Ich habe gegessen* (Ger); *he comido* (Sp); *ho mangiato* (It); もう 食べました (mo u ta be ma shi ta) (Jap) (2) Sequencing information: *first – then – next – finally* (Eng); *d'abord – puis – ensuite – finalement* (Fr); *yn gyntaf – wedyn – nesaf – yn olaf* (Welsh)

also find that most idiomatic phrases do not translate literally into other languages, for example:

faire un canard (Fr) (lit. *to make a duck*) = *to hit a wrong note*

ins Gras beißen (Ger) (lit. *to bite the grass*) = *to bite the dust*

βρέχει καρεκλοπόδαρα (vréhi kareklopódara) (Greek) (lit. *raining chair legs*) = *to rain cats and dogs*

сесть в лужу (sest' v luzhu) (Rus) (lit. *to sit down in a puddle*) = *to fail, make a mess of things*

ميت فل واربع تاشر (meyt fol w'arbataasher) (Arabic) (lit. *100 jasmine flowers and 14*) = *everything's just perfect!*

taro deuddeg (Welsh) (lit. *to strike twelve*) = *to ring true*

In the early stages of language learning, you may well find that your mother tongue or another language you know will interfere with what you are trying to say. This means that words may sound or look the same but have different meanings, e.g. *burro* in Italian means butter, but *burro* in Spanish means donkey. Don't be put off by this. It happens to many learners and will gradually diminish.

DEVELOPING SKILLS TO HELP YOU LEARN

Making and keeping notes

For many activities associated with language learning you may wish to make notes. Some, such as notes on specific grammar points, will serve as a more or less permanent record for future reference. Others, such as notes to help you prepare a talk or an essay, will be of a more temporary nature and can often be discarded once they have fulfilled their purpose. Some notes are work in progress and will need regular updating, e.g. vocabulary notes on a specific topic or outlines for reports.

There are different reasons for making notes. They can help you:

- build up language knowledge, for example in vocabulary or grammar;
- guide you, for example through a spoken task or writing of an essay;
- make sense of what you are hearing or reading in the language you are learning;
- increase your cultural or historical knowledge and understanding on a particular topic;
- reflect on your learning and your progress and help you work out your strengths and weaknesses.

Different ways of making notes

As with all methods of learning, there are different ways of making notes in different circumstances and depending on what sort of learner you are. Past educational experience may have taught you to make notes in a certain way, but it is sometimes good to try new ways. If they don't work for you, then discard them. Different settings will also dictate what sort of notes you are able to make, as you may be constrained by time or space. Making notes covers the simple jotting down of vocabulary or noting keywords, as well as more elaborate activities such as classifying or connecting ideas.

Vocabulary lists
This is traditionally one of the most common ways to note and learn vocabulary. Split your page into two columns, writing the new words in one of these columns and the equivalents in your own language alongside each one, in the other. Always note the gender of the word if it has one, so that you learn this at the same time. If the word has an irregular plural jot this down as well. Take *a street* for example:

Une rue (Fr)	*Eine Straße* (Ger)
Una calle (Sp)	*Una strada* (It)
улица (ulitsa) (Rus)	街道 (jiē dào) (Mandarin)
ένας δρόμος (enas thrómos) (Greek)	*an t-sràid* (Gaelic)
通り (to o ri) (Jap)	شارع (shari'a) (Arabic)

You may want to group words by topic, in which case dedicate a page to it and only enter words linked to this topic; Figure 3.1 shows an example of French vocabulary for card games.

At some stages in your learning you may want to write monolingual not bilingual notes. This can help avoid the trap of translating words literally from your own language. Your definition will therefore be in the same language as the word you note. Look at the following examples:

alt – nicht neu/nicht jung (Ger)
vieux – pas neuf/pas jeune (Fr)
viejo – no nuevo/no joven (Sp)
old – not new/not young

Some learners prefer to draw a picture for their definition as this too prevents interference from their own language.

☺ = happy (Eng); *heureux/heureuse* (Fr)
☹ = sad (Eng); *triste* (Fr)

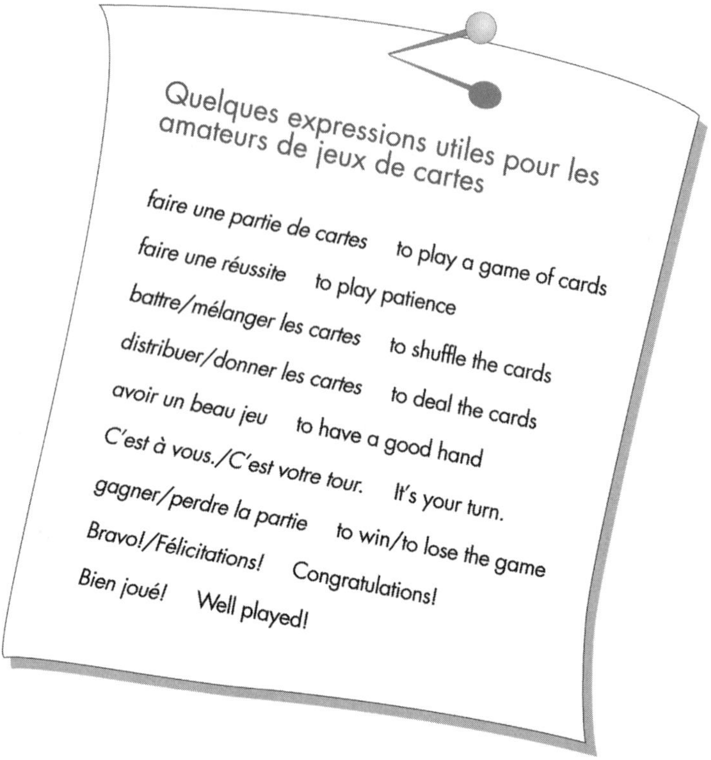

Figure 3.1 Organizing and grouping words by topic.

Chapter 6, 'Remembering and activating your vocabulary', provides other ideas on developing your vocabulary.

Key words and bullet points
Another useful technique is to pick out key words for a presentation and organize these in a way that suits your purpose. These can be listed in order of importance, in the order in which they will appear or according to main headings and subheadings. Arrows can be used to link connecting points if this is appropriate. Different size or colour of typescript or handwriting can also help to distinguish main points from subsidiary points, as in the following examples in German and Spanish.

morgens/ *por la mañana*/ in the morning:
aufstehen; duschen; Kaffee trinken; arbeiten
levantarse; ducharse; tomar café; trabajar
get up; shower; have a coffee; work

mittags/ al mediodía/ midday:
nach Hause kommen
volver a casa
come home

nachmittags/ por la tarde/ in the afternoon:
einkaufen; Deutsch lernen
ir de compras; estudiar alemán
go shopping; learn some German

abends/ por la noche/ in the evening:
fernsehen, Freunde treffen, ins Kino gehen
ver la televisión, encontrarse con amigos, ir al cine
watch TV; meet up with friends; go to the cinema

Alternatively, you may wish to work with bullet points which will usually be sequenced in the order in which you are presenting key points. This learner was giving a talk on education in France:

- *obligatoire 6–16 ans;*
- *école primaire/collège/lycée;*
- *brevet de collèges;*
- *le baccalauréat;*
- *redoubler;*
- *lycées professionnels;*
- *laïc;*
- *écoles privées.*

Abbreviations and codes
Shortened forms of words or sentences or symbols or numbers instead of words or ideas are both very useful when making notes quickly. You may wish to make notes this way when you are listening to a spoken piece of language on audio/video cassette or on CD/DVD, or when you don't have time to write every word or sentence out in full. Make up your own abbreviations and codes but try to choose ones that you will remember. For example, words ending in *–tion/sion*, *–science* or *–ic* could be abbreviated as follows:

^{N} = *tion/sion*, e.g. institu ^{N} (institu**tion**)
^{CE} = *science*, e.g. con ^{CE} (con**science**)
^{C} = *ic*, e.g. pragmat ^{C} (pragma**tic**)

Graphics or numbers can also provide useful shortcuts. For instance, arrows up and down can indicate positive or negative factors. Backward- and forward-facing arrows can also be used to indicate when events took place or will take place in time. For recurring ideas you can assign a number. For example, on every occasion that 'economic development' appears in a text or talk on that topic, you simply write 1 in your notes. Further shortcuts can be made by missing out vowels, or using numbers or symbols which sound the same. Those who are adept at texting on mobile phones may find this easy to do, for example:

tomorrow and Saturday = 2mrw + sat

Mind maps and flow charts

Mind maps and flow charts are useful for connecting ideas and establishing relationships or categories. They can also be used when preparing notes for a spoken presentation or when making sense of the main ideas in a written or spoken text. For example, you have been given the topic 'The origins of the tango' and have to give a 3-minute talk on this. You wish to group your main ideas quickly and so that they are visually easy to grasp while you are talking. Figure 3.2 is one example of how you might do this using a mind map.

Mind maps or 'spidergrams' are also useful for noting related vocabulary to help you to memorize and recall words more easily. Some learners use them for organizing verb forms, particularly tenses, or to show uses of a particular pronoun, as in the French example in Figure 3.3.

A flow chart is useful if you have been given a text on a subject and wish to trace the sequence of the author's main ideas in graphic form. The example in Figure 3.4 traces someone's plans for next weekend, which are dependent on the weather.

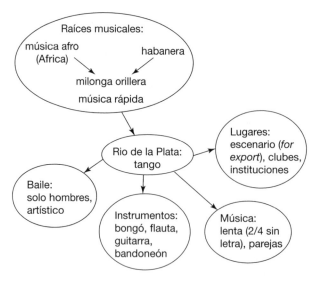

Figure 3.2 Organizing your ideas for an oral presentation.

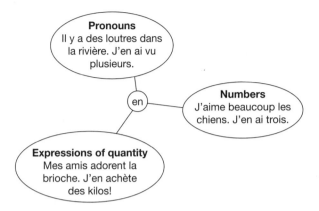

Figure 3.3 Organizing grammatical information.

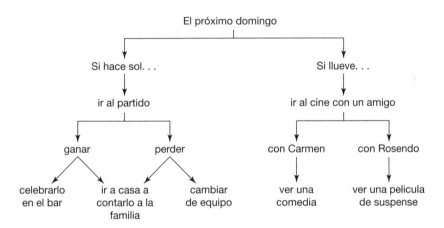

Figure 3.4 Organizing future plans and making choices.

Temporary and permanent notes

When learning with others or on your own, there will be occasions when you want to make notes fairly quickly for immediate or future reference. It will help your learning if you revisit these notes soon after the event and organize them into a more permanent format; for example some items may go into your personal grammar reference book or online file, others into your vocabulary store or into a cultural section. There is no need to keep temporary notes, as you will have to rationalize how much material you keep.

Using a dictionary

A dictionary is an essential tool when learning a language. It can offer you much more than just the meanings of words. If you are following a taught course, a particular dictionary may well be recommended. If not, your choice of dictionary will very much depend on the layout, the size of print, the clarity of presentation and the amount of information covered. You should consider using a variety of dictionaries and renew your dictionary every so often as language changes and new words come into use. There are various types:

- Bilingual dictionaries are most commonly used when beginning language study. They provide the meaning of single words or phrases in both languages.
- Monolingual dictionaries give the meanings of words and phrases in the same language. They are useful when you want a definition of a term in the same language or when you need to express a word or phrase in a different way. For this reason they also help to expand your vocabulary, which is particularly crucial at more advanced levels. Even in the earlier stages of language study, learners find it very useful to double-check meanings via a monolingual dictionary.
- Pocket dictionaries, phrase books and electronic translators are also available and are handy for immediate use when travelling abroad, for example, but be aware of their limitations.
- Pictionaries show you graphic representations of meaning. Some students find it easier to memorize new vocabulary by linking it to an image.
- Specialist dictionaries are useful if you have a particular interest or need specific terms for your professional or personal life. They are more commonly used at more advanced levels of language study. They give you more detailed information in your search for the correct term or meaning.
- Online dictionaries are another option if you have access to a computer.

Dictionary features

Good dictionaries have a variety of features beyond the simple meaning of the word. They indicate:

- the function of a word in a sentence (noun, adjective, verb, etc.) usually in an abbreviated form, e.g. n, adj., v. Make sure you are familiar with the abbreviations in order to be able to choose the correct part of speech;
- the pronunciation of a word. Often they use the letters of the International Phonetic Association (IPA) to present specific sounds

and these will be listed in the introduction to the dictionary. You may find it helpful to familiarize yourself with these. With a bit of practice you will soon be able to make sense of it. IPA characters are normally inside square brackets. You can test yourself by looking up some words in your mother tongue and checking which characters are used for their pronunciation;

- the use of the word in context, for example in a short phrase or sentence. Meanings can differ depending on the context so it is important to read the whole entry for the word;
- idiomatic uses of the word, e.g. *Hals-und Beinbruch* (Ger: wishing someone good luck; lit. break your neck and leg! The *your* is implied here);
- specialist terms. There may be occasions when you are looking for engineering terms, medical terms, cookery terms, musical terms, etc.;
- verb **conjugations**, i.e. the different verb patterns and their endings, e.g. in English: *I talk* but *she talks*. Complete verb tables are particularly useful for irregular verb forms;
- the register of the word, for example, whether it is used for formal or informal purposes, whether it is colloquial or unacceptable in certain circumstances;
- cultural information such as festivals, for example:

KARNEVAL
Karneval is the name given to the days immediately before Lent when people gather to sing, dance, eat, drink and generally make merry before the fasting begins. **Rosenmontag**, the day before Shrove Tuesday, is the most important day of **Karneval** on the Rhine. Most firms take a day's holiday to enjoy the parades and revelry. In south Germany **Karneval** is called 'Fasching'.
(*Collins German Dictionary Plus Grammar*, 2004, p. 188)

Task 3.4 Using all the features of your dictionary

Check whether your dictionary contains some of the following, putting a tick or cross against each one as appropriate.

- shows which part of speech the word is (verb, noun, adjective, etc);
- shows how words are used in the target language;
- has separate grammar section;
- has separate verb tables;
- gives guidance on pronunciation;

- lists specialist words (to see if it includes technical vocabulary, try *mouse* or *soundcard*);
- gives idioms;
- indicates the register of the word;
- lists cultural information.

Comment

A good dictionary will have many of these features. If yours does not, consider buying a different one or taking advice on this from other language learners or tutors if you can.

- Read through the introduction to your dictionary as a quick route to understanding the conventions adopted.

- When searching for a word in the target language, check its entry in the other half of the dictionary. In this way, you can make sure that you have chosen the most appropriate word for your needs.

- Use your dictionary to extend your vocabulary. Words are remembered in context, so 'read around' the word you are looking up and note down related words/expressions which are of interest to you.

- Try to work out the meaning of a word or phrase from the context. You can check your interpretation later in the dictionary before committing the word to your permanent vocabulary store.

- Some students like to trace their progress in acquiring vocabulary by highlighting all the words in the dictionary they have ever looked up!

DEVELOPING STRATEGIES TO IMPROVE YOUR LEARNING

One step further is knowing when and how to apply the skills and approaches above, how to remedy problematic situations and how to enhance what you do with the language. Some analogies from other areas of life might help to illustrate this. When cooking, for example, the recipe book will tell you what ingredients you need, the order in which to mix them, the cooking time and the required heat. But you may want to cook food for a longer or shorter time to suit your own particular taste. Perhaps you like spicy food and will want to add chilli powder to most dishes to give extra piquancy. Diagnosing what action to take allows you to achieve success in your cooking in the way you desire it. In the same way, playing the piano requires more than being able to read the music and play the notes. You also need to be able to interpret the piece, understand the phrasing and compensate in finger technique for the instrument you are playing. It is the same in language learning. Different situations require different approaches and adjustments. You may come up against an accent or speed of conversation that is not the one you are used to or be able to read a text perfectly but not understand the cultural references which are crucial in fully making sense of the text beyond the words. It is not enough to be acquainted with the study skills; you need to know when and how to apply them. Here are some strategies which will help increase your learning awareness and move it on to a different level.

Knowing how to prepare yourself

. . . for predictable situations

Being equipped and at ease with the vocabulary, phrases or grammatical structures you need for a specific and predictable situation will depend on the strategies you employ in advance. Repeating and rehearsing what you want to say or write is a technique chosen by many learners to increase their familiarity with language they will need. Rote-learning of vocabulary works for some people when they want to feel secure and have quick access to the word or phrase they need. This saves reference to dictionaries which may not be possible or too time-consuming. Other learners prefer to practise using specific language in different spoken or written contexts. This helps to free up the use of particular words or structures so that they are not tied to just one situation and can be used flexibly. The more you use and reuse language in different contexts, the faster the vocabulary and structures will become fixed in your long-term memory and able to be used automatically, without conscious thought.

. . . for unpredictable situations

While you may not feel the need to be prepared for the unpredictable in your own language, you will discover that the greater your readiness to accept the unpredictable in the target language situation, the easier you will find it to cope. Being aware that unpredictable things may happen is half way to coping with them when they arrive. Even in unpredictable situations there are strategies which you can apply both in advance and on the spot. These are generally referred to as **compensation strategies**. With the written form of the language you probably have time to work out meaning with the help of the clues available to you. In spoken situations you have to act more spontaneously and may feel constrained by a limited amount of knowledge at your stage of language learning. In these cases, you can use guesswork as a way of understanding the whole message by putting together both your understanding of the words, the tone, the context, the body language and any visual clues there might be. Even in spontaneous situations it is often possible to predict what someone is going to write or say. This may give you time in advance to listen or look out for specific meanings, such as words or phrases linked to the topic or to the way the person is feeling, which in turn may enable you to use an appropriate response that you already have in your repertoire.

There are of course many situations where guesswork is not enough and it is crucial to understand fully the response to a question you have asked. These may be practical, for example asking for directions, for items in a shop, for travel information, for medical or other emergency help, or they may involve understanding people's opinions on certain issues or personal information about them. Often, although you are able to ask the question, the response may catch you unawares if the language or expression or accent in spoken language is unfamiliar.

Task 3.5 Compensation strategies for understanding and being understood

If you have asked a question but don't understand the reply, what could you do?

If you want to express something but don't have all the words you need, what could you do?

Comment

You may have listed one or more of the following strategies for understanding. Ask the person to

- repeat;
- speak more slowly;
- express the idea in a different way;
- write or draw to help illustrate what they are saying.

You can also be honest in telling them that you don't understand or ask them follow-up questions to further aid your understanding. You need to make sure from an early stage that you are equipped with the necessary language to do these things.

For speaking you may have thought of the following to make yourself understood:

- draw;
- mime;
- rephrase.

When you are in the early stages of language learning there is a temptation to be too complex and to think in your own language first. Try to avoid this and use only phrases you know in the target language, however simple they may seem to you.

Maintaining your confidence

Keeping up your confidence levels usually plays a major part in the progress you make in any endeavour. Language learning is no exception. Chapter 1, 'What does learning a language involve?', emphasizes the importance of reminding yourself of the amount of knowledge and the variety of skills you will have already acquired as an adult in a vast array of contexts. Yet everyone has feelings of inadequacy from time to time. These may not always be linked to competence levels but to how confident or not you feel at that time. Do not underestimate the influence of how you feel psychologically or socially when learning a language, particularly in a group setting.

If your study includes scheduled classes or you have the opportunity to work with others, there may be occasions when you feel that your fellow students are better than you or are more confident. If you do find yourself in a situation where this occurs, try to rationalize how you are feeling. If it still gets you down or you cannot overcome it, then try one of the following:

- moving pair or group;
- sitting elsewhere (for the next activity or the next class);
- asking the tutor to assign you to a different pair or group for the next activity.

Some people get stressed because of the pressure of the course they are following, the teacher they have, the goals they have set themselves, or their view of their success or failure. Stress in general can be relieved by employing relaxation techniques. This can be as basic as playing music that makes you feel good, to going to yoga classes or stopping for a cup of tea! Doing something you know will give you some distance and that you enjoy doing is the best relief for anxiety induced by study. It will also alter perspectives in a positive way.

In real-life situations you may not have these options. Be aware that you are not the only language learner to feel ill at ease in a social or work context where the language is being used. As well as knowing what linguistic strategies help you feel more confident, it is also good to know how to cope psychologically and socially. Helping with the practical aspects of a social event, such as offering to hand out drinks or food if this is possible, can alleviate feelings of anxiety or exclusion caused by language barriers, as you are focusing on something other than the language. This will also usually help break the ice with other members of the group. You should try, however difficult it might be for you, to move on and not let any negative feelings overwhelm you. Sometimes it can be better to ignore the fact that you have not understood everything and try to keep the conversation flowing, rather than make the person you are talking to repeat the same thing umpteen times. In social contexts you do have the right to leave if you feel linguistically excluded or uncomfortable. This may be more difficult in a work situation. In this case, it is best to make it clear to others that you do not understand what they are saying and be reassured that no one at work is going to think any the worse of you.

Task 3.6 Strategies to relieve stress and help you cope

List other relaxation techniques which have helped you or people you know reduce anxiety or stress.

Comment
The list could be endless and there is no right or wrong answer. It is chiefly about what works for you.

Managing low points

- Do not become seriously discouraged by setbacks but accept them as part of the learning process.

- Accept that the way you are feeling generally within yourself at the time may have a strong part to play in your reaction to the setback.

- Accept that, at times in language learning, you will feel that you have reached your peak and are not improving. This is a common experience. Be assured that you are progressing and not at a standstill. Concentrate on what you have already achieved.

- Accept that it is alright to say 'good enough' on occasion rather than push yourself to an impossible limit. Often learners are encouraged to aim for a native speaker target when in fact even native speakers do not speak a perfect version of their own language.

WORKING WITH MODEL ANSWERS AND KEYS

When learning independently, it is not always easy to get feedback on your performance. This is why some course materials provide answer keys and model answers, and include useful feedback for the activities provided. Activities vary in their function, as does the nature of the answer keys. For some activities (e.g. those providing intensive practice on a newly taught item of grammar), the key will simply indicate the right answers with, perhaps, some brief explanations. For others, it might be a model answer, or a checklist of the 'Did you remember to include . . . ?' type, such as in the more open-ended activities that place what you have learned in a wider context. For example, if you have just been taught the structures needed to describe a building, you may be asked to use them to describe your own house. Obviously, each student will give a different answer, so in this case the key can only give general advice and help. This can be a source of frustration for independent learners, who can sometimes feel hampered by the lack of on-the-spot feedback geared to their own needs. However, there are ways of overcoming this problem. If your difficulty is a specific one (e.g. doubts about the correct form of a verb), you will almost certainly find the answer in the course materials (by using the index or study guides), your grammar book or dictionary.

The ability to identify and correct your own mistakes is extremely important in language learning, but you have to make a conscious effort to develop it. Use the key as a starting point for diagnosing your weaknesses, or listing topics that need revision. If the difficulty is more general in nature, e.g. 'What should I emphasize in the conclusion?', you should find model answers, where provided, helpful. You could also discuss your answer with another student: for example, you could swap answers, compare them with models in the key and give each other feedback. Other people can often be more objective than you yourself can, identifying shortcomings in your work that were not apparent to you. Self-help groups are another source of advice and support (see Chapter 10, 'Making the most of support from your fellow students'). Finally, seek assistance from your tutor if, despite all your efforts, you are unable to resolve the problem. Chapter 4 goes into more detail about how you can monitor your progress.

TAKING RISKS AND LEARNING FROM MISTAKES

Language learning is never complete; we can always extend our knowledge and skills. This sometimes involves making mistakes, both inside and outside the classroom. Making mistakes should not be regarded as something negative; it is part and parcel of language learning and can also help your tutor give you feedback on a point you have not fully grasped. Nevertheless, many of us, when learning a new language as an adult, are on occasions unwilling to take the risk. It is reassuring to know that even native speakers make mistakes!

Task 3.7 Taking risks in language learning

When you have to speak the language you are learning in front of others, either in class or in real life, how do you react? Tick the statements below that apply to you:

1   I only speak when I can be sure that what I am saying is correct.
2   I try to say what I want to, regardless of whether it is absolutely accurate or not.
3   I only speak if others seem to be making mistakes as well.
4   I only speak if I have rehearsed something a lot.
5   I worry about speaking in case I can't understand the reply.
6   I try to draw on what I *have* understood.
7   I try to check that what I am saying makes sense.

Comment
If 2, 6 or 7 are true for you, you are probably more risk-oriented in your learning.

If 1, 3, 4 or 5 are true for you, you may be more reluctant to take these risks. This may not be a problem, but if you are learning a language in order to communicate with others, it is important to take risks when speaking.

The advantages of risk-taking

Taking risks means doing something without being sure of the outcome. Real-life communication involves uncertainty, and dealing with the unexpected. Taking risks in language learning means being prepared to have a go at saying or writing something even if you are not exactly sure how to do it, without worrying that you might get it wrong.

The student in Figure 3.5 was prepared to take the risk of talking without understanding everything. When you interact with other speakers of the language, there are likely to be situations where you have to deal with the unexpected. Even when you have planned what you want to say, you will not be able to anticipate what other people will say and how they will react to your questions and comments. Through practising in the 'safe' environment of the classroom, where others can help you understand and make yourself understood, you may become more confident in dealing with real-life situations.

When we went to Madrid I got into a conversation with an elderly gentleman in a restaurant, and I could understand about a third of what he said, but he could understand most of what I said, so we sort of carried on quite a sensible conversation because I picked up enough to give him answers. . . .

Figure 3.5 A student view.

Task 3.8 Responding to a challenge

You are in a group where everyone else seems to speak better Spanish, for example, than you do. Do you regard this as an opportunity or a threat? Why?

Comment
If you saw this as an opportunity, you are probably prepared to take risks without feeling inhibited. If you saw this as a potentially threatening situation, you are probably in the majority! Try, however, to see it in a more positive light, for example:

- You can learn from a good performance by listening to others and possibly imitating what they have said at a later date.
- If you make a mistake, listen carefully to what your tutor or other students are saying and you may well be able to correct yourself.
- Concentrate on taking the chance to improve your oral fluency without worrying about grammatical accuracy. Measure your performance not in terms of mistakes made (or avoided) but how much you were able to contribute, or the length of time you talked. If you are still anxious about being 'judged' on your accuracy by the tutor or other students, you could explain your goal if that reduces your anxiety. (See also Chapter 6, 'Accuracy and fluency').

Many taught language courses incorporate formative assessment tasks (see Chapter 9, 'Formative and summative assessment'). These may not count towards your final grade but you may receive feedback from a model answer or from your tutor. These offer you the chance to take risks with both written and spoken work and to try out new ways of communicating your ideas and language without fear of losing marks.

DEVELOPING AN INDEPENDENT APPROACH AND TAKING RESPONSIBILITY

Successful learning can happen when you are least aware of it. However, there is no doubt that it will also happen when you have developed self-reliance and are prepared to take responsibility for your learning. Searching for the answer will help you learn and embed the knowledge. However, it also means being prepared to ask questions of yourself, the tutor, your fellow students and other people and to use the resources you have at your disposal. Take responsibility and use feedback to move forward.

Lots of different metaphors have been applied to learning. In trying to get from Point A to Point B what are your tactics? Do you build bridges bit by bit? Do you create tunnels exposing more light as you go? Do you find diversionary routes which take you off the path? Do you close your eyes and take a leap? Do you go back over old ground to make sure foundations are safe? Do you rely on others to get you there?

In language learning a mixture of all of the above may be inevitable. Sometimes you may want to plan meticulously in advance; sometimes you may simply want to take a leap in the dark. Whatever method you employ, here are some useful tips for making progress:

- If you are following a course which is assessed, check your work against the given criteria and establish reasons for errors yourself.

- Personalize your language and cultural notes. Make up examples which are of relevance to you and not abstract.

- Record useful words and phrases on your own cassette or disc. Include aspects of pronunciation and intonation.

- Learn vocabulary and revisit it.

- If you know you have made an error then correct it yourself if you can, wherever you are.

- Be assertive when working with others, e.g. Say *Hang on a minute* if you need more time to participate in a task.

- Discuss with others how they study, share tips, watch others.

- Step back and think. The first response may not always be the best one.

- With spoken language take the risk and say it.

Summary of key points

- Language learning takes place in many different contexts on your own and with others.

- Taking a proactive approach to your learning will mean that you will become a successful language learner and will be able to use the skills you acquire in many other situations.

- Building on your knowledge of your own and/or other languages and on your own life experience will greatly enhance your learning of a new language.

- Making notes plays a key part in learning. The more skilled you become at making notes in different ways and for different purposes, the easier it will be to manage your study material, to organize your thoughts and to produce language.

- Successful use of the dictionary will be of invaluable help in your language learning.

- Checking your own work against model answers and keys in course books or with other students provides an additional opportunity for enhancing your language learning.

- Making mistakes and taking risks is a key part of language learning.

- Being in charge of and taking responsibility for your own learning will make it more effective.

4

Reflection and self-evaluation

Linda Murphy, Mirjam Hauck, Margaret Nicolson, and Helga Adams

Reflection has become something of a buzzword in recent years. Why do so many people feel that it is important for learning in general and language learning in particular? What does it actually mean to reflect on your learning and why should you do it? This chapter explains what is involved in reflection and how you can increase your effectiveness as a learner and boost your self-confidence by setting aside some time to think about your approach to learning, what you actually do and how you do it. Time spent on this can save you more time in the long run.

WHAT DOES REFLECTION MEAN?

Chapter 3 explains the need to develop an independent approach and take responsibility for your learning. Reflection is an important part of that process. Every learner 'takes stock' from time to time and considers what they have learned. You may remember particular words or phrases you want to use next time there is an opportunity, or that you find easy to recall because they remind you of expressions in your own language. Or you may resolve to revise particular verb forms because you need to be able to use them more often. Perhaps there is something you discovered about the country or the people who speak the language you are learning which you found particularly interesting and you want to find out more.

Reflection means becoming aware of your learning and everything connected with it, including how you are learning and how you learn best. Once you are aware of what you are doing when learning, reflection also means questioning and challenging your habits and assumptions. In this way you can gain new knowledge and understanding, learn more about yourself and your learning and make appropriate decisions about how to move on. In order to reflect effectively, though, it is not enough to just 'think back' over events in an unstructured way; a more systematic approach is needed. The first part of this chapter sets out the different areas in which you need to develop awareness and how you might achieve this. The second part looks at ways of questioning and challenging yourself in order to learn more effectively.

DEVELOPING AWARENESS

To help you become an effective language learner, you need to develop awareness of:

- yourself as a language learner;
- the context in which you are learning;
- features of the language you are learning;
- the choices you make about your learning and their implications;
- your performance and progress.

How can you develop your awareness in each of these areas as you learn your chosen language?

Awareness of yourself as a language learner

People have different beliefs. What you believe influences what you do, how you do it and what happens to you. As a result people may react differently in the same situation. For example: Do you avoid doing things that don't interest you, or get involved to motivate yourself? Do you prefer to have an overview or do you need lots of details? Similarly, each learner experiences the language learning process differently. To learn effectively, it is important to be aware of the beliefs you have about language learning, how you approach your language learning and the assumptions you make. It also helps to be aware of other possible approaches so that you can try them out to see how helpful you find them for yourself. There are examples of possible approaches and language learning techniques for you to try throughout the book.

Your beliefs about language learning can either limit or assist the learning process. If you believe, for example, that your learning is influenced by your ability (along the lines of: *I am no good at . . .*) or your teacher alone, then you have no control. If, on the other hand, you look at it as something influenced by the amount of time, effort and interest you put in, you retain control and can make a difference. Your beliefs and assumptions are likely to depend, at least to a certain degree, on your past experiences. They are also likely to have an impact on your attitudes towards new situations such as, for example, learning a language at a distance and/or in a virtual learning environment via the Internet. Becoming aware of them can help you make decisions about learning and enable you to become more flexible in your approach.

Chapter 1 asks you to consider your learning styles and preferences, that is, whether you are a visual, auditory, tactile or kinaesthetic learner or maybe even a bit of everything. If you worked through tasks 1.6 and 1.7, you may have been surprised by the outcome of the task or found that your answers confirmed your beliefs and assumptions about yourself.

Awareness of the context in which you are learning

Chapter 2 encourages you to spend some time organizing your resources and your learning environment. The most important resource you have is yourself. The previous section explained why it is important to understand more about yourself and the way you learn. It is also important to look more closely at the qualities or personal resources which you bring to your language learning and how best to manage them. Successful self-management means that you:

- understand the conditions/circumstances under which you can accomplish a certain (language) task, i.e. you are aware of what is needed;
- can create those conditions for yourself and make best use of the resources you already have.

Task 4.1 may help you understand the qualities you demonstrate in the activities you manage successfully on a daily basis, i.e. which personal resources you use. You will want to draw on those resources to become equally successful as a language learner.

Task 4.1 Becoming aware of your personal resources

- Make a list of all roles you play in life, e.g. business partner, mother/father, neighbour, counsellor (for friends' problems), plumber, cleaner, artist, mathematician (children's homework, tax return), Open University student, etc.
- Imagine each of these roles is a job you are applying for. Write down the personal qualities you bring to each job, keeping in mind that you really want this job. Write down the qualities which will help you get it (but be honest!).
- By now you have probably realized that you are quite talented. Now add those qualities that you are aware that you have but don't seem to be using at the moment.

■ When you have finished, look at the 'jobs' for which you don't seem to have many qualities and see whether you could use any qualities from other 'jobs'.

■ Which of all these qualities do you think can be useful in language learning?

Source: adapted from J. Revel, and S. Norman,
(1997) *In Your Hands*, Saffire Press, p. 71
http://www.saffirepress.co.uk/content/?page=1

Comment

You will have identified a wide range of personal resources which you draw on in certain contexts. Having identified them, you will be able to draw on them in other contexts such as learning a language. For example, if you are able to do several things at once, are creative and good at making contact with people, look for ways of using these resources. You might revise vocabulary while putting the children to bed, create memorable examples for new language learned or get in touch with a speaker of your target language who has moved into your neighbourhood.

It is important not to confuse 'personal resources' with 'skills'. As a language learner you may not have the skills yet to speak another language as fluently as you would like, but you have the ability to learn and, as you can see from Task 4.1, you already have a vast array of resources which will help. You will probably know people who have similar qualities and who have learned to speak another language very well. Take inspiration from them!

Most people tend to be aware of the things they are not good at. However, once you start analysing the qualities or personal resources you have, you are likely to be able to transfer these positive attributes from one particular context in your life to another, for example language learning. Becoming aware of your personal resources and qualities so that you can access them when you need to is the first step.

Awareness of features of the language you are learning

Even before you started to learn your chosen language, you probably had some general impressions and ideas about it. Here are some people's responses when asked about their impressions of German:

- has lots of long words;
- *w* pronounced as *v*;
- it can sound rather 'throaty', all those *ach* sounds;
- strange word order with verbs at the end of the sentence;

- many words like English words: *Bier* (beer), *Wein* (wine), *Butter* (butter), *Mutter* (mother);
- some words used in English: *Kindergarten*; *Schadenfreude*; *Zeitgeist*;
- language of musicians (Bach, Brahms, Beethoven);
- language of science, technology: *Vorsprung durch Technik*!
- spoken in Germany, Austria, Switzerland, N. Italy;
- Bavarians speak a dialect that even other Germans can't understand;
- German is a hard language to learn.

If you look at this list and at your own list, you will see that the items can be grouped under various headings: sounds of the language; word formation; pattern of the sentences or longer pieces of language; and social or cultural role of the language, as well as different forms of the language. These groupings indicate the main aspects of the language you need to be aware of and are examined in more detail in the following sections with suggestions to help you increase your awareness.

Task 4.2 Impressions about the language you are learning

Make a note of the following:

- the language you want to learn;
- your impressions/ideas about this language (e.g. its sounds, its influences on other languages, etc.).

Comment
Depending on the language you have chosen, you will probably have a wide range of impressions. Some of them may be based on fact or experience, others more on stereotypes handed down through the years.

How the language sounds

Each language has a set of distinctive sounds because of the way it is pronounced, and its intonation patterns, i.e. the patterns of emphasis or stress on different parts of words or phrases and the way a speaker's voice rises and falls, in other words, the 'music' of the language. You learn the **pronunciation, stress** and **intonation** patterns of a language by listening and trying to imitate them yourself, by using the language, rather than by reading about the rules that govern its various features. Chapter 5 explains the importance of becoming familiar with the sounds of the language you are learning and Chapter 6, 'Pronunciation and intonation', gives advice and techniques to improve your speaking skills. It is helpful to look out for patterns as you learn so that you can make sense of them and remember them.

Patterns of stress and intonation have a big impact on meaning and differ from one language to another. If the patterns are distorted or altered in this way, it makes spoken language very difficult to understand. This can cause more problems than mispronouncing individual sounds. Spend time listening to the stress patterns in the language you are learning. At the same time, listen to the way a speaker's voice rises and falls. This intonation affects meaning, for example indicating surprise or a question, as in the English exclamation: *Another piece of cake!* or *Another piece of cake?* In some languages, such as Mandarin or Vietnamese, a change of intonation changes the meaning of individual words. To increase your awareness of the sound patterns in the language you are learning try the following:

- Note any pairs of sounds that you need to distinguish, e.g. *u* and *ü* in German or *è* and *é* in French. Collect examples of words with these sounds. Practise repeating them and record yourself. Play back later and see if you can decide which word was which. Examine the words to see if you can spot any patterns in the use of these sounds.
- Listen to short examples of the language on your course CDs or cassettes. Mark on your transcript (if you have one) the syllables which are emphasized. Does the emphasis follow a particular pattern? When you learn a new word, make a note of where the emphasis falls, e.g. in English: interesting, celebration (see also Chapter 6, 'Intonation').
- Check your dictionary to see how stress patterns are shown.
- Listen to a short audio extract and concentrate on the rise and fall of the speaker's voice. Read the transcript as you play the audio and copy the intonation patterns. You can mark this on the transcript with arrows to remind you. Try to spot examples of where the intonation has an effect on the meaning or examples of certain patterns which are used for particular effects, such as to express surprise.
- Listen to the patterns of sound in your own language and look out for similarities to or differences from the language you are learning.

Word formation and sentence patterns

When you learn a new language it can seem as if you are being swamped with new words. Being aware of patterns can make things easier and reduce the amount you have to remember. Certain patterns may always indicate a verb or a noun, certain conventions will transform a noun into an adjective, for example in English adding a y can make the noun *sand* into the adjective *sandy*, or *wind* into *windy*. (See Chapter 6 for ways of remembering and activating vocabulary.)

You should also be aware of how words are combined in the language you have chosen to study. The rules for combining words are known as the syntax or grammar of a language, as described in Chapter 1, 'What does learning a language involve'. In many languages, including English, word order is very important for conveying meaning. Apart from word order, languages use many other ways to express key ideas, for example, word endings, words and phrases to indicate time, location, amount, etc.

At first you will be more concerned with how to put together short sentences or pieces of speech. As you learn more of the language, you will need to be aware of how longer pieces of spoken or written language are put together. Chapter 6, 'Making your speech writing flow', examines how to use linking devices and how to make sure that the structure of what you say or write is appropriate for your intended purpose.

Task 4.3 Increasing your awareness of word formation, and sentence patterns

Note down any patterns you have noticed in the way words are formed or transformed in other languages and look out for further examples in the language you are learning as you go along.

What are the similarities to or differences from the word formation and sentence patterns in your own language?

Comment

As Chapter 3 explains, making use of prior knowledge of any aspects of the language, including words that are the same (cognates) and ways in which it is different from your own, can provide you with a strong foundation for learning a new language and even make the task easier.

To increase your awareness of word and sentence patterns: when you learn a new grammatical point in your course or learn how to convey particular ideas, make a point of looking for more examples both in the course material and elsewhere. Try creating your own examples too.

The social and cultural role of the language

Language is a very important part of our identity and when you learn another language you are learning much more than words and syntax. Apart from learning about the social and cultural life of the people who speak the language you have chosen to study, you will become aware of different ways of using the language, for example the Bavarian dialect mentioned earlier, or the ways in which Spanish is spoken in different parts of the world. You may learn how different groups of people use the language for particular purposes. There are powerful cultural associations such as the impression of German as 'the language of musicians'. A language may be a strong focus of regional identity and culture, for example in the Basque and Catalan regions which straddle the French/Spanish border. It may be used by particular groups of people, for example the government in China uses Mandarin rather than other Chinese regional languages. Learning and speaking some languages or dialects may also be used to make a political statement, for example the use of Gaelic in Scotland or Ireland.

Within every language there are further associations and cultural connotations attached to words and phrases, for example, if English is your first language, what images are conjured up by the words *lads* or *cool*? Are you aware of changes in the connotations of these words? At the same time, there is usually a difference between spoken and written language and there may be more or less formal forms of address depending on the circumstances and status of the people involved. This is referred to as **language register**. (See Chapter 5, 'Engaging with the cultural content', and Chapter 6 for further explanations of style and register.)

MONITORING YOUR PROGRESS

Chapter 2, 'Keeping records', explains the importance of reviewing your progress in order to keep yourself motivated. This also ensures that any tasks you undertake are successfully completed, that they have increased your knowledge and understanding of the language and helped you to improve your use of it. Systematic monitoring is therefore crucial for developing an independent approach and taking responsibility for your learning. The following sections explain some ways of monitoring your progress.

Keeping a learner diary or learning log

A learner diary, notebook or log is a useful tool to help you think about your learning in a structured way and assess your own needs and progress. In your diary you could do the following:

- Make a note of your achievements in a specific skill, topic or grammar point. Evaluate your performance by giving an indication of how well you have done. You can choose your headings, for example: very well, moderately well, not so well.
- Make a note of your general strengths and weaknesses.
- List improvements. These are not always apparent in language learning. Look for evidence. For example your tutor's comments on your work will be useful. You may also be able to gauge improvement yourself. For instance you may notice that you are now using a grammatical structure you once found difficult.
- Make a note of things you need to do. These will often emerge as you evaluate your own performance. Try to discriminate between what you

really need to do and what you enjoy doing. Try to achieve a balance in your list so that you retain motivation.

- Make a note to reuse idioms, expressions and phrasing that have worked well for you.

Here are two examples:

(1)

Aim	Points to work on	Success rate	Further work
Participate in a group conversation.	How to pause while making a point.	Learned some fillers but still too slow presenting ideas so I get interrupted.	Listen to/watch debates on radio and TV.
Get reflexive verbs of daily routine right.	Irregular verb forms for first person and third-person singular.	Still some problems with word order of reflexives in the past tense when speaking but definitely getting better.	Describe my own routine out loud for the next few days. Record if I have time.

(2)

Monday: Got tutor feedback. Need to work on agreement of adjectives. Reread grammar note. Good on colours but not size, shape, etc.

Tues: Try to write descriptions of 10 things in the house making sure adjectives agree. Concentrate on size and shape.

Wed: Test myself without looking at the descriptions.

It is important to find a style and format that suits you and your purpose for learning. As well as recording what you have done and how it went, make a note of anything you want to follow up or questions you want to ask your tutor. You could also jot down things that you found particularly interesting about the language or the people who speak it (for example, word or sentence patterns).

Using checklists

Another way of monitoring your progress is to use the checklists of key learning points or intended learning outcomes which most courses provide at the beginning or end of course units or class sessions. Look at the items and try to decide how well you have done. What sort of evidence do you have for your judgements? Try to get into the habit of making a quick check at intervals during your course.

Table 4.1 is a completed example. You can use this method for a single session or for your study of a course unit or chapter over a period of time.

Table 4.1 Using a checklist of key learning points to monitor progress

Intended outcomes: by the end of this unit you will:	In general, how well did I do?	What evidence do I have for my judgement?	What have I improved since last time? How do I know?	What else do I need to work on? How am I going to do it?
• understand and be able to use names of a number of common dishes and drinks	OK, I found it quite easy to remember these	I was able to supply names when the teacher showed us pictures. She praised my pronunciation!	I've practised some sounds using the CD and it has obviously paid off	
• be able to order a meal from a menu	I gave an order in a role-play	The other student who took my order appeared to understand what I wanted!	I didn't feel so stupid trying to say longer things. I felt pleased with myself for having a go!	The test will be trying it out for real, but that will have to wait until my next trip.
• be able to ask for the bill and pay for the meal	I think I did this OK	Again, the other student appeared to understand and I managed to give an amount of money to cover it	I understood some of the prices this time but I couldn't catch the total. I just had to hope I'd given enough	I need to get more used to understanding numbers. I'll listen to the activities on the CD again. Perhaps I can persuade a few colleagues to try a game of bingo?
• know the usual restaurant etiquette and how it compares with your experience	I had some previous experience, so I think I knew this already	I know what to expect from my previous visits	I'm more aware of the differences from what I am used to and the importance of the polite forms	Can't wait to go again!

Task 4.4 Monitoring your progress by using a checklist

Look at the key learning points or intended outcomes for one of your own course units and try this approach.

- What are the key learning points for this section?
- In general, how well did you do?
- What evidence do you have for your judgement?
- What have you improved on since last time? How do you know?
- What else do you need to work on? How are you going to do it?

Comment
Looking at your performance in this way can help give value to the positive aspects of your performance rather than allowing negative feelings about one or two things to dominate.

Using the language you have learned

A good way of checking your progress can be to use the language for real! If you have the opportunity, talk to speakers of the language where you live, look at a magazine or a satellite TV channel if available. Engaging in 'real' communication in any form is a good way to measure your progress, whether this is face-to-face, by phone or via the Internet (see Chapter 8, 'Using CMC in your studies'). Ask yourself these questions: Did the others understand you and respond in a way that you hoped? Were you able to understand the gist of a conversation or an article? Were you able to contribute anything, or even a bit more to a conversation than you did last time? Were you aware of how cultural differences or similarities affected your interaction with other speakers of the language? You can use a similar framework for reviewing your learning in these situations to the one suggested above for intended learning outcomes. Engaging in real communication can be an enormous source of encouragement. As one learner exclaimed, after successfully negotiating accommodation for a visit: 'Yes! I *can* do it!!'

Developing awareness is the first stage of reflection and the basis for challenging your habits and assumptions, so that you are ready to make the choices and decisions that are beneficial to you throughout your language learning. This includes reflecting on your preconceptions and attitudes towards the other culture(s) and asking yourself whether your language learning experience has increased your understanding of that culture and challenged any previous attitudes and assumptions you held.

ASSESSING YOUR STRENGTHS AND WEAKNESSES: SETTING GOALS

Assessing your strengths and weaknesses involves asking yourself key questions as in Task 4.5. Answers to these will refer both to your performance in the language and to your approach to learning it. It's all too easy to get bogged down by the things you find difficult and to take your strengths for granted, so always make a point of asking yourself what you do well first.

Task 4.5 Assessing your strengths and weaknesses

Answer the following questions as fully as possible:

- What do I usually do well?
- What do I often find difficult or need to improve on?

Comment
You may feel happy doing grammar exercises because you always get them right. Perhaps you are good at pronouncing new words and remembering them. You may feel you have a good system for storing new words because you can usually find what you need easily. On the other hand, it could be that you find it hard to join in a conversation because you have difficulty understanding when others speak fast. You may need to concentrate on getting the gist rather than on understanding every word (see Chapter 5, 'Reading or listening for information').

Having a general idea of your strengths and weaknesses is fine up to a point, but if you are going to build on your strengths and address your weaknesses, you will need to be more specific. You can't work on everything at once so it is important to set yourself short-term, manageable steps or objectives as suggested in Chapter 1. These steps are stages on the way to reaching your longer-term goal, whether this is to be able to go shopping on your next visit to the country, or to complete the next spoken or written assignment for your course. Examine what you will need to be able to do in order to achieve your longer-term goal and consider your strengths and weaknesses in relation to these short-term objectives. Table 4.2 gives an example for a beginner and a more advanced learner.

This approach is similar to the one suggested for monitoring your progress in Task 4.4; in that example, you started from a set of key learning points or intended outcomes. These examples start from the elements which, in combination, will allow you to achieve a particular goal. Either framework can be used for assessing your strengths and weaknesses. In each case, it is important to consider what evidence you have for your

Table 4.2 Identifying strengths and weaknesses

Longer-term goal	Short-term objectives To achieve this longer-term goal I need to:	OK	Needs a bit more work	Difficult, not there yet
Beginner level:				
I want to be able to shop on my next visit so I need to:	know and say vocabulary for items to purchase	✓		
	know how to ask for things		✓	
	understand and say numbers			✓
	know how people behave when shopping (e.g. will shop assistants ask me what I want or will I be left alone?)	✓		
More advanced learner with formal assessment:				
for my next written assignment I need to:	understand the gist of the source materials	✓		
	pick out specific information required	✓		
	structure ideas into a clear plan		✓	
	spell accurately			✓
	include all the information required in my own words		✓	
	use appropriate grammatical structures accurately			✓
	use a range of vocabulary and linking phrases to give variety	✓		
	keep to the word limit			✓

judgements so that you have a sound basis for ticking 'OK', or 'difficult, not there yet'. There are several sources of evidence which you can draw on. Using language for real communication as mentioned earlier can provide useful feedback. Your fellow learners, your tutor and other speakers of the language will provide feedback on your performance in a number of ways. They will respond to what you say or write in ways that indicate that you have succeeded in conveying the message you intended, or ask for clarification when the meaning is not clear. In conversation, they may also repeat words and phrases in a way that shows you how they should have been said, or how ideas might have been expressed more appropriately. Sometimes they will point out inaccuracies or mistakes.

Feedback of all types can help you form a judgement about your strengths and weaknesses in relation to the elements of your immediate short-term objective or the key learning points in any piece of learning material. Simply being aware of them is very important, but not the end of the matter. You also need to ask yourself the following questions: Which of the items in the 'needs a bit more work' and 'difficult, not there yet' columns are the priorities? How shall I tackle them? When shall I do it by?

Task 4.6 What do you need to be able to do to achieve a longer-term goal?

Choose a longer-term goal. The examples in Table 4.2 should give you some ideas.

Decide what you will need to be able to do in order to achieve this goal.

Assess how good you are at these things already and which you may need to work on. What evidence do you have for your judgement?

Comment
If you are not sure about the things which you need to be able to do to reach your goal, talk to your tutor, discuss it with a fellow learner or with someone who has learned the language before.

DEFINING YOUR PRIORITIES IN ORDER TO DRAW UP AN ACTION PLAN

Chapter 2 looks at establishing priorities and making selections in order to cope with large amounts of course material and make the best use of your study time. To help you prioritize, consider what is likely to make the most difference to your performance. Work out what would be relatively quick and easy to do and therefore give you an immediate boost for relatively little effort. In Table 4.2, writing and spelling accurately might come into that category. Perhaps you could make use of a spellchecker? Maybe you need to adopt a systematic technique for checking your work? Ask yourself if you need to spend more time on understanding how particular structures work and where exactly the difficulty lies. Concentrate on one or two structures.

Once you have selected a limited number of priorities, these will become your short-term goals or objectives. Decide how you are going to work on them and what your timescale will be. If you are not sure how to achieve a particular goal, or need further resources, seek advice from your tutor. Table 4.3 shows how the answers to these questions can form an action plan to help you work on the priorities. Once you have worked through your action plan and you see the evidence you are looking for, you will have every reason to feel pleased with yourself.

Table 4.3 Short-term action plan to achieve priorities

Priorities	How?	When?	Evidence of achievement?
Spell accurately	Install spellchecker on PC.	By the end of the month	Reduce the number of tutor comments about accuracy of spelling by half on next assignment and to virtually nil by the one after that!
	When handwriting, check systematically.	From now onwards	
Use imperfect and perfect tenses accurately and appropriately	Concentrate on exercises related to formation and use of these tenses in course book.	Over the next two weeks	Feel more confident. Be able to explain the formation and use to others.
			Get the answers right (check in book).
	Do the exercises again.	In three to four weeks time	Ask tutor to check examples.
	Write 10 examples of my own using each tense separately.	From now onwards	Take them along to show colleagues and discuss.
	Look for and collect examples of both tenses used together.		Get it right in the next assignment!

Task 4.7 Drawing up an action plan for your own priorities

In Task 4.6 you identified some areas which you need to work on to achieve a particular goal in your language learning.

  Choose two or three of these as your priorities and draw up an action plan similar to the plan in Table 4.3.

Comment
Some learners find it keeps them motivated if they decide how they will reward themselves once they have achieved a priority goal. If you do, you could add another column for that purpose.

REVIEWING YOUR GOALS

Achieving the short-term goals or objectives which you have prioritized is an important step, but it is not the end of your journey. You need to regard it as an ongoing process, and regularly draw up new priorities. If you are following a course with assignments or coursework, you can take the opportunity to get some specific feedback from your tutor about how your work on these priorities has affected your performance. When you submit your assignment or coursework consider including information for your tutor along the following lines:

- the priorities you have worked on for this assignment;
- the things you think you have done well in the assignment and why you think so;
- the things you had difficulty with and why;
- any other questions or comments about your work.

This will help your tutor to provide relevant feedback on issues which concern you and relate to your individual priorities. If you do not have to complete coursework or have more practical goals like those shown in the first part of Table 4.2, then you might seek feedback from another speaker of the language, either locally or when you next visit the country, or from your tutor at one of your classes.

To review your goals, you will need to pull together information from a number of sources:

- your longer-term goals, motivation for learning the language and short-term objectives;
- your assessment of your strengths and weaknesses in relation to the short-term objectives;
- feedback on your performance from the sources described above.

You are then ready to select your next longer-term goal and identify the steps which will help you achieve it, select your priorities and work out an action plan to achieve them. Of course the process may not be clear-cut, and at times you may feel you still need to work on elements which were included in your previous list of priorities. The important thing is to make decisions and actively plan how you will spend your time rather than 'drift' along. Make sure that once you are aware of what you want to achieve your tutor or others are aware of it too, so that they can give you really useful feedback.

DEVELOPING GOOD LEARNING HABITS

Becoming aware of yourself as a learner, deciding on your long- and short-term goals, monitoring your progress, assessing your strengths and weaknesses, working out an action plan and regularly reviewing your goals are all good learning habits to cultivate. It is also worth reviewing your study patterns and learning strategies from time to time. Challenge yourself with some of these questions:

- Does my study pattern work? Am I achieving what I want to this way?
- Why do I study this way? Might there be a better way? What do others do?
- What strategies do I use to remember vocabulary, or improve my listening comprehension, for example? Are they working? Are there other techniques I could try?
- Am I getting all the support I need? From my tutor? From my family/ work colleagues? From others? Who do I need to talk to about this? What do my fellow learners think?

This approach may be very different from anything which you have tried in the past and it is not something which everyone finds easy at first. However, it is worth working at as the benefits are long-lasting and can save time in the long run, making the effort really worthwhile.

PERSONAL DEVELOPMENT PLANNING

Chapter 2 talks about the value of keeping records. If you are following any kind of formal learning programme in a college, institute or university, you will probably be expected to keep a record of your long-term goals and your progress towards them in the form of a Personal Development Plan (PDP). Many other organizations use them too. The plans usually include:

- a summary of your educational and career history;
- your long-term goals (what you want to achieve in your educational programme or your career);
- a self-appraisal (examination of the qualities and personal resources and skills which you have gained and those which you need to develop to achieve your long-term goals);
- an action plan to enable you to achieve these goals;
- regular opportunities to review and evaluate your progress and to revise your goals.

As you can see, they follow the processes described in this chapter. The concept of a personal development plan has been adopted by educational institutions to help learners engage individually in a structured and supported process of reflecting upon their own learning performance and/or achievement for their personal, educational and career development. The aim of these plans is to help learners to become more effective, independent and self-confident learners. Such plans can be a great source of personal encouragement, by helping you to see how much you have achieved over a longer period of time, as well as providing the motivation to continue. They may also help you to provide evidence for potential employers, depending on your circumstances. The European Language Portfolio may be worth considering as a framework for your own PDP. Full details are given at: http://www.cilt.org.uk/elp.htm

You will find more information on how portfolios are used for assessment in Chapter 9, 'What tasks constitute the assessment?'.

Many colleges and universities have their preferred methods for drawing up personal development plans, but you could use a notebook, a computer file or a set of file cards. Table 4.4 shows an example related to language learning but it could include a wider range of personal and professional goals and draw on evidence from study, work, domestic and leisure contexts.

Table 4.4 Example of part of a Personal Development Plan

What do I want to achieve and when?	What relevant qualities, personal resources and skills do I have already?	What do I need to do to reach my goal and how will I do it?	What will be the evidence for achievement?
Learn enough Arabic to be able to 'get by' in day-to-day situations in Egypt by the end of next year.	Past experience of learning another language; the motivation of a possible job on an archaeological project in Egypt; determination; Arabic-speaking friends.	Sign up for beginners' course; get the book; decide when I can put time aside for study; contact an Arabic-speaking friend and set up a regular 'conversation session' perhaps in return for some help with English; read more about modern Egyptian culture and customs.	Certificate of course completion; being able to engage in conversations with my friends on day-to-day topics, getting positive feedback from them about my performance.

The process outlined in this chapter can help you to manage and control your learning even when you are short of time. If you have a clear idea of your priorities, you will be able to make decisions about what to concentrate on and what to leave for the time being. You can ask for feedback specifically on these points rather than being overwhelmed with other things to think about. It may not seem easy to start with, but with practice, it will pay off by saving you time and making your learning more effective.

Summary of key points

- Question yourself about your learning, your approach to study and the progress you are making.

- Identify priorities to enable you to achieve your short-term goals.

- Prepare an action plan showing how and when you will work on your priorities and what evidence you will look for to show achievement.

- Share your priorities with your tutor and/or others who can give you feedback on them.

- Monitor your progress and review your learning in order to revise your priorities.

5

Developing competence in the language (1)

Reading and listening skills

Felicity Harper, Pete Smith and Tita Beaven

When you are learning a foreign language, listening and reading have a dual purpose: any material you read or listen to is (1) a piece of information from which you need to extract meaning – even if you are reading purely for pleasure, and (2) a tool for improving your familiarity with and ability in the language you are learning. It is worth keeping this distinction in mind, as approaches which help you to work out the meaning of a given extract may well be different from those you might use to improve your understanding of the way the language works or how it sounds. Whatever your purpose in listening or reading, the more you know about the processes involved and the strategies you can use to support these processes, the more successful you are likely to be.

BEING A REFLECTIVE LEARNER IN THE CONTEXT OF READING AND LISTENING

As explained at the beginning of Chapter 4, becoming a reflective learner is about developing an awareness of how you learn and using that knowledge to improve your learning. Course writers make use of their knowledge about what language learning involves when designing learning materials. Language tutors also use this knowledge to help them adapt materials to the interests and needs of their group. Sometimes, however, it is not made clear to the learner why things are being done in a certain way. The aim of this chapter, therefore, is to give you some useful information to enable you to improve your reading and listening by:

- understanding what they both involve;
- analysing a specific task;
- familiarizing yourself with strategies that support the processes involved;
- selecting the right strategies for the specific task;
- evaluating the success of the strategies you choose.

WHAT DO READING AND LISTENING INVOLVE?

Reading and listening as processes

Although reading and listening are often referred to as 'passive' or **receptive** skills, in reality both involve complex mental processing in order for the reader or listener to make sense of the material. When you listen, for example, you do far more than merely absorb sound. You may well have experienced a situation where you have asked someone to repeat something you did not hear, only to work it out before the other person has a chance to repeat it. This is because your brain is busy processing what you have heard and trying to make sense of it. You will be very skilled at this in your own language, because you have a vast repertoire in your memory of things people say in certain contexts, and the vocabulary and phrases related to given topics. You also have an intuitive awareness of the way your language works grammatically and structurally. This means that when you listen to your own language, you do not need to hear every word, because you are able to make sense of the whole. The same is true of reading.

Task 5.1 Filling in the gaps

Have a look at the following news extract from which some words have been deleted. Can you supply suitable words for the gaps?

CCTV cameras have _____ _____ at a local shopping _____ in a _____ to crack _____ on hooligans _____ the area. Over the _____ year, shopkeepers have _____ numerous attacks on their _____, with the estimated cost to local trade in _____ of £60,000. The local council _____ the cameras will act as a _____ to would be _____. If vandalism does _____, police will be able to use the _____ to _____ who is responsible.

(Answer at the end of this chapter.)

Comment

You may have been surprised at how many words you were able to supply. This is because repeated exposure to this type of news report has embedded the frequently used phrases, vocabulary and structures in your brain for this type of text.

When you read or listen to material in the target language, even if you do not understand every word of what you see or hear, you can often get the general meaning from structures and vocabulary with which you are already familiar. If you imagine the text above to be in the target language, for example, and the gaps to represent the words you have not seen before, you can see that it is possible to work out what a word might mean, even if you do not recognize it.

It is helpful to read or listen to a number of examples of the same type of material in the target language and to note down the phrases and vocabulary that regularly occur. This will help you to build up context and topic-related vocabulary.

As well as information from your knowledge of the language and the context, if you are able to see the speaker, you will also have other clues, such as body language to help you work out what the speaker is saying. For both reading and listening you may also have images or other information which can contribute to providing a fuller picture.

What do reading and listening have in common and how do they differ?

Linguists talk of approaches to reading and listening as 'top-down' and 'bottom-up'.

- Top-down processing refers to activating prior knowledge of the subject and using contextual clues, such as pictures, to aid comprehension, as well as knowledge about how the language works structurally to predict and interpret the content.
- Bottom-up processing is about using the input itself, recognizing individual words and building these into phrases and then sentences.

Task 5.2 Top-down and bottom-up processes in action

1   Read the situation described below. Can you explain how the student arrived at his answer? Why might the other students have been unable to supply an answer?

A group of 12-year-olds is having a French lesson, their faces screwed up in concentration. They are coming to the end of a teaching unit about buying clothes. Their teacher has told them that they are about to hear a recording of a conversation in a clothes shop. What they have to do is tell her what it is the customer asks for. During the extract, the sentence: 'Je voudrais un jean' occurs ('I would like a pair of jeans'). At the end of the extract, the teacher looks around the class hopefully, but is met by a sea of blank faces. Eventually, a hand goes up tentatively at the back of the class. 'Yes?' says the teacher eagerly. 'Is it . . . is it gin?' the student asks.

Comment

This (true) example shows how important it is to combine top-down and bottom-up processing to have the best chance of understanding something. Knowing that the conversation took place in a clothes shop (contextual clue) was not enough for most students to know what the customer required. On the other hand, the student who ventured *gin* had processed the input *je voudrais un*, recognized it as the key phrase prior to the content he required and, hearing clearly the word *jean*, had used a strategy of thinking of what it sounded like in English. But he did not check his idea against the whole context. It made sense in terms of the sound input and of buying something in a shop, but not of buying something in a *clothes* shop.

2　The example below is of a young child reading aloud in her first language. Can you explain what is happening here?

> Sentence in reading book:
> *He'd opened the door and blown out the candles before Pip could get there.*

> Child's version:
> *He opened the door and blown – blew out the candles before Pip could get there.*

Comment

This is a good example of how our brain tries to make sense of the input depending on our expectations, even disregarding the evidence of our own eyes to do so. In this case, it doesn't matter at all in making sense of the story, but it shows how a slight slip in processing the input (here, misreading *He'd* as *He*) can affect how we read the rest of the sentence. The child here knew that *He blown* was wrong, so changed *blown* to *blew* despite what the printed word said. This is worth bearing in mind when you are reading or listening in the target language.

In reading, bottom-up processing builds up from words to sentences; in listening, however, it starts with *sounds* which you try to build into words or phrases. One of the difficulties learners of a foreign language sometimes have is being able to break up the stream of sound into words or phrases. Even if you do not need to understand every word, you still need to hear and recognize a sufficient number of words and phrases to be able to make some sense of what is being said. In fact, because of the way most people learn a foreign language, you may find yourself in the reverse situation to that of young children learning to read. While children may understand words and phrases that are spoken to them but not recognize these same words written down, you may do the opposite, particularly if the words are spoken quickly and are embedded in a long extract. For this reason, it is useful to practise working out how words and phrases you have noted from written material sound in speech. This is sometimes referred to as developing a 'listening vocabulary'. Try to ensure that development of your listening vocabulary keeps apace with the written forms.

Another key difference between listening and reading is the time you have available to process the material. With reading, you can reread a section several times. With listening, on the other hand, unless there is an opportunity to hear the extract a second time or you are involved in a conversation where you can ask for clarification, you will have to recognize words and phrases almost instantly, so that you do not miss what comes next.

It is worth remembering that written and spoken language can be different. Tourist brochures, newspaper reports and books generally include chunks of text made up of complete sentences and well-thought out paragraphs, as well as eye-catching headlines and slogans that can be difficult for the foreign language learner to understand. Spoken language, in contrast, is full of repetitions, false starts, hesitations and incomplete sentences. When you listen, you need to recognize which phrases carry meaning and which are 'filler' words and phrases used to plug gaps or to indicate hesitations. You can then build up a repertoire of these fillers to incorporate into your own speaking as appropriate (see Chapter 6, 'Giving yourself thinking time: using fillers').

WHY DO WE READ OR LISTEN AND WHAT MATERIAL DO WE CHOOSE?

Reading

You may be an avid reader in your own language, in which case your challenge is selecting *what* to read. On the other hand, reading may not come naturally to you. In this case some strategies for simply getting down to the task of reading and improving reading speed and comprehension may be useful. When you are choosing your own materials, be selective –

look for variety, short publications, including children's books and illustrated volumes, and possibly books with audio versions to accompany them (see Chapter 7). Tourist brochures, leaflets and other documents or texts that are familiar formats in your first language can also be good starting points where you will find common ground or cognates, such as *taxi*, *bus* and *cinema*, as discussed in Chapter 3, 'Making use of prior knowledge'.

- Keep adding to the range of material you read in your own language to match what you need to read in the target language. This will help you to become familiar with the typical structure of a range of material, so that you know what to expect in the target language equivalent.

- Venturing into specialist areas, such as food and wine or environmental protection, or reading material from more highbrow publications, such as serious newspapers or magazines, may also help to increase your vocabulary.

Task 5.3 Why are you reading?

Have a look at the following list, and decide which of the statements you agree or disagree with:

My reading in the target language is:

1   for enjoyment, e.g. fiction and poetry;
2   for obtaining information;
3   to be done in a studious, private way;
4   quite hard work;
5   primarily a question of vocabulary;
6   not necessary for improving my language skills;
7   generally confined to books with serious content;
8   something I prefer to do on my own;
9   an activity that involves absorbing words from pages.

Comment
If your study requires you to cover set books from the literary repertoire of the language in question, then statements 1, 3, 4 and 8 amongst others could well be true. If you are interested in tourism or travelling in the country whose

language you are learning, then statements 2 and 9 might be more relevant, while 1, 5 and 6 will be less valid. How and what you read depends on your purpose, and you will know yourself that the different reasons for reading include:

- purely for pleasure;
- gathering information;
- learning about the target language culture;
- research to inform ideas for writing tasks;
- seeing the language in action;
- learning new vocabulary in context;
- pronunciation;
- communicating with others (letters, emails, text chat).

There is no single right or wrong way to read, and how you go about it will be a mix of elements that brings together your past experience, your knowledge of the subject area, the time and resources you have available, the nature of the reading you choose to do, or *have* to do, and your preferences as a learner. Computers and the Internet are bringing about rapid changes in the way we see and read text, and as it is still a relatively unexplored area of study, it is not entirely certain how these new forms of text are affecting us in terms of reading. If you think about what you do when you are online, it is often quite different from 'traditional' reading – it can involve moving graphics, or audio and visual accompaniment, several screens of text at the same time, links which are not linear but are 'web-like', and it is quite possible that you approach these using different skills. You might like to compare how you read a book with what you do on the Internet and see if there are any differences.

Listening

Although you are open to hearing what is going on in the world around you, at times you will be able to select what you actually listen to. This could be deciding to listen to a conversation taking place in a shop while you wait in a queue or choosing a particular documentary to watch or a specific section of your course material to listen to. At other times there will be no such choice: you might need to pay attention to an announcement in a railway station or you might be asked a question. When someone addresses you directly, you will need to use additional strategies to help you clarify what was said (see Chapter 3, 'Developing strategies to improve your learning', and Chapter 6, 'Getting the message across' for some examples).

One thing to bear in mind is that your ear may be so accustomed to your own language that you may not perceive some of the sounds in another language. As well as adjusting to the rhythm, pronunciation and intonation of the target language, you might also need to develop your ability to hear the full spectrum of sounds it contains. Chapter 4, 'How the language sounds', suggests some techniques to increase your awareness of the sound patterns in the language you are learning. However, just as babies are surrounded by the sound of their native language before they speak, so, as a learner of a foreign language, you might benefit from just absorbing the sound in parallel to or before working on improving your comprehension. Remember that all humans have a 'silent period' of up to two years while there is input but no coherent output. As an adult learner, if you reduce this to a matter of months, it represents a remarkable short cut!

- Subtitled videos, DVDs or films on television may be helpful, whether the original version is in the target language or your mother tongue. When the original version is in the target language, you have an immediate version in your own language in the subtitle.

- With video and DVD you can replay scenes to capture pronunciation and useful phrases (see also Chapter 7). As you advance in the language, you can hide the subtitles and then listen again with the subtitles visible to check for anything you missed. You can even turn off the sound and try to supply your own target language soundtrack from the English subtitles.

- Subtitles are also often provided in the same language as the film for the benefit of those with hearing difficulties, which can be of enormous help to the foreign language learner. Where the original version is in your mother tongue, on the other hand, and the subtitle in the target language, you can pick up a lot of useful phrases. In an English film subtitled in Spanish, for example, you might hear the word *horse* and see the word *caballo*.

HOW READING AND LISTENING ARE APPROACHED IN COURSEBOOKS

Below are some descriptions of a number of different purposes for which you might listen or read, and, where appropriate, some examples of the types of exercises often devised by course writers or tutors to develop the specific skills required in each case. Awareness of which skills are being developed through specific exercises may help you to notice areas where less practice is available and provide you with some ideas of how you can work on improving these skills yourself.

Reading or listening for information

You often read or listen to something in order to find out some information. 'Listening for information' can be broken down into three different categories:

Reading or listening for gist: getting an overview

When you listen to a newscast or documentary or even a conversation between speakers of the target language, you may be interested not so much in the precise details of what you are hearing but rather in the overall sense. The same is true when you read news reports or magazine articles. You often automatically disregard the details in order to keep a sense of the whole. Typical exercises associated with reading and listening for gist include:

- summarizing in one or two sentences what the extract is about;
- ordering pictures as you listen or in accordance with the written text;
- selecting an appropriate title or a brief description from a list of possibilities;
- making very brief notes (e.g. one word per paragraph);
- matching a heading to an extract (e.g. a headline to a short news item);
- identifying key points in paragraphs;
- putting jumbled pieces of a text in a suitable order.

Reading or listening for detail: engaging with the arguments

If you are trying to follow a complex argument, it matters that you understand the detail. This can be a demanding task in the target language. With listening, you need to be able to understand and make sense of what you hear as you hear it in real time, so that you can keep up mentally with the discussion. In reading, you need to be able to understand what you are reading and keep it in mind as you go on to read further. This type of listening and reading is sometimes called 'critical' listening or reading. Typical exercises associated with listening for detail include:

- writing detailed summaries;
- questions or incomplete sentences requiring detailed responses;
- true/false questions which distinguish subtly between alternatives;
- essay-style tasks synthesizing the information gleaned;
- selecting the correct second half of a sentence from subtly different possibilities;
- completing a cloze exercise (a text with words or phrases blanked out);
- making notes as you listen or read (e.g. 10 words per section).

Reading or listening for specific information

If you are waiting for a train and an announcement is made which mentions your train, in your own language you are likely to 'switch on' to the rest of the announcement to hear what is said. This is the essence of listening for specific information. It does not matter what the announcer says about any other trains, you just need to listen out for your train. Similarly, if you are looking at the opening times of a museum, you only need to recognize the words related to conveying that particular piece of information. To practise this type of reading and listening, (coursebooks often use real-life material which might be beyond your level of comprehension if you had to under-stand all of it. Typical exercises associated with practice in listening and reading for specific information include:

- focused questions with one-word or short-phrase answers
- filling in tables with missing information
- completing sentences with a word or short phrase.

Exposure to new styles, vocabulary and linguistic practice

Another reason for choosing to listen to or to read a particular extract is to improve your knowledge of vocabulary and structures, either to increase your comprehension or to improve your own speaking or writing skills. When listening, try to choose material which is relevant and which you find easily accessible. You will then be able to focus your attention not so much on understanding what you hear but rather on assimilating appro-priate words and phrases that you can reuse when you speak. Listening awareness also includes developing a familiarity with the sound of the language. Reading texts, on the other hand, provide an excellent resource for finding out about the structure and grammar of the target language, and you can learn a lot by analysing how things are written.

Exercises commonly associated with encouraging awareness of language include:

Listening and reading

- finding the exact words used to express an idea;
- finding examples used to express opinion, disagreement, etc.

Reading

- deducing rules and usage of grammatical forms by identifying these in the text;
- working on improving your vocabulary by reading a text and look-ing for cognates, **collocations** (words that go together in a particular order, such as *chalk and cheese; an almighty crash; pitch black*), and words related to each other, e.g. *collide, collision; decide, decision* (see Chapter 3, 'Making use of prior knowledge', and Chapter 6, 'Remembering and recalling words and phrases');

- working on improving your ability to deduce what words might mean by working with cloze texts;
- developing your awareness of word formation or patterns between languages to help you work out the meaning of words you have not previously encountered.

Listening

- ordering phrases which occur in the extract;
- matching beginnings and ends of sentences;
- using exercises with transcripts or cloze texts;
- focusing on stress or intonation;
- focusing on the sound of words, e.g. comparing and contrasting similar vowel or consonant sounds;
- improving your listening vocabulary by working on recognition of common phrases, 'fillers' and expressions of hesitation.

Before and after you read or listen

Prominence is now given to teaching people *how* to listen and read and to helping learners to develop conscious strategies for improving these skills. One key aspect of this is what you do before and after you read or listen to something. Typical exercises include:

Pre-listening and reading

- preparing to listen or read by anticipating vocabulary and phrases that might occur;
- predicting what might be in the text from contextual clues;
- predicting answers to the questions set;
- analysing questions to consider how the answer might be phrased;
- setting your own questions or specifying what you want to gain from the extract;
- predicting what the content might include from contextual clues, e.g. pictures, titles, topic knowledge.

Post-listening and reading

- practising or extending examples of linguistic structures or grammatical forms found in the text;
- reusing some of the language encountered, e.g. recording your own version of what you heard, writing a letter based on the content of the extract;
- analysing errors made, e.g. in listening, comparing completed cloze

exercises with the original and noting misheard sounds to bear in mind in the future;

- evaluating how successfully each task was achieved and considering where the difficulties lay.

ACTIVE READING AND LISTENING

Prior knowledge of the topic, vocabulary and type of material

Chapter 3 shows you how you can make use of any prior knowledge you have to help you learn a new language. If, when trying to understand something, you know what the topic is or you know what type of material is involved, you already have a wealth of information available to you to help you. Before you read or listen to material in the target language, therefore, it is worth considering what sort of format or structure it is likely to have and the sort of vocabulary you should expect to find.

Task 5.4 Using what you already know

Imagine you are watching the television news after a national team, in this case, England, has just lost the World Cup. When this item is treated on the television news:

- What structure will the report have? How will it be introduced?
- Who will you be listening to and what contribution will each person make?
- What sort of information will you expect to be given?
- What vocabulary or phrases would you expect to hear?

Comment
In terms of the format, you might expect some interaction between the reporter and the newsreader: *Yes, John, a terrible day for England* . . . some interviews with key people such as the players, the coach or the manager, and possibly some banter and some jokes.

You would expect to find out how the match developed and what the decisive moments were, as well as an overall summary of the standard of play. There will probably also be a discussion about who might be sacked.

There are certain words and phrases you might predict, such as: *very disappointing for the lads, just couldn't bring it all together on the day* and maybe *dismal performance* for your team and *on top form, a stunning tackle,* etc. for the other.

Prior knowledge of commonly used words and phrases

As well as the topic-related vocabulary, there will also be phrases which signal a change in the focus or a change of direction. In the football report in Task 5.4, for example, these would include the phrase used by the newscaster to hand over to the sports reporter, and phrases to signal the beginning of an interview and the end of it. Such phrases are called **discourse markers** and many are common to different contexts. Examples to be found in discussions include phrases such as *Let's start with you, Mike* . . . and *All in all then.* . . . Awareness of these helps considerably with finding your way through spoken and written material. As well as discourse markers, spoken language abounds with words and phrases which occur frequently in all types of exchanges. Examples include 'filler' words like *surely, actually, yes, but, the point is* as well as expressions of hesitation, such as *well, um, let me see*, etc., as explained earlier in this chapter.

Using clues and exercises to aid comprehension

If you are studying the language using a coursebook, you will probably find that listening exercises are preceded by some activities that prepare you specifically for the extract you are about to hear. A similar approach is used if you are about to tackle a particularly challenging written text. Typically, pre-listening and pre-reading exercises will stimulate your prior knowledge of the topic as well as of the language that is likely to occur in the extract. The exercise questions also provide information on the structure and the content of the material as well as on the language you might expect to hear or read. In listening, for example, if a question asks: *What time does the train leave for Paris?* you already know that part of the extract concerns a train going to Paris. In this case, before listening, it would be helpful to consider the different ways *depart* and *arrive* might be expressed and listen out for these specific phrases in the material. This is generally easier than trying to understand a large chunk of language. Similarly, questions beginning with the word *Why?* suggest you could look out for part of a sentence beginning with a phrase such as *because*, or *owing to*.

Making predictions

A further step is to predict the answers. This is particularly helpful in listening, if you have difficulty hearing what people say, as it helps to reduce the number of possibilities to listen out for. It can also help if you are reading a text. You will have to consider appropriate vocabulary and structures for expressing the answers, and this helps to activate prior knowledge and focus your mind on checking for precise phrases. In the listening example above, you would need to consider the ways time might be expressed in the target language in a railway announcement, and, if you are working at a more advanced level, consider the possibility that the departure time could be announced as a delay. In French, for instance, you would expect to hear the word *heure* in the middle of the time, as in *dix heures quinze*. Because you now expect to hear that phrase, if it occurs in the passage you are more likely to perceive it. This is a strategy you can also use in a conversation in which you are requesting information or in which responses are likely to follow a typical format with largely predictable vocabulary.

It is important that while you are listening, you constantly check your interpretation – in other words, you need to monitor the extent to which your predictions were correct and consider what would make sense in terms of the extract itself, as you discovered in Task 5.2.

Hypothesis-testing

In your own language, you are constantly making predictions of how a sentence will unfold, using your knowledge of what would 'fit' and revising it as new information comes in. This depends on you having access to a range of possibilities. In the target language, you may not actually have encountered the vocabulary concerned before, so you may find the following approach helpful. Imagine you are listening to an extract in the target language about the conditions for renting a holiday home, which include leaving it clean and tidy. You manage to hear *Guests are asked to _____ the kitchen floor with a _____*. If this is a new area of vocabulary for you, a good way to approach this would be to start with an educated guess in your own language, look up the word in a dictionary and check whether the target language equivalent fitted with the sound input. Alternatively, you could consider *all* the possibilities for one of the gaps in your own language, look these up in a dictionary and listen closely to see which word was actually used. In the first gap, this might turn out to be: *sweep, polish, clean* or *wash*. Once you have established which it is, then you can consider what you might have to use to complete the second gap. If you are reading an extract without the help of a dictionary, the context may help you to work out the meaning of an unknown word. Often, the precise meaning of individual words will not be important, but on those occasions where it is, you may be able to use knowledge of word formation and how words are related between languages to help you decide which of various possibilities is the meaning of the unknown word.

Strategies for understanding written material

There are a number of strategies you can try that are particularly useful with longer and more challenging texts of particular interest to you. In a classroom situation, you could work with other students or your tutor, but even if you are learning independently, these strategies can still be of value and it is worth trying them out for yourself. Despite their technical titles, they describe processes that are quite simple to do:

- *semantic mapping* involves describing the development of the main sense units of a text – in other words what different sections of the text are about and how these develop;
- *structure glossing* is a process of producing a diagram or chart of the length of the text, the number of paragraphs, the type of language and the development of the themes (or topics) in it;
- *generative précising* involves summarizing key ideas, which serves as a springboard for comprehension.

Another way to engage with ideas is a strategy called Experience Text Relationship (ETR) in which you match what you know with what you find in the text, in a way that consciously involves using your own experience. A common variation of this for classroom-based learning involves discussing the title or theme before reading the text, and leads to a similar engagement with the ideas it contains. These mapping approaches are associated with the notion of 'reading as a psycholinguistic guessing game' where you generate a hypothesis (or 'educated guess') about what you are going to read, following which you read and test out the theory, and then you revise it in light of what you find. There are various ways you can go about this, including:

- making margin notes of keywords either before or as you go through the text;
- brainstorming and mind-mapping the topic before reading, comparing the text with these afterwards and adjusting your mind map accordingly. This also provides a summary on the way;
- jotting down what you expect to encounter in the text, and revising it as you go through;
- mapping out the 'semantic structure' of the text before you read it – a sort of flow chart of what you think might be the main themes or ideas.

All of these strategies are essentially processes that help you prepare to read in more detail and become an *active* reader. You might like to try these strategies with simpler texts with which you are familiar, for example tourist brochures, letters and magazine articles, in order to develop an understanding of how the processes work.

- Some research has shown that the reading strategies you have in your first language do not automatically transfer to the language you are learning. This explains why reading can be frustrating in a foreign language, and why some different strategies may well be necessary.

BECOMING FAMILIAR WITH THE SOUND OF THE LANGUAGE

Language learners often feel that the language they are learning is spoken much faster than their own, but often it is just that all the words seem to merge into one another. The difficulty is in perceiving and recognizing individual words or phrases. There are a number of reasons for this and a range of strategies you might adopt to try to improve your ability in this area.

Reconciling sound and spelling of the target language

In most cases, there is a difference between your own language in terms of the relationship between sound and spelling and that of the language you are learning. If you come across a new word, you will want to be able to check its meaning in a dictionary or use other strategies, such as seeing if it is a cognate, in order to find out what it means. So it is important to spend time considering the way words are spelt and listening to how they are pronounced.

A simple way to begin is to read the transcription as you are listening to material and then replay the extract with your eyes shut. This will help you to associate the written and spoken forms of the language and gradually improve your ability to understand spontaneous speech.

Changes in pronunciation of words in different contexts

It is useful to note that words may be pronounced differently when they occupy different positions in a sentence. They may 'liaise' with adjacent words, so that the final consonant sounds like the first letter of the next word or so that the first letter of the following word sounds like the last letter of the previous word, as in Task 5.5. Sometimes final consonants or even syllables disappear completely.

Task 5.5 How do words sound?

The following sentence in English illustrates some of these features. Try reading it out loud:

Of the two of you, do you think it will be you or Marion who goes to the Olympic Games in the end?

You may have noticed that:

- The word *of* could be pronounced *ov* or *euv* in its first occurrence, but in its second occurrence it will almost certainly be pronounced *euv*
- *of you* is likely to sound more like *a view* and *do you* is likely to sound more like *dje*
- *Olympic Games* may sound like *limpi'gaims* and *the end* like *theeyend*.

Comment

As you can see, the pauses between sounds that you might expect to mark individual words might not actually be between words at all, e.g. *a / view*. This means that you may think you recognize a word or phrase and then try to construct a meaning for the rest of the sentence around it, when it isn't actually there. These or similar influences on pronunciation occur in most languages, though the examples here are in English.

- The range of possibilities for interpreting what you hear is one of the reasons that listening to a text can be more difficult than reading the same text. There are a few simple rules, however, about how sounds might change depending on the surrounding language, and once you have become aware of what these are, you can try out different ideas if you are having difficulty deciphering what you hear.

Task 5.6 Hearing the right thing

Look at the sentences below. In each case the listener has misinterpreted part of what was said. Try reading each sentence aloud and see if you can you supply the correct phrase. What caused the misinterpretation in each case?

1 It's a lot harder than I thought, mine due.
2 It was nice to see her eyes to the occasion.
3 The man resisted a rest.
4 There is wonky consideration here.

Comment

1 The listener was probably unfamiliar with the phrase *mind you*, so wrote two words that exist in English and match the sound.

2   The *r* of *rise* is swallowed, producing *her eyes*, which is also a more
    common phrase. The listener was presumably unfamiliar with the phrase
    to rise to the occasion.

3   The listener recognized the word *a* as introducing a noun. She or he was
    probably unfamiliar with the phrase *to resist arrest*.

4   The listener may have always pronounced *wonky* as *won* and *ky*, so hears
    this instead of *one key*. He or she was also seemingly unfamiliar with the
    frequent use of the phrase *one key* . . . in various types of speech and
    writing, and unaware that *wonky* is too informal for the context.

The importance of stress patterns for recognizing word boundaries

Fluent speakers of a language know where to break up a stream of sound, but for those learning the language, this can cause considerable difficulty. One reason is that you may unconsciously apply the rules about the stress and intonation patterns of your own language to the target language. In English, for example, the stress tends to be placed on the first syllable of nouns or compound nouns, which can lead English native speakers to assume that any stressed sound signals the first syllable of a word, and to misplace the word boundaries. Chapter 4, 'How the language sounds', considers the impact of patterns of stress and intonation on meaning and suggests activities to make you more aware of these patterns. Another useful approach is to listen to how speakers of the language you are learning use stress patterns from their own language. You will quickly notice where the stress falls incorrectly in their pronunciation of your language and you can apply that stress pattern when you are speaking their language.

ENGAGING WITH THE CULTURAL CONTENT

Awareness and appreciation of linguistic varieties

If you are about to listen to an interview with an Andalusian flamenco dancer, you might expect them to speak with an Andalusian accent, and being mentally prepared for this – marshalling all your prior knowledge about what that linguistic variety of Spanish sounds like – may help you make sense of it faster. When developing your listening skills, it is important that you listen to people with different accents and to different varieties of the language you are learning, so that you develop strategies to cope with this.

Awareness of style and register when reading and listening

Chapter 4, 'The social and cultural role of the language', explains what is meant by language register, e.g. the differences between spoken and written language, and the use of formal and informal language. When developing your listening or reading skills in a target language, you will need to develop an awareness of style and register. For instance, if you are reading a letter, it is important to know if it is formal or informal, as this will contribute to your understanding. Similarly, being familiar with different registers will enhance your understanding of the target language. For example, if, as a learner of English, you hear something like *Bear with me while I put you through*, you will make more sense of it if you are familiar with the expressions and idioms used in 'telephone language'. In your language studies, you will be exposed to a whole variety of styles and registers to widen your linguistic repertoire.

Discovering and analysing linguistic and cultural content

This is a skill you will develop throughout your studies, but it is important that you start thinking from the start what you can learn about the language and culture from a written text or piece of spoken language.

For instance, you might want to ask yourself:

- What linguistic variety does the speaker use, and what does that tell me about their background (geographical or social)?
- What is the style of the passage? Is the text literary, technical, factual? What is the effect of any rhetorical features used, i.e. language used to persuade or influence? (See Chapter 6, 'Style and register' for rhetorical devices used for effect.)
- What can I tell about the register? What sort of text is it? Is it a telephone conversation, an announcement, a formal presentation? Is it a newspaper advert, a letter from the bank, a dedication in a book? (See again Chapter 6, 'Style and register'.)
- What cultural information can I gain from the passage? If you are listening to a customer ordering a meal in a restaurant, you will be learning about the language used for ordering food, but ask yourself what you can learn about the culture too: How formal is the language? How is politeness expressed? Is the food ordered similar to or different from the food in your country?

Understanding socio-cultural references and their implications

When learning a foreign language, you can explore listening and reading material for all sorts of information about the culture and society in which the language you are studying is spoken. You will also find that it works the other way round: the greater your knowledge about the society and culture, the more you will understand listening or reading material in the target language.

Task 5.7 Linguistic or cultural knowledge?

Look at the menu below. A learner of English has underlined all the elements they couldn't understand. How would you explain them? Are the difficulties linguistic or cultural?

A menu for a pub lunch:

The Royal Oak
The Green, Little Horwood
Menu

All-day breakfast

Jacket potatoes

Sandwiches

Ploughman's lunch

Bubble and squeak

Sausage and mash

Sunday roast from the carvery

Ask your waiter for our selection of sweets from the trolley

Comment
You probably found that the meanings of the words used were dependent on cultural knowledge. In other words, learners of English would be able to find a definition of all the words in a dictionary, but that would not help them to understand what they mean on this menu. They would need to know, for example, that an all-day breakfast is a cooked breakfast and that the Royal Oak is a common name for a pub.

DEVELOPING STRATEGIES

Some of the strategies you will try out when you are listening and reading will be useful where your main aim is specifically to *understand* what is being said. Such strategies include drawing on what you know about the topic in your own language and listening or reading for specific information. Other strategies, however, are designed to *improve your overall ability* in listening to and reading the target language.

Creating your own activities for extra practice

Whatever your learning situation, you may find it helpful to create extra activities to give you more practice in specific areas. Not only will you become more skilled at the aspects you have chosen, but also you may well find out more about the way you learn best.

It is helpful to begin by deciding what sort of material you would like to use and what you hope to achieve. The Internet and digital broadcasting have increased access to real-life material for a range of languages (see Chapters 7 and 8), but even if you are limited to the material provided with your course, you can still devise extra practice activities using the material you have. You may at first want to concentrate on improving your skills within a very specific context – understanding numbers or directions, for example, or you might want to focus on a specific form of language use, such as advertisements or reports.

Selecting and evaluating your strategies

The focus of practice exercises in reading and listening can be:

- understanding what you are reading or listening to at the time, as might be your aim in a real-life situation;
- improving your skills and language knowledge overall, possibly using exercises that would not be suitable in real life.

Two examples are given below which show how you can use strategies to develop these two aspects. Although reading is used to illustrate the first and listening the second, the processes suggested apply to both skills and can be adapted to suit the slightly different demands of each as described earlier in the chapter.

Example 1: selecting strategies to understand what you are reading
Table 5.1 shows a method you can try to help you decide how you are going to approach a text, depending not only on what you hope to gain from reading it, but also on how much you know about the topic and the difficulty of the text.

Table 5.1 Approaching a reading text

1 The pictures and headings	• provide a number of clues about the content; • provide some indication about the content; • are not very helpful.
2 The first two sentences suggest that this text	• contains mainly structures and vocabulary I will understand; • contains some structures and vocabulary I will understand; • contains many structures and much vocabulary I will find difficult to understand.
3 This is a topic	• I know a lot about; • I know about in general terms; • I know virtually nothing about.
4 When I have read this text, I hope to have	• identified some key points; • found out some specific details; • got the gist of what it was about; • answered some specific questions set in advance; • found out enough to talk or write about the content in some detail.
5 The strategy / strategies I am going to adopt to read this text is / are	• make margin notes of keywords as I go through the text; • brainstorm and mind-map the topic before reading, and then compare the text with it afterwards and adjust my mind map accordingly; • jot down what I expect to encounter in the text, and revise it as I go through; • 'map' the structure of the text before I read it; • read the text and make a summary at the end of what I found in it; • write some questions to answer in advance; • think of specific details I want to find out before reading; • read the text quickly once, then adopt one of the other strategies above.
6 I expect to have to read the text	• quite superficially, looking purely for specific information; • quickly, just to get a rough idea of what it is about; • carefully, trying to find detailed information; • carefully, trying to understand virtually everything; • critically, following arguments and forming my own view; • once; • several times.

Task 5.8 Choosing appropriate strategies

1   Choose a text you would like to read. Look at the first column in Table 5.1 *Approaching a reading text* and select the phrase from the second column that most accurately describes what you think.
2   Try out the strategies you have identified as being appropriate in response to item 5, Table 5.1. When you have finished, ask yourself:

- Did the strategies I chose help me to achieve my aim in reading this text?
- Did the strategies I chose help me to do other things I hadn't planned for?
- What other strategies could I have used?
- Would the strategies I used be helpful in another context?

Are there other questions you could ask yourself before deciding how to go about reading a text?
How could you adapt this table to help you approach a listening extract?

Comment
Once you have become familiar with this method, you should be able to scan a text and make these decisions automatically.

Example 2: improving your skills and language knowledge overall
This second example shows how you can use a range of exercises with listening material related to one topic. Different exercises help to develop specific skills, all of which contribute to you becoming a better listener overall. The topic used here is one most suitable for beginners, but this can be varied as appropriate. At higher levels you might want to choose various types of listening material all related to one topic.
    The approach follows the sequence below:

1   select a topic and decide what your purpose in listening is;
2   select appropriate pre-listening activities;
3   select appropriate listening activities;
4   select appropriate post-listening activities;
5   review how successful the approaches (strategies) you chose were in helping you to achieve your purpose.

Selecting a topic

A topic which occurs early on in many course materials is the weather. This is an ideal area to start with for the following reasons:

- If you have access to the Internet, you will be able to find weather forecasts in written form, generally with picture support and possibly speech.
- You can find written reports in newspapers.
- You may be able to hear weather forecasts on your radio.
- If you have satellite or cable television, you may be able to watch weather forecasts at home.
- If you are studying a course, you will probably have material in your coursebook which you could refer to or reuse in a different way.
- Weather forecasts generally follow a standard format and use a limited range of structures and vocabulary.
- Weather forecasts follow a similar pattern in a number of languages.

Selecting appropriate pre-listening activities to suit your purpose

Before you select activities to do before listening, consider why you might be listening to something and what you hope to gain from it. Make sure you include reasons why you might do so in real life as well as reasons you might do so for practice. Examples relevant to a weather forecast could include:

- I want to know what the weather will be like in a certain area tomorrow afternoon.
- I want to know where within a two-hour drive it will be dry all day tomorrow.
- I want to learn and be able to recognize the sort of phrases that weather reporters use.
- I want to become better at hearing what they actually say even if I do not fully understand what it means.
- I want to become familiar with the structure of spoken weather forecasts.

Task 5.9 Selecting pre-listening activities

Study the list below of typical pre-listening activities you might encounter in course materials:

- 'Word storm': write down any vocabulary that comes to mind related to the topic, consulting a dictionary for expected but unknown vocabulary.
- For a topic with a limited range of typical phrases (e.g. booking a hotel room), write a list of these to listen out for and tick them off as you hear them.
- Note typical phrases in your own language to listen out for in the target language.
- Note down the key points of a talk you would give about the topic.
- List the sorts of phrases people might use to structure the material (discourse markers).
- Set yourself some questions to answer in advance.
- Read something related to the topic.
- Look at any clues provided in advance. Note down what they tell you about the extract and what they indicate you can expect to hear. A news event, for example, will contain information about when, where, why and how it happened and who was involved. Note down the phrases that might be used to express this information.
- If you have a transcript available, create a cloze text by scanning the text into a computer cloze programme, or by blanking out the last word of every line yourself, making sure you don't read it too carefully. Then, either listen to the extract and try to fill in what is missing or start by reading your cloze text and predicting what goes in the blanks. This second activity helps you to activate top-down processes (thinking about what would make sense grammatically and in terms of the context) before you listen and then to modify your predictions in the light of the sound input.

Now ask yourself:

- Which activities would be useful before listening to an extract?
- Are there any that could be adapted to make them useful?
- Are there any other ways of preparing?
- Can any pre-listening activity be used as preparation or does it depend on what you hope to gain from listening to the material you have chosen?

Comment
Predicting what goes in the blanks of a cloze text can help prevent you becoming overloaded, while trying to process what you hear at the same time

as new input is coming in. If you have predicted something and you hear it, then the exercise helps to increase your listening vocabulary; if, on the other hand, what you hear does not match what you thought, then you will have to think again. This involves exactly the sort of top-down process so important in making sense of material, but you are helping your brain along by having already considered consciously what sort of word or phrase would fit.

It is important that you vary the activities you use, as this will help you to work out when particular exercises are more beneficial and will ensure you develop a range of skills necessary for understanding the spoken language in real life. Reading a transcript before listening, for example, may help you develop your ability to hear exactly what people say, but it does not help you improve your ability to focus on key points. A better option would be setting yourself some questions to answer in advance or noting specific aspects to listen out for.

It is worth making a note of any other activities you come across that you find useful. Try out ideas of your own – this is all part of being a reflective learner and taking charge of your own learning.

Selecting appropriate listening activities

Some learners find it helpful to listen to the whole extract first to 'get a feel for it' whilst others prefer to start straight away on doing some sort of task. It may well depend both on such preferences and on the difficulty of the material and what you are hoping to understand.

Task 5.10 Which activities for which purpose?

Below are some suggestions for activities you could use when listening to recorded material. Have a look back at the various reasons why you might want to listen to a weather forecast. Which activities below do you think would be most useful in each case?

Using your pre-listening activities

- Tick off as you hear them words and phrases from your word storm, opinions you predicted, discourse markers, e.g. *The outlook for the evening, on the other hand . . . , All in all, then . . .* or the key points of your talk.
- Decide whether there were points you would have included but which were omitted.

- Answer the questions you set in advance.
- Complete your cloze exercise.
- Listen out for the specific aspects you identified in advance.

Focusing on what you hear

Working on content

- Write down all the weather you hear mentioned and only that.
- Play the recording once without pausing and afterwards note down what you remember about it/what words you heard.

Working on language

- Write a short transcript of a section or note down some phrases you hear. Compare them to written forecasts and look for phrases which appear to correspond.
- Note new vocabulary.
- Concentrate on pronunciation and stress.

Working on cultural aspects

- Note who presents the forecast (age, gender, etc.).
- If you are watching a television broadcast, note the body language and style of the presentation.

Using contextual clues

Make use of any visual clues during the extract. Note down or bring to mind phrases and vocabulary related to the visual clues. A television weather forecast, for example, will not only normally have a map with symbols but also a presenter pointing to the precise part of the map to which he or she is referring.

Prediction and educated guesses

Use your knowledge of phrases and collocations (such as *heavy rain, gale-force winds, thunder and lightning*) to consider what might work in the gaps you cannot decipher, e.g. *Temperatures will soar to a _____ high this afternoon. (record)*. Check your ideas by listening again.

Transcription

Write a transcription of a small section of what you are listening to. Write down what it sounds like the first time you hear it. Listen again and when you feel you have understood as much as possible, write a second transcription. When you have finished listening to the whole extract and have finished the other exercises, go back and listen to the small section again and write a final transcription. Compare your first with your final transcription and consider the differences. If you have a transcript available, compare this with your interpretation. Highlight the differences and look for patterns. For example, did you make the same type of mistake twice or more? What was the mistake and what can you learn from it? Make a note of these mistakes and your conclusions and when you listen to something else, apply what you have learnt from your previous exercise.

Using a computer to play your extract

If you have a precise counter display, you may be able to replay an exact section of text you are at first unable to understand, even down to a single syllable. You can also break up the extract into different chunks, trying out new places where a word might begin, for example. If you vary the length of the chunk of sound you replay, you may even find that it suddenly comes to you what the person is saying – this is because your brain is using all the contextual and linguistic information available to try to make sense of the extract. You can think of it as like looking at a photograph of something taken at an unusual angle – a tiny piece of new information can make a tremendous difference and suddenly it becomes clear to you what the picture is.

Checking your interpretation as you go

As you listen and begin to understand what you are hearing, check whether your interpretation makes sense grammatically and in terms of the content. If you think you hear a heatwave and snow storms forecast for the same region on the same day, you will need to think of some explanations. Was the forecaster using the past tense to talk about snow storms at this time of year in 1953 or did you confuse snow storm with thunder storm?

Comment

The essential thing is to remember that different activities develop different listening skills. Whenever you listen, think of how best you can achieve your particular aim at the time.

Selecting appropriate post-listening activities

Try to stay alert to what else you can learn while you are listening. If you noticed that you tend to hear a *p* as *b* make a note of it, so that you can consciously check when you listen to material in the future. You could also record yourself saying part of the extract or particular phrases, doing your best to mimic the native speaker so that you fix in your mind how they sound. Try to pick out some key structures, phrases and vocabulary that you can include in your own language. If you have come across new vocabulary and structures that might occur in future material but which are beyond what you would hope to use yourself, you will also want to make a note of these.

Here are a couple of examples of ways you can reuse the vocabulary and phrases you have encountered to fix them in your mind:

- Write a postcard to a friend incorporating the information and structures in the extract, tell him/her about your holiday, what the weather is like and what your plans are for the rest of the week based on the forecast.

- Record a weather forecast from the television. Watch the sequence with no sound and try to provide the soundtrack yourself, either spontaneously or by making notes first.

Reviewing how successful your strategies were

Finally, ask yourself as before:

- Did the strategies I chose help me to achieve my aim in listening to this text?

- Did the strategies I chose help me to do others things I hadn't planned for?

- What other strategies could I have used?

- Would the strategies I used be useful in another context?

Task 5.11 Adapting listening strategies for reading

Have a look back at the listening example (Example 2: improving your skills and language knowledge overall). How could you adapt this approach to apply to reading skills? Some listening activities concentrate on the *sound* of the language. Can you think of any exercises that would be specific to reading?

Comment
You might want to try some reading activities that consider the formation of words, e.g. identifying all the cognates in a passage and considering how they differ from their equivalents in your mother tongue – is there any pattern? You could also work with cloze texts or use material familiar to you in your own language to build up your vocabulary or awareness of grammatical structures.

Summary of key points

- There is a difference between reading and listening in real life and doing so for practice.

- You can use listening and reading material to focus on:
  - understanding what you are reading or listening to in order to grasp the global meaning or to understand specific information;
  - improving your overall ability in the skill you are practising;
  - developing other language skills, such as writing and speaking;
  - learning about the language – its syntax, grammar and vocabulary;
  - increasing your awareness of the cultural aspects of language and the target language culture.

- You can use your knowledge of the mental processes that reading and listening involve to make conscious decisions about how you read and listen depending on your purpose.

- You can transfer and adapt the general principles to other areas of your language learning.

Answer to cloze text in Task 5.1

CCTV cameras have <u>been installed</u> at a local shopping <u>centre</u> in a <u>bid</u> to crack <u>down</u> on hooligans <u>in</u> the area. Over the <u>last</u> year, shopkeepers have <u>suffered</u> numerous attacks on their <u>premises</u>, with the estimated cost to local trade in <u>excess</u> of £60,000. The local council <u>hopes</u> the cameras will act as a <u>deterrent</u> to would be <u>vandals</u>. If vandalism does <u>occur</u>, police will be able to use the <u>footage</u> to <u>identify</u> who is responsible.

6

Developing competence in the language (2)

Writing and speaking skills

*Lina Adinolfi, Christine Pleines, Felicity Harper,
Tita Beaven, Pete Smith, Xavière Hassan,
Helga Adams and Margaret Nicolson*

While Chapter 5 focuses on how to improve your understanding of the language, Chapter 6 is about the skills of speaking and writing, which form the other side of the coin when it comes to successful communication. Speaking and writing are often called active or **productive** skills, which complement the **receptive** skills of listening and reading. Being able to express what you want to say can be one of the most rewarding achievements when studying a language. Whether you are a complete beginner or an advanced learner, this chapter aims to help you find effective ways of doing so.

The first sections of this chapter contain information about acquiring vocabulary for active use, improving the accuracy and fluency of your language and interacting effectively. Later sections concentrate on structuring your speech or writing and on making you aware of different conventions and styles. Some of the ideas and techniques introduced will be particularly useful at the earliest stages of language learning, while others are aimed at more advanced learners who are dealing with more complex situations and tasks.

Finally, and most importantly, the chapter presents strategies for developing different aspects of your speaking and writing and for evaluating your skills.

REMEMBERING AND ACTIVATING YOUR VOCABULARY

Building up a store of vocabulary is an essential aspect of developing your speaking and writing skills, as it will enable you to express yourself more effectively and appropriately in the range of different situations that you will encounter.

Passive and active vocabulary

Learners often assume that they either know or do not know a particular feature of the language they are mastering. However, there are different levels of knowing language. In your mother tongue you may be able to follow a seventeenth-century play, read technical instructions and understand speakers with accents different from your own. You are not, however, likely to produce this range of language yourself. This is entirely normal and applies to the languages you are learning as well. You will always be able to understand more than you can say in any language, whatever your level of ability. A distinction is therefore often made between your **passive vocabulary** – the words and expressions that you recognize but do not actually use – and your **active vocabulary**, the subset of these items that you regularly produce.

Much of the vocabulary that we acquire – whether in our mother tongue or a new language, for either passive or active use – is picked up from the spoken or written language that we encounter around us. There are many different sources of this input, as it is known. Learners following a course often rely on the course materials for most of their input. Yet valuable, wide-ranging language is also available from many other sources, such as films, songs, conversations, letters or literature.

Being selective

When reading and listening, you will be concerned with your understanding of particular vocabulary and expressions. When speaking and writing, in contrast, you will need to recall and produce some of this language. Yet, rather than attempting to learn every new word or expression you come across, it is important to be selective in identifying which items will be most immediately useful to you at your current stage of learning. For general purposes, frequently occurring items or those which cover a wide range of meanings are more likely to be useful, particularly at an early stage. Your individual interests and needs will also influence your choice.

Task 6.1 Being selective

Make a note of the areas of language that you are most likely to find immediately useful at your current stage of learning. Depending on your level and needs, this may range from buying goods from a market stall, to negotiating a business deal on the phone, to exchanging emails on a particular hobby via the Web. You may find that you require certain forms of language for speaking activities, and others when writing is involved.

Pairs and strings of words

Although words are usually listed as individual items in dictionaries, they very rarely occur in isolation in real life. Chapter 5, 'Exposure to new styles, vocabulary and linguistic practice', introduces the concept of collocations – words that have strong connections with other words – and how knowledge of these can often help you understand what you hear: *Sweet dreams! a deep breath; stop dead; Happy Birthday!* are all common examples. There are no rules; they simply sound right, whereas plausible alternatives, such as *Merry* or *Enjoyable Birthday!* sound odd. Look out for examples in the language you are learning; the use of simple collocations can make a relatively new learner sound very natural.

It is not only idiomatic pairings that matter; there are longer strings of words too. English is full of expressions like *how d'you do? keep in touch; not at all; by the way; hang on a minute; Kind regards.* Every language contains large numbers of set phrases such as these. They occur in both spoken and written language, though some will be specific to one or the other. Common examples in other languages include: *Wie geht's?* (Ger); *Non mi piace . . .* (It); *Qu'est-ce que c'est?* (Fr); *¿Cómo te llamas?* (Sp) Τι να κάνουμε; (Ti na kánoume?) (Greek) = *What can we do?* استنى دقيقه (Istana daqeeqa!) (Arabic) = *Just a minute!*

Competent speakers of the target language rarely compose sentences from scratch, one word at a time. They do not have to think about the language they need to communicate a message, and regularly incorporate set phrases into speaking and writing. As with collocations, set phrases are integral to language use and the key to accuracy and fluency. The trick therefore, from the earliest levels of learning, is to look beyond individual words, to take note of their common combinations with other words and to try to use them actively when you speak or write.

Remembering and recalling words and phrases

It is reassuring to know, as pointed out in Chapter 1, that you can get quite far with the 1,000 or so most frequently occurring words in a language. You should not expect to be able to meet a new word or expression and immediately incorporate it into your active vocabulary. This may happen sometimes, but more often it is the words and expressions that you have already come across several times that eventually 'stick' and become part of your own repertoire. You can help this process along by using a range of techniques to record, organize, practise and recall the words and expressions that you identify as important to you. A number of techniques are listed below. You will need to experiment with different techniques to find out what works best for you. If you respond better to aural stimuli, for example, you will tend to focus on the sounds of the language that you are learning and remember items best when you hear them or repeat them orally, or say them aloud to yourself when you read them. If you prefer visual stimuli, you will respond better to written forms of language, recalling them best through reading on the one hand and writing them down on the other. You may wish to review Chapter 1, which describes the importance of identifying what type of learner you are so that you can study to your best advantage, and Chapter 4, which encourages you to develop your awareness of what works best for you.

Noting words and phrases
There are many different ways of recording and organizing new vocabulary and expressions. You will need to decide whether to record new vocabulary in written or oral form. This will depend partly on your preferred learning style and partly on whether you are more concerned with writing the language or speaking it. Written records may be kept in a dedicated note-book or computer file, while oral records will need to be recorded onto a cassette or mini disc. It is, of course, possible to combine both methods. Chapter 3, 'Different ways of making notes' gives ideas for storing vocabulary, through the use of lists and mind maps. In some cases, instead of translations, it is possible to note down synonyms (words that mean the same as other words) alongside particular words or expressions. Synonyms for the word *happy* in English might include: *contented, pleased, delighted, glad, thrilled*, and in Italian: *contento, felice, lieto, allegro*. Some words will also have opposites or antonyms such as this example in Spanish: *económico* (economical) – *costoso* (expensive). Be careful here, however. In the same way that the opposite of the English word *light* could be *dark, heavy* or *serious*, so may words in other languages have more than one antonym, depending on their meaning in a particular context.

Organizing words and phrases
Whether recording vocabulary in writing or orally, there are several possible ways of organizing it in order to recall the words and phrases you need more easily. Whichever way you choose, it should be easy to add new items as you meet them. Here are some examples:

- Organizing vocabulary and expressions according to particular topic areas or situations. These will depend on both your level and interests. Examples of groupings might be food and drink, modes of transport, environmental issues, etc.
- Grouping vocabulary in terms of word families. In English the words *believe* (verb), *(dis) belief* (noun), *(un) believable* (adjective), *unbelievably* (adverb) and *beyond belief* are all part of the same family. Other examples might be: (1) based on the word for *rich* in Italian: *ricco* (rich), *la ricchezza* (wealth), *arrichirsi* (to get rich), *ricco di vitamine* (full of vitamins); (2) based on the word for *head* in German: *Kopf* (head), *Kopfweh* (headache), *kopfrechnen* (to do mental arithmetic), *Hals über*

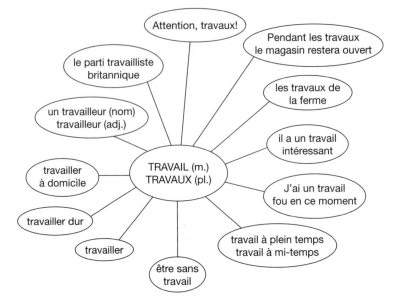

Figure 6.1 Grouping vocabulary according to word families.

Kopf (head over heels). You could set out these word families as in the example in French in Figure 6.1, based on *travail* (work), *travailler* (to work) and *travailleur* (worker).

• Organizing language in terms of its structure or use. This might be particular verb types, for example. You could also group discourse markers in the foreign language: *first of all, however, in contrast, the point is, in conclusion* (see Chapter 5, 'Active reading and listening'), and expressions of hesitation corresponding to *well, you see, you know, um.*

Memorizing words and phrases
Try to take every opportunity to reinforce the vocabulary and expressions that you have recorded, for example:

• Repeat items aloud or write them out several times to fix them in your memory from the start.
• Make associations between these words or expressions and any others you know, whether in your mother tongue or the target language itself, to aid recall, e.g. *conseiller/un(e) conseiller(ère)* (Fr); *to counsel/counsellor* (Eng).
• Use regular mini self-tests to reinforce the recall of new language:

  – re-translation: if you have recorded items with a translation, you can use the translation as a prompt to recall the original word or phrase. You can do the same with opposites or synonyms;

- brainstorming: the random recall of items relating to a particular topic, such as sport or music, or those associated with a particular structure such as verbs which combine with *mit* in German;
- collocation pairs: test yourself by using one part of a collocation to elicit the other part e.g. *Sweet . . . dreams! a remote . . . possibility*;
- set phrases: a number of set phrases are associated with particular situations. Test yourself by matching a situation with a given phrase, e.g. for introductions: *Freut mich Sie kennenzulernen* (Ger); Μια χαρά (*mia hará*) (Greek). Alternatively you can test yourself by matching one set phrase with an appropriate set response e.g. *Muchísimas gracias – De nada* (Sp); *Many thanks – Don't mention it/ you're welcome* (Eng).
- using the items in context: this will help both your accuracy and fluency (see the section on this later in this chapter). A useful exercise is taking a particular word or expression and inventing a new sentence in which it might be used. Again you can say the sentence aloud or write it out, as you wish.

Using knowledge of your mother tongue
If English is your mother tongue, you can make use of the history of the English language when learning some of the other European languages. What is generally considered 'everyday' vocabulary tends to come from German, while more formal equivalents or related terms often come from Latin or French, to which Spanish, Italian, etc. are related:

begin	**commence**
beginnen (Ger)	*commencer* (Fr), *comenzar* (Sp)
King	**royal, royalty, regal**
König (Ger)	*roi* (Fr), *rey* (Sp), *rex* (Lat)
answer	**reply, respond, response, responsive**
antworten (Ger)	*répondre* (Fr), *responder* (Sp), *respondere* (Lat)

Highlighting all the cognates in a text in the target language and writing out the equivalent in English or another language you know can help you identify patterns in the way spelling changes between languages. You can draw on these when trying to remember or 'construct' items of vocabulary. Using the cognates above, for example *répondre, responder*, you might wonder whether the French *é* generally corresponds to the Spanish *es*, a theory you could then check and refine or refute by looking for further examples, such as *école – escuela (school)*.

Sometimes, where French and Spanish verbs consist of one word, German uses a separable verb or a verb followed by a preposition. English often has the equivalent of both to express the same concept. You can 'put up with' something or 'tolerate' it, for example.

Task 6.2 Using cognates

Have a look at the table below and fill in the gaps with the alternative verb in English.

English phrasal verb or verb with preposition	German	English single verb	French	Spanish
	austeilen	distribute	distribuer	distrubuir
try out	ausprobieren		tenter	tentar
	hereinkommen	enter	entrer	entrar
talk about	sprechen über		discuter	discutir

Comment
Make use of any knowledge you have of word formation in the foreign language and what you know about cognates to help you work out or 'create' the word you need. Practise paraphrasing (expressing things in different ways) in your own language as well as in the target language, so that you become adept at thinking on your feet as you speak.

PRONUNCIATION AND INTONATION

Pronunciation

Unlike other elements of a foreign language, such as grammar and vocabulary, which you will encounter progressively throughout your language studies, pronunciation is an aspect of language learning in which you are, as it were, thrown in at the deep end. However, don't forget that in most languages, there are only between 30 and 50 different sounds, and that most of them will be familiar to you already from your mother tongue. You may nevertheless encounter completely new sounds that don't exist in your own language, such as the French *u* in *super*, or the Spanish *rr* in *terraza*. You will also find that the subtle differences in familiar sounds can be just as problematic, such as the *o* in Spanish *rosa* which is similar to the *o* in *cot*, but which English speakers tend to pronounce like the *oe* in *toe*.

Intonation

Practising pronunciation is important because it enables you to get to grips with the specific sounds of the target language. But intonation, too, plays a central role, as illustrated in the following examples. It can:

- indicate emotions: intonation can express anger, interest, impatience, openness and many other attitudes and emotions. Try to express your emotions in the foreign language to make your speech more varied and less monotonous. You could try the following English sentence for practice, using the appropriate intonation to express anger, interest and impatience in turn: *What are you doing?*
- provide information on the grammatical structure of speech. For instance, it can be used to differentiate a statement from a question, e.g. *You're coming* and *You're coming?* or used to indicate an unfinished sentence: *Well, I don't know what to say . . .*
- give prominence to specific elements by stressing certain words, e.g. *He's meeting the director in Sheffield on Wednesday morning* or *I didn't say it was wrong* (I think it might be right) and *I didn't say it was wrong* (someone else did).

Improving your pronunciation and intonation

You will probably encounter a whole range of approaches to developing your awareness and your ability to reproduce sounds and words in order to communicate. These might include:

- 'Listen and repeat' exercises or drills: these exercises may focus on specific words or longer units, such as phrases or sentences. They are useful in helping you get your tongue round new or unfamiliar sounds or combinations of sounds. You might want to look at yourself in a mirror, feel your mouth and your throat when you practise new sounds, or record yourself and listen carefully to check your pronunciation. There are a number of electronic resources you can use to practise your pronunciation, including CD/DVD-ROMs, and web-based (CALL) materials (see Chapter 8).
- Phonetic training: explanation of how particular sounds are articulated, often illustrated by a diagram of the (relative) positions of the mouth and tongue, as in Figure 6.2.
- Use of the phonetic script, a way of representing the sounds in language – often used in dictionaries to help with pronunciation.
- Awareness-raising activities such as those suggested in Chapters 4 and 5: comparing the similarities and differences between the sound systems of your own language and the foreign language, or focusing on specific sounds in words.
- Reading aloud or listening to mini-dialogues to become aware of or practise pronunciation or intonation patterns in, for example, questions or statements.

Do not feel you have to measure yourself against the fluent speakers you are exposed to as models in the course materials. It is perfectly acceptable

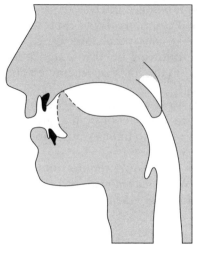

Articulación de [rr]

Figure 6.2 Diagram of how the sound [rr] is pronounced in Spanish.

to have an accent that is not identical to any given native accent, and indeed trying to imitate precisely the pronunciation of a mother tongue speaker can be a demotivating and unrealistic goal: it is far more important to concentrate on making yourself understood. It is also important to remember that native speakers may use a whole range of different varieties of the language, and have different accents, all of which are equally valid. A good language course should be presenting you with a variety of regional accents so that you are able to communicate with any speaker of the language.

ACCURACY AND FLUENCY

The terms accuracy and fluency are often contrasted with one another when referring to speaking or writing in another language. Accuracy refers to the use of correct grammatical forms and vocabulary. Fluency is concerned with communicating spontaneously and with ease. The two are complementary – each having a role in making yourself understood.

In the past, approaches to language teaching focused primarily on accuracy or 'getting things right', through formal exercises or drills, for example. Learners often found that real-life communication was difficult, even though they might 'know the rules'. By contrast, people who have learned a language through living in an environment in which it is spoken are often able to use the language fluently and spontaneously, if at times not entirely accurately. Typically then, if you focus exclusively on accuracy, you may jeopardize some of your fluency and vice versa. With practice and over time both will become more closely aligned, so that increasingly you are able to speak or write both accurately and fluently. Contemporary language courses recognize the importance of balancing the two, incorporating tasks which focus on producing language accurately, as well as those which encourage freer language production. It is important that you work on getting the sounds of the language right, but you must also think about the other elements that will make you sound fluent, such as being able to use common set phrases and discourse markers, as described earlier. The following are some activities you could try.

Using model texts

Model texts may take the form of oral recordings or written scripts. They can range from individual phrases to longer texts such as dialogues or speeches. Some recorded texts are designed to allow time for you to repeat given phrases, perhaps providing you with a further repetition of the expression for comparison. Even if this is not the case, you can still pause and repeat selected phrases yourself, and then listen to your efforts to see where you can improve.

Spoken and written model texts may also include gaps for you to complete with suitable words or expressions. This may involve changing words from singular to plural or masculine to feminine, as a means of practising agreements. Alternatively you might be required to transform verb forms from one tense to another, from active to passive voice or into 'reported speech'. Once you feel confident with these activities, you might try to reconstruct short texts from memory, whether orally or in writing. For more complex oral or written texts, you might find it helpful to note key points or expressions before attempting to reconstruct them yourself. Alternatively you could use given models as the basis of your own adapted versions, whether spoken or written.

Strategies for improving accuracy, fluency and pronunciation

Build your speaking skills from your listening. Focus on how the language sounds and the sort of things people actually say rather than learning just from the written word. Printed dialogues, for example, will normally omit hesitations and fillers, but these are a fundamental aspect of how people talk in the target language.

Sometimes it is helpful to concentrate on how the language sounds before seeing the printed word, as it can be tempting to pronounce words as you would in your own language rather than how they are pronounced in the target language. This is particularly the case when words look very similar, e.g. télévision (Fr), televisión (Sp).

continued

If you are studying a course that sometimes presents new material in the form of a spoken dialogue, you could try the following approach:

- Listen to the dialogue before reading it; this will help you focus on what the language sounds like.

- Listen to a short section and record yourself repeating it; this will help you to pronounce the sounds correctly.

- Read the dialogue silently and ensure you understand it; this will ensure you know what you are saying.

- Record yourself again, using the written dialogue as a prompt if necessary; this is the stage where you are combining knowing what you are saying with sounding fluent.

- Compare the model dialogue with your two recordings, and work on improving your version if necessary.

INTERACTING WITH OTHERS

Sounding and looking like a competent speaker of the target language

Do your best to sound, feel and look like a fluent target language speaker. Notice and adopt the typical gestures you have observed people using when speaking. Listen out for the routine expressions and utterances that target language speakers use. Try to mimic these, copying their pronunciation and intonation, and incorporating them into what you say.

Giving yourself thinking time: using fillers

When you are trying to work out how best to express yourself, you can use 'fillers' to good effect to stall and at the same time avoid long silences that break up the flow (see also Chapter 5, 'What do reading and listening involve?').

- A simple technique for English speakers is to replace the English *um* with the target language equivalent, e.g. *Do I think it's his best film . . . ? Well, I don't know . . . I . . . uh . . . I . . . didn't . . . I . . . uh . . . I haven't seen her . . . uh . . . his third film yet. So, um . . . I'm not sure, really.*
- Similarly, using various equivalents of the English filler *Well . . .* at the beginning of a response can be very effective in lending your speaking a fluent air: *Eh bien . . ., Alors . . .* (Fr); *Also . . ., Na ja . . .* (Ger); *Bueno . . ., Entonces . . .* (Sp), *Allora . . ., Così . . .* (It).

- Other typical English fillers include short set phrases such as: *That's an interesting question; Absolutely; I'm not sure, but . . .; To be honest . . .; I don't know; Yes, I think so; Really? Surely not!* The target language may not have direct translations of these phrases, but there will be others that fulfil the same purpose, e.g. in Arabic *Really?* is صحيح؟ (Sahiya?) and in French *Vraiment?*

- Make sure you know some set phrases relevant to the sort of conversation you might have, so that you can pull out ready-made chunks of language, rather than trying to construct something from individual words. Some phrases crop up in all sorts of conversations: *I wonder if you could help me?*

- Draw directly on the language directed at you in conversation. For example, if someone asked you: *Did you leave it in the bar?* you could respond with *Hm . . . Did I leave it in the bar . . .?* or even *. . . in the bar? . . . um . . .*

- Spend a little time early on in your language studies learning phrases to use when you are not sure you have understood: *Can you say that again, please? / I didn't quite understand / Where exactly . . .?*

You should also listen out in general for key items of vocabulary, pronunciation and grammatical forms, so that you have them in your 'language store' for when you need them.

Improving your accuracy and range

During a conversation, it is likely that if you make a mistake, the person you are speaking to will reformulate what you said in the correct form, not necessarily deliberately to correct you, but as a way of clarifying what you said. If you asked an English speaker, for example, *Excuse me, what time finishes the spectacle?* the question might be reformulated into *What time does the show finish?* as part of the reply. Although you may at first find it difficult to concentrate on the form as well as the content of what people say to you, a conversation is a very good opportunity for you to try out language, hear the correct form and reuse it, or at least store it away for future use. Often, a question asked of you can be answered using a similar structure. The following conversation illustrates how this might work with a learner of English (L) talking to a fluent speaker (F):

L: *That's where I falled off my bike . . .*
F: *You fell off your bike? What happened?*
L: *I don't know what happened. I turned too fast and suddenly I fell off.*

GETTING THE MESSAGE ACROSS

Using language in context

Many activities you do as part of your course are intended to prepare you for communication by focusing on specific aspects of the foreign language: the appropriate use of words or phrases, a particular grammar point or your pronunciation. But to communicate effectively in the language, you also need practice in coping with real-life tasks, that is, situations which involve using language in context. In real-life interactions the most important thing is getting your message across, rather than concentrating on correct verb endings or 'perfect' pronunciation.

When language is used in context – whether in your mother tongue or the language you are learning – several different things happen at the same time:

- You are aware of the situation in which you find yourself: who you are speaking to, where and when.
- You have an idea of the content of what you want to communicate.
- You put together the words or phrases you want to say.
- You articulate these words.

In your own language the elements lower down the list, such as finding the right words and saying them, are automatic, allowing greater attention to be paid to the content of the message. In the foreign language, focusing on situation and content, rather than struggling to formulate a 'correct' sentence, can help you communicate effectively.

Using the language you know

Learning a foreign language has similarities with learning your mother tongue as a child. Sometimes children may want to say something but may not yet have the right words or the complexity of language to do so accurately. They therefore try to make themselves understood with whatever linguistic means they have at their disposal. The reaction they receive is their best feedback and will influence their use of language in the future.

Chapter 1 points out the frustrations and difficulties you may experience as an adult language learner, because of the mismatch between the ideas you want to express and the language you have available to do so. Like children, you will at times have to 'make do' with what you can say. Although it is important to experiment with language and take some risks with what you say and write (see Chapter 3, 'Taking risks and learning from mistakes'), trying to go too far beyond your language level will not generally pay off. Remember too that complex concepts can often be expressed in simple words.

How not to get your message across

You are an English speaker on holiday abroad and have to drive to the nearest station to meet a friend. You would like to ask: *What's the best way of getting to the station?* and want to sound as polite and sophisticated as in your own language (a somewhat problematic notion as politeness is expressed differently in different cultures). Even if you have time to reach for your dictionary and attempt an exact translation, this is not likely to lead to the best possible result. In this particular case the first word already proves to be a major hurdle: *What* has several meanings and can usually be translated in different ways. Moreover, the whole construction is quite complex.

A much better approach would be to start not with the precise wording but with a general idea of what you want to say and then search your store of the foreign language for ways of expressing this idea. Depending on your level of language you might come up with just the name of the place you are looking for or a set phrase you know, e.g. *La gare, s'il vous plaît? Où est la gare, s'il vous plaît?* or *Pour aller à la gare, s'il vous plaît?* (Fr); *Der Bahnhof, bitte? Wo ist der Bahnhof, bitte?* or *Wie komme ich zum Bahnhof, bitte?* (Ger); *¿La estación, por favor? Perdone, ¿dónde está la estación?* or *Perdone, ¿por dónde se va a la estación?* (Sp). All of these are suitable ways of getting your message across. Using the language you know will make you much more comprehensible to a speaker of your target language than trying to translate unfamiliar items which can often lead you into a 'translation trap' (translating words literally).

Task 6.3 Using the target language

Think of two situations where you are likely to use the target language. Start making a list of useful expressions and sentences that you would use in these situations.

	Situation	What you might want to say
1	For beginners: booking a hotel room	
2	For more advanced learners: complaining about the state of your hotel room	

Understanding the reply

Getting your message across effectively is of course very satisfying, but it can lead to yet another difficulty: the other speaker may treat you as an advanced speaker of their language and may give a reply that is incomprehensible to you, because it is too fast or too complex or contains difficult vocabulary, or because you are simply not used to the accent or intonation. A successful exchange is one where you get your message across *and* get the information you need in return (see also Chapter 3, 'Knowing how to prepare yourself', on compensation strategies and Chapter 5, 'Before and after you read or listen', on anticipating what you may hear.)

Steps to successful communication

- Think about the situation (or, in a language learning context: make sure you have understood the task).

- Decide what needs saying.

- Draw on the language you have learned to formulate what you are going to say.

- Practise saying it in your head.

- Think about possible replies you might get.

- Prepare a response (e.g. *thank you*).

- Prepare an appropriate set phrase in case you have not understood.

- In cases of partial understanding: repeat back what you did understand.

- Try to incorporate useful expressions you hear during the interaction into your own replies.

PREPARING WHAT YOU WANT TO SAY OR WRITE

Making time to prepare

In your native language, it is helpful to know what you hope to say or write before you begin, particularly in an unfamiliar situation or one in which it matters how you put across your points, for example making a complaint, requesting a service or dealing with a sensitive topic. Whatever level you are working at in the target language, you will find that you communicate much more effectively if you take time to organize and structure your ideas in advance.

Conventions in speaking and writing

When you start learning a foreign language, it is not long before you notice differences in the way things are done in comparison with your own language. These can range from the way people answer the telephone or ask for goods in a shop to the way they structure a formal talk or letter.

Task 6.4 Reasons for writing and speaking

Consider the following common reasons for writing and speaking. Each of these situations has its own conventions – a specific structure, typical phrases and an expected tone. In each case, think about what these would be in your own language:

- a letter complaining about poor accommodation in a hotel;
- a telephone call to a friend who has just received bad news;
- a telephone order for goods from a catalogue;
- a job review meeting where your salary may or may not be increased;
- an email to a colleague with instructions on how to get to your house;
- a conversation with your neighbour's children about their new toys;
- a birthday card to a relative;
- a conversation at the doctor's about an illness;
- a conversation with a friend explaining a recipe.

Comment
Becoming aware of the conventions in your own language will help you to recognize those of the target language when you encounter them. If you become sensitive to this in the early stages of your language learning, you will find it easier to become attuned to more subtle and complex conventions as you progress.

Developing good reading and listening skills is, of course, central to improving the productive skills of speaking and writing, as discussed in Chapter 5. Even in a conversation, where you are faced with dealing with the unexpected, focusing not only on *what* people say to you but also on *how* they say it will help you to increase your range and accuracy and also to adopt an appropriate register and tone when you speak.

What applies to the real-life situations listed in Task 6.4 is also true for the tasks you may be asked to do in the course of your language studies. Many of the spoken presentations or pieces of writing that you are asked to produce as a language learner simulate real situations and their conventions, styles and formats. In preparing, planning and then drafting, where appropriate, it is important to recognize and be aware of the format that is expected – whether it is a short thank-you speech, an interview, a report, a description, an essay, an article, a letter or a poem.

Thinking about the content

Planning a spoken or written contribution very often starts with thinking around the topic. In some cases all you need to do is note down a few important points, but if, for example, you have been asked to write an essay, more extensive research may be needed.

Whether it be brainstorming the topic, discussing it with someone else, reading around it, or searching via the Web, the initial information-gathering stage is useful in drawing together what you know already with other ideas that emerge. You will find links and themes developing, and whether your brainstorming evolves into a list, a table or a mind map, it will be a useful way to generate ideas. For example, if you were asked to compare people's shopping habits in the western world now with twenty years ago, you might come up with a mind map or a table resembling the following:

Twenty years ago	Now
Corner shop	Online shopping
Paying cash	Credit cards
Knowing the shopkeeper personally	Big department stores
Quality products	More choice
Being able to ask for a credit	Special products, e.g. diet, organic
. . .	Cheaper products
	. . .

Thinking about the structure

Even short spoken or written contributions benefit from a coherent structure that has been thought through beforehand. For more complex tasks you may want to write a detailed plan. In the case of writing an essay or preparing an oral presentation, the title and task will usually give clues as to the format needed, and this will allow you to start plotting the lines of reasoning you will use. For example, it might imply an analytical approach, where you define the issues, summarize the main themes, present an analysis and critique, and end up with a viewpoint on the topic that may be your own or a synthesis of other viewpoints. Alternatively, it may be a narrative-type task that invites you to describe events chronologically and descriptively but without critical analysis.

It is a personal decision whether to produce a very detailed plan or whether to approach the task in a more spontaneous, organic way that involves perhaps more drafting and redrafting. There are different schools of thought on this, and trends have changed with the use of word-processing and other ICT tools. It is unlikely that you will produce a well-structured essay or presentation, however, without some form of plan. This may be keywords on a scrap of paper to help you remember the items that you will talk about spontaneously to a group, or it may be more detailed notes on a developed line of reasoning for a speech you are giving or recording. When writing, you may find that you keep revising your initial plan. On the computer you can do this with relative ease by cutting, pasting and rearranging parts of the text.

This does not mean that your initial plan was not useful. A plan can be a good antidote to the proverbial writer's block – it can help to break down what seems to be a daunting undertaking into smaller more manageable tasks. A plan is also a lot easier to redraft than an extended piece of written or oral work.

Beginning with the basics: a beginning, middle and end

When presenting a topic orally or in writing, the beginning is used to present the topic, the middle to develop and expand on it and the end to come to some sort of conclusion. This is standard in planned presentations and essays, but you may also find a similar pattern when listening to conversations, watching news reports or reading letters or newspaper articles. If you are writing or speaking in a situation where there is no opportunity for interaction, such as writing a letter or giving a brief presentation to express your views about something, it is important not only that you introduce and conclude what you have to say but also that your middle section is clear and coherent.

At more advanced levels when you are dealing with complex material, particularly if you are trying to put forward a case for something where there may be opposing views, it helps to think of your 'text' as a discussion. One way of doing this is to imagine you are talking with a group of people. You put forward an opinion, and someone challenges you with a counter-argument. Someone else accuses you of being biased for various reasons. Another person introduces a whole new angle on the topic. Giving a talk or writing an essay is about gathering together all these characteristics of a discussion and presenting them coherently. Because your audience cannot raise objections and ask questions directly, you have to anticipate and address these in what you say or write.

Awareness of audience and purpose

You would not normally talk in the same way to a close friend as you would to a complete stranger. Similarly, your purpose in writing or speaking, such as requesting information or complaining about how you have been treated, will have a bearing on what you say and how you say it. Consider the following questions:

What is your purpose?

- Are you trying to persuade, inform, complain, ask for advice . . .?
- What does your role in a conversation involve? What is the context?
- What are the linguistic resources you need to achieve your purpose? Do your textbook, grammar book or dictionary provide appropriate expressions?

Who is your audience?

- What tone, register and forms of address are appropriate for your audience?
- How will you make sure your audience follows you and is interested in what you have to say?
- Do you know how to interpret the body language of your audience and how to adjust yours accordingly? In some cultures, for example, interest is shown by looking at the speaker, whilst in others it is considered disrespectful to do so. You will need to become aware of these conventions by paying close attention to what you read, hear and see in the target language as well as by noting any information provided in your course or other materials.
- Sometimes you might have to anticipate how your audience is going to react. You may need to explain a complex term, use rhetorical questions to interest the audience in what you are about to say or pre-empt any counter-arguments.

A good way to prepare is to imagine yourself as one of the people you are addressing, which means that you will need to pay attention to any cultural conventions that differ from your own. Ask yourself some of the following questions:

- How would I like to be addressed?
- What sort of tone would I respond most positively to?
- How would I like the topic to be presented to gain my interest?
- What sort of arguments would convince me?

Strategies to develop planning and sequencing skills

1 Draw up a plan which reflects the structure of one of the following:
    - a recent discussion you have heard;
    - a documentary you have watched;
    - a letter you have read;
    - a newspaper article.

2 Make a photocopy of a text in either the foreign language or in your own. Without reading it, cut it up into paragraphs. Lay all the paragraphs out, read them and put them into a logical sequence. Compare your finished product with the original. Which sequence works best and why?

3 Read or listen to some material in the target language and create a detailed plan which reflects its overall structure. Rewrite or record your own version following the same plan, and compare your version with the original, noting in both versions phrases and vocabulary that you particularly like.

Strategies to help with composition

To avoid the problem of thinking in your mother tongue and translating your ideas literally:

1 Work from the plan you have prepared in the target language. This will contain the key linguistic elements and ideas and possibly some set phrases you can include.

2 If you are using a word processor, open various documents at the same time: a target language plan, lists or tables of useful phrases and a blank document for composing your text. You can then copy and paste as necessary.

3 Keep a list to hand of key differences between your own language and the target language that you have particular difficulty with. If you are a native English speaker, for example, these might include how to express the English continuous tenses *I was going, I am going, I will be going*, etc. and formation of the future and conditional tenses: do you add endings to the verb or is there a separate word for *will/shall* and *would*?

continued

4 Try to ensure that what you write is grammatically possible. Rephrase complex sentences into chunks that you know to be correct, e.g. *My ideal holiday would be spent lying on the beach on a sun-drenched island*, to *I would spend / my ideal holiday / on a sun-drenched island*.

Strategies to encourage self-correction

1 Draw up a list of key grammatical areas to check, e.g. verb agreements, adjective agreements, tenses, genders, etc., remembering to include particular difficulties you have. Check for one category of error at a time, leaving as much time as possible between composing and your grammar check.

2 Check that the language you have used is accurate, e.g.:

- Do my nouns and verbs agree?
- Are my adjective endings correct?
- Are the tenses I used consistent?
- Is the word order correct?

3 If you have access to a foreign-language grammar and spellchecker on a computer, use these to check your work, remembering that neither is perfect.

4 In revising work, focus on one area you know you have difficulty with, for example, a certain tense, adjective agreements or word order.

5 When you have used the methods above for spotting errors or have received some feedback from a tutor, try to categorize your errors to help you learn from them (see Chapter 9).

SPEAKING AND WRITING FROM NOTES

Making notes to organize your thoughts

As Chapter 3, 'Making and keeping notes', explains, notes are useful for supporting your language study in many different ways. You may be making very quick notes in preparation for a spoken exchange or writing more detailed and sequenced notes for a lengthy essay or report to be submitted at a later stage. In the latter case, you will probably go through several stages in your note-taking. As you gather more information on the topic from either written or spoken sources you will add points which may be more relevant and delete others which have become redundant. You will also change the structure of your notes as you think through the task and refine your approach. At a later stage you may also choose to jot down specific phrases, idioms and vocabulary which you wish to use in the final piece of work. The more adept you become at all of this, the better your final piece of work will be.

Task 6.5 Using notes

List a few situations in your everyday life where you use notes to help you focus your thoughts in preparation for a task. Have you got any examples of notes you made recently?

Comment
You will probably find that your notes are structured in different ways depending on the nature of the task. For instance, you might have listed the points in order of importance or in a logical sequence. You may have grouped items under headings or put questions you want to ask during a telephone conversation in chronological order.

The type of work you need to produce undoubtedly influences the way you organize your notes. In early stages of language learning, you will be dealing with basic situations and tasks and your notes may simply reflect the content points you wish to include, which you can tick off as you cover them. If you are a more advanced learner planning to produce an oral report or discursive essay, your notes will have to reflect the structure you wish to follow. If you are involved in comparing views then be sure to indicate both sides of the argument clearly. You have already seen that charts or tables are often good for this. Here is another example of notes, this time preparing a first draft of arguments on the advantages and disadvantages of shopping in supermarkets.

Pros	Cons
large selection of products	staff not always friendly
cheaper than local shops	excessive packaging
all in one place	accessible only by car
saves time	further away than local shops
parking spaces	no fresh local produce

The next stage might be to take each of the advantages and disadvantages in turn and to develop a mind map round each of them. Figure 6.3 shows an example:

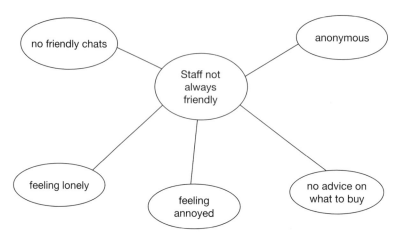

Figure 6.3 Brainstorming ideas for an essay.

You may prefer to write your notes in the target language from the start, so that you start thinking in the language and avoid the trap of translating words literally. Of course, you may occasionally want to jot down some ideas in your own language, but generally target language notes give you a head start by providing the linguistic basis for your speaking or writing.

Using your notes

When speaking or writing from notes, you will need to consider the conventions described above and make your contribution interesting to your audience. In written contributions your audience usually expects fully formed sentences which are grammatically correct and coherent. Formulating spoken language from notes is quite a different process, as the language contains some features that are unacceptable in written language, such as repetitions, incomplete sentences and unconventional word order. At the same time, you have other means at your disposal to get your message across and capture your audience: stress, intonation and gesture are as important as the words you choose.

Incorporating language from other sources into your speech or writing

When making a longer contribution, such as giving an oral presentation or writing an essay, you will probably base some of your content on source materials, for example a radio programme or an article. You can incorporate some of the language used in these materials into your own speech or writing, such as vocabulary relevant to the topic, set phrases or structures that you have come across in your reading and listening.

Reusing language from source materials does not mean copying whole sentences word for word. Indeed, in institutional settings you will be penalized for doing this, unless you use quotation marks. Noting down key points first and then formulating your contribution from your notes will help you find your own way of expressing yourself rather than directly copying from other texts.

Delivering oral presentations

Oral presentations are required in many language courses, as well as in other environments. They require planning and structuring, and the language is expected to be more 'polished' than in informal spoken interaction.

Tips for oral presentations

- Think of your audience first: what are they likely to find interesting? How does it need to be structured? What visual aids should you use?

- When preparing your notes, index cards are useful for each section or point you wish to cover. Large sheets of paper are not as easy to use as you can lose your way.

- Try not to make your notes too detailed or too complex or your writing too small, as visual clarity is very important when you are speaking with notes. Full sentences are not helpful, as you won't have time to make sense of them if you are put on the spot. In addition, if you read from them without looking up, your presentation will become monotonous and your intonation inappropriate. If it is an assessed language task you may also lose marks.

- As note-taking tools, mind maps have an added benefit (see Chapter 3, 'Different ways of making notes'): they can help you memorize the points you wish to make. This will make you more assured when giving your presentation and you will be less reliant on your notes.

- Flow charts can be more useful when adopting a chronological or linear sequence (see Chapter 3, 'Different ways of making notes').

continued

- Highlighting key words or those that you find difficult to say can also be helpful.

- If you are interpreting points from written texts, you may have to modify the way you express these points to suit the spoken medium.

- You may also wish to make a note of when to pause and breathe to allow your audience to absorb your points.

- Speak slowly and clearly and stress important facts and arguments, otherwise vital information may be lost on your audience.

- Look at your notes only if you need to and at your audience as much as possible.

MAKING YOUR SPEECH AND WRITING FLOW

Keeping to the point and presenting a coherent argument

In any number of situations in the world outside your language studies, you may need to be able to put forward a clear case, for example you might want to complain about a faulty shower in your hotel, discuss lack of progress on alterations to your property or write a formal letter to the appropriate body to protest about something. Whether you are dealing with a real situation or doing a language task, it is important to check that what you write or say is coherent, consistent and relevant. Each section needs to follow logically from the previous one and your conclusions must be in agreement with what you have already said and be derived from the points you have made previously. To check this, there are some key questions to consider when planning and reviewing:

- Do I know what my view or argument is?
- How clear is this to my audience?
- Have I shown my audience how one point follows on from the next?
- Have I used evidence to support what I have said?
- Does everything I have included refer to the overall question or point?
- Does my conclusion follow logically from what I have said before?
- Am I sure that my presentation or writing does not contradict itself?

Using 'discourse markers' to help your audience find their way through

As mentioned earlier ('Remembering and recalling words and phrases'), discourse markers are an excellent device for structuring your work and improving fluency. If you use them appropriately to guide your audience, they will not have to work out for themselves how one point relates to another and your arguments will come over clearly and coherently.

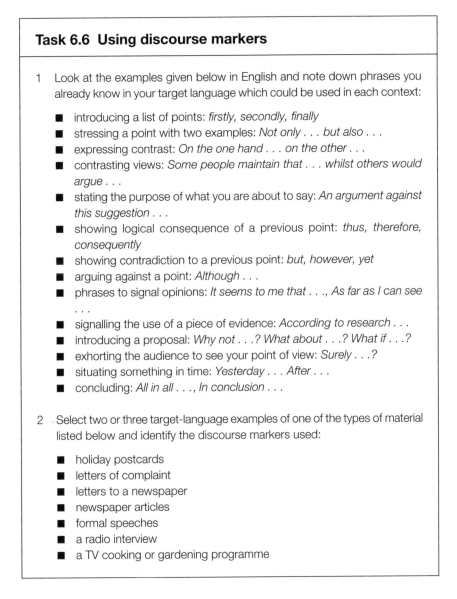

Task 6.6 Using discourse markers

1   Look at the examples given below in English and note down phrases you already know in your target language which could be used in each context:

   ■   introducing a list of points: *firstly, secondly, finally*
   ■   stressing a point with two examples: *Not only . . . but also . . .*
   ■   expressing contrast: *On the one hand . . . on the other . . .*
   ■   contrasting views: *Some people maintain that . . . whilst others would argue . . .*
   ■   stating the purpose of what you are about to say: *An argument against this suggestion . . .*
   ■   showing logical consequence of a previous point: *thus, therefore, consequently*
   ■   showing contradiction to a previous point: *but, however, yet*
   ■   arguing against a point: *Although . . .*
   ■   phrases to signal opinions: *It seems to me that . . ., As far as I can see . . .*
   ■   signalling the use of a piece of evidence: *According to research . . .*
   ■   introducing a proposal: *Why not . . .? What about . . .? What if . . .?*
   ■   exhorting the audience to see your point of view: *Surely . . .?*
   ■   situating something in time: *Yesterday . . . After . . .*
   ■   concluding: *All in all . . ., In conclusion . . .*

2   Select two or three target-language examples of one of the types of material listed below and identify the discourse markers used:

   ■   holiday postcards
   ■   letters of complaint
   ■   letters to a newspaper
   ■   newspaper articles
   ■   formal speeches
   ■   a radio interview
   ■   a TV cooking or gardening programme

STYLE AND REGISTER

Style

Writers or speakers can shape what they are communicating and influence their audience by using different stylistic features. You can change the focus of what you are communicating by giving prominence to specific elements of a sentence – by changing the word order, by highlighting specific elements using adverbs or other devices, or by using a passive instead of an active construction. For instance, in the sentence *The president has been assassinated by freedom fighters*, the use of the passive stresses that it is the president who has been killed; in the sentence *Freedom fighters have assassinated the president*, which uses an active construction, the 'doers' of the action, i.e. the freedom fighters, are given prominence.

At higher levels you can use **rhetorical devices** to persuade people, or to engage them in what you are communicating. Below you will find some of the most common rhetorical devices, with examples in English. You may find similar devices in authentic texts of the language you are learning or you may become aware of others not used in English:

- Choice of vocabulary: this will depend on the tone, the purpose, or the context, for example.
- Sound patterns, such as the use of alliteration (*six sizzling sausages swimming in a pan*) or onomatopoeia (*Bang!*) for specific effects.
- The use of metaphors, e.g. *You are my sunshine*; similes: *as pretty as a picture*; personification: *She's a great little car*, etc.
- Rhetorical questions: these are commonly used both in speaking and writing to introduce an argument or a topic and are often used as the final sentence of one paragraph, with the subsequent paragraph addressing the issue raised in the question. Rhetorical questions do not always have to be answered. In some cases they are used to end a presentation or an article in order to leave the audience with a question in their mind, for example: *But at what cost? When will we know for sure? Is this really what we want for our children's children? What changes will you be making?*
- Structural devices that organize the discourse. These include:
  - using repetition for stress: persuasive speaking often uses repetition to stress a point. This can often be heard in speeches made by politicians and may even be accompanied by banging fists on the table for extra emphasis, for example: *We will cut crime, we will cut violence and we will cut fear.*
  - using contrasting mirror sentences: a mirror sentence is one where the structure of both halves is identical. If the two halves have identical structure but contrasting content, then this can create a powerful effect, for example: *Mankind must put an end to war or war will put an end to mankind* (John F. Kennedy).

Register

Register, as Chapter 4, 'The social and cultural role of language', briefly explains, describes the variations in language according to use:

- The mode: either written or spoken. The conventions used in these two modes vary. Think, for instance, of how you end a telephone conversation as opposed to a letter.
- The manner: the relationship between the participants, which can be formal or informal. Compare for instance an email to a friend, which will be informal and personal, and an essay written for an exam, which will be more formal and not seek to develop a personal relationship with the reader.
- The field: the area, the subject matter. In a report about the ecological threats of mass tourism, for instance, you could use vocabulary specific to environmental science, which would not be appropriate or relevant in other contexts.

It is important, to remember that features of style and register differ across languages and cultures, and that what is appropriate or effective in one is not necessarily valid in another. The passive is used in English much more than in Spanish, for example, so a direct translation of that form is not always appropriate.

Improving style and register

1 Select a text. Highlight in different colours all the phrases the author uses to show:

  a an opinion;
  b a generally held view;
  c the use of evidence;
  d an appeal to the reader;
  e a link between ideas;
  f time and location.

2 Practise using some of these phrases in writing and speaking with topics of your choosing: e.g. *Not only* was the campsite dirty *but also* noisy and overcrowded. *Surely* you do not expect anyone who has stayed here to recommend this site? *In my view*, the reality did not match the description in the brochure at all. *On page 6*, for example, it is described as 'peaceful and relaxing'. *In the circumstances*, I request a 50 per cent refund.

continued

3   Create handwritten grids or set up tables in a word-processing document, as follows:

  - synonyms for common words, e.g. *be, have, like, want*;
  - phrases to express agreement, disagreement, evidence, etc.;
  - phrases for certain contexts, e.g. welcomes, thanks, business letters.

4   Print or write out the useful phrases in 3 above on pieces of card, with your mother-tongue equivalent on the back if that would help, and make up various ways to practise them.

EVALUATING YOUR WRITING AND SPEAKING

This involves being aware of the accuracy and fluency of your language, the clarity of your ideas, and the factors influencing style and register, such as your audience and the purpose of your communication. You should also incorporate feedback from your teacher or from others into your subsequent speaking or writing.

Checklist: monitoring and evaluating your work

- What was the purpose of my writing/speaking, and have I fulfilled it?
- Have I taken my audience into account?
- Have I answered the question/carried out the task fully?
- Have I got my message across?
- Have I kept to the point?
- Are my arguments coherent?
- Are my ideas well organized with appropriate links?
- Is the language I have used fluent?
- Have I used natural-sounding collocations and set phrases?
- Is the language I have used accurate?
  - Do my nouns and verbs agree?
  - Are my adjective endings correct?

    – Are the tenses I have used consistent?

    – Is the word order correct?

(You may wish to create your own checklist, depending on the language you are learning and your level.)

Summary of key points

- Language does not occur in isolation. The context in which it is used forms an integral part of its meaning.

- You will always understand more language than you can actively use.

- Being exposed to language on the one hand and practising it on the other will together help develop your ability to understand and produce it.

- Collocations and set phrases are key features of natural language use.

- You can practise language either by concentrating on individual elements (for example a grammar point) or by simulating more realistic situations. Both are important to make your language more accurate and fluent and to prepare you for language use in real contexts.

- Different situations and audiences call for different uses of language in terms of style and degree of formality.

- When preparing a presentation or extended piece of writing, the time spent on planning and note-taking will be invaluable.

- You can use a variety of strategies to improve your spoken or written language in order to capture and maintain the attention of your audience.

7

The world as a classroom

James A. Coleman and Uwe Baumann

Language learning can be greatly enhanced by what you do outside the classroom or beyond your study materials, whether or not you are following a formal course. What is learned is not necessarily the same as what is taught. It can be much more or much less, depending on whether you seize the opportunities available to you and use the language you are learning.

In many ways, learning a language is like learning to play tennis, or to drive a rally car. Formal tuition in whatever form can take you so far, but only real-life practice can speed up your reactions and make your responses fluent and automatic. This chapter shows you what real-life resources are available to you, and how you can use them to build your confidence and your capacity to deal with the kind of written and spoken language a competent speaker of your target language would use.

WHY USE REAL-LIFE MATERIALS?

You have probably found out for yourself that spending hours over grammar books or vocabulary lists contributes only so much to developing your competence in the language you are learning. Memorizing the rules governing word endings, tenses or adjective agreement provides you with knowledge of how certain features are used, but it may not always help you when you want to respond spontaneously. Of course, knowing how language rules operate is vital for anyone learning a foreign language. You can use this knowledge to analyse the meaning of what you hear or read, and to check that what you write or say is as correct as you can make it. However, remember the advice in Chapter 6 about the need for a balance between fluency and accuracy, and the importance of not emphasizing accuracy at the expense of fluency. There is more to learning a language.

After all, how much do most of us know about the formal grammar of our own language? For example, how many people who speak English as their mother tongue could explain to a learner of English the difference between these sentences, when one or the other might be more appropriate, and why?

Often I've been to the cinema.
I've often been to the cinema.
I've been often to the cinema.
I've been to the cinema often.

The fact is that using a language well is a matter of *feel* as much as *knowledge.*

There are at least two approaches to foreign language learning.

- The first recognizes that because adults have fully formed brains, they cannot learn a foreign language in the same way as they learned their mother tongue as children. This approach initially requires *conscious learning* of grammar and vocabulary (e.g. verb forms, word order, agreements and so on) but suggests that, through practice, the things you learn consciously can gradually become more automatic, more intuitive (see Chapter 1, 'What does learning a language involve?').
- The other approach is similar to that of a baby *unconsciously absorbing* the language. As you hear and read the foreign language, seeking meaning above all, your brain discerns and stores patterns which you recognize more easily a second time. Over time, these patterns can not only be effortlessly deciphered when others say or write them, but they become part of your own growing repertoire when you speak or write.

In both approaches, learning happens through use. The more you use the language, both receptively (reading and listening) and productively (speaking and writing), the more effortlessly you will be able to handle it. Real-life language resources increase your opportunities to use the language. There are lots of them readily available once you start looking. They can not only improve your language skills but also increase the enjoyment and motivation you derive from language learning.

A FEW PRINCIPLES

The first principle is to take advantage of opportunities. It is surprising how much foreign language material is available. You are likely to be able to find books, newspapers, magazines and product descriptions or instructions in the language you are learning without having to travel to a country where it is spoken. You may also be able to access cable television channels, websites or see foreign films at a local cinema. There may be speakers of your target language living nearby. It is up to you to make the most of all the opportunities available.

People who have learned a language well often get annoyed to be told, 'you're lucky to be able to speak such good Italian/Japanese/Norwegian'. Luck has little part in learning a foreign language. Indeed, research has shown that there is probably no such thing as luck in our everyday lives. What is called 'luck' is a combination of opportunities and the readiness to take advantage of those opportunities.

Principle 1: identify and seize the target language opportunities available to you.

Task 7.1 Identifying target language opportunities

Make a short list of target language opportunities available to you under these headings:

What have I got at home/access to from home?

What is available locally/within a reasonable distance?

Comment
Your list is a good start. Keep a look out for other opportunities which may arise.

Some learners use these opportunities as a background to their language learning, for example, leaving an Italian radio station playing while they do the ironing, or reading *Paris Match* once a month. This can be effective, allowing them to gradually absorb language as described earlier, but it can take a long time.

You can speed things up by taking an *active* approach to the language in the world about you. Set yourself an active task and you become more involved, your attention is more focused, your brain busier. Your imagination is the only limit to the tasks you can devise. You could summarize a film plot for a friend, explain the latest political scandal in a newspaper to a colleague at work or list the adjectives used in TV adverts. Chapter 5 suggests ways of creating your own activities using real-life reading and listening materials, while Chapter 6 describes some strategies for improving your fluency and coping in real-life interaction with other speakers of the language. There are more suggestions later in this chapter, and you will no doubt add others of your own.

Principle 2: take an active not a passive approach.

Task 7.2 Active tasks

Think of three more active tasks you could carry out using target language TV or radio programmes, newspapers or magazines.

Comment

If you need some more ideas, look at the following sections on using TV, radio, newspapers and magazines.

This may sound like hard work. It is, or at least it can be. That is why it pays off. But this is all the more reason to make it as attractive as possible. If you do not keep up your own motivation, you will soon be tempted to do something easier and spend less time on your language learning. Have you ever wondered why, when UK high street bookshops sell thousands of foreign language packs every year, all promising to have learners speaking Greek, Russian or French in three weeks, many people continue to speak in English when they go abroad? It comes down to effort and confidence. Effort is a matter of motivation. Keep up your motivation, and you will find the time necessary to improve. As you notice improvement, so your confidence grows, increasing your motivation at the same time.

Maintaining motivation means finding tasks and materials which are right for *you*. If you are keen on gardening or photography, order a specialist magazine in the language you are learning. If you like romantic fiction, buy a few titles in the target language from a bookshop or an Internet retailer, or ask your library to get them for you. If you are interested in politics, check the websites of the main political parties or look at the political columns in a newspaper. If celebrities fascinate you, find photos and magazine articles about them or look at the websites for their fans and email your own contribution.

Level is important too. It can be demotivating to struggle with material which is too advanced or complex. But that does not restrict you to basic textbooks with audio material. There are real-life materials which are accessible to even absolute beginners. Holiday brochures, children's picture books or cartoons in the language you are learning can offer you authentic material which is relatively easy to understand. If you have moved on from being an absolute beginner you could use videos or DVDs which often come with optional subtitles or soundtracks. You can watch the film in your own language with subtitles in the foreign language or vice versa, or watch *and* have the subtitles in the foreign language at the same time. Many books are published with parallel mother tongue and foreign language texts, or you may be able to obtain your favourite novel in a target language translation. Even radio and television programmes can be accessible. The formats for popular quiz shows have been sold across the world, and the language used is fairly predictable. You will be surprised at how much you can understand, and this will make you feel good, strengthening your sense of achievement and hence your ongoing motivation.

Principle 3: keep up your motivation by choosing real-life materials and tasks which reflect your own interests and level of proficiency.

The final principle follows on from the question of motivation, and is a matter of personal preference. When you are using real-life materials, should you focus on the meaning or on the language forms? In other words, how far should you try to forget that you are learning Japanese, Hindi or Greek, for example, and simply seek to enjoy a film without worrying about understanding every word? Chapter 6 explains the need to balance accuracy and fluency, but in general, meaning and fluency come first when you are using real-life language opportunities. After all, your reason for learning the language in the first place is to understand or communicate meaning.

This does not mean that attention to language is unimportant. Your textbook or language classes will often involve work with texts or video, initially focusing on meaning, but then looking in more detail at the language forms used, for example, to express opinions, or to link one idea to the next. You can do the same with real-life spoken or written texts, adding the conscious learning approach to the unconscious learning approach by looking at how speakers of the target language use a particular form of the language you are studying to express a particular meaning. For instance, if a character in a detective story asks a question, such as *Why did you go to Barcelona by car yesterday?*, what matters first is to grasp the relevance of this question to the plot. Then, for example, if you are learning French and have been studying question forms, you might look at how the question is asked. Does the character use inverted word order or just intonation? *Pourquoi êtes-vous . . .* or *Pourquoi vous êtes allé(é) à Barcelone en voiture?* Why might this be? Alternatively if you are learning German and have been studying the order of adverbs, look at how the question shows the 'rule' in practice, i.e. time before manner before place, *Warum sind Sie gestern mit dem Auto nach Barcelona gefahren?*

Principle 4: focus primarily on meaning, but look out for examples of the forms you have learned and how they are used to convey meaning.

The four key principles for using the world as a classroom

1   Identify and seize the target language opportunities available to you.

2   Take an active not a passive approach.

3   Keep up your motivation by choosing authentic materials and tasks which reflect your own interests and level of proficiency.

4   Focus primarily on meaning, but look out for examples of the forms you have learned and how they are used to convey meaning.

Task 7.3 Applying the key principles

Look at the opportunities you identified in Task 7.1. Then look at Chapter 4, 'Defining your priorities'. Choose one of your priorities and answer these questions:

■   Which real-life language opportunity will you use to help you reach your goal? (Think about your interests and your level of language.)
■   In what ways can you make *active* use of this opportunity? (Look at your ideas in Task 7.2.)
■   When are you going to do this and how often?

Comment
By making these decisions, you are forming an 'action plan' to achieve your goal by using real-life language opportunities. Your own plan depends on your circumstances and interests, but here is an example:

A beginner learner of Italian decided to get some brochures from tourist offices in Italy because she was planning a holiday. She aimed to summarize the places of interest in each city over a period of two weeks and make a chart to help her decide where to go. While she was looking at the brochures she noticed some adjectives used to describe the cities which she could use in her language class where she was learning how to describe places. She made a note of them.

TELEVISION AND VIDEO

Getting started

If you live in an area that has cable TV or if you have satellite TV, foreign programmes including films are available. Many foreign language channels are available to subscribers at no extra cost, so check what is on offer. Alternatively, for a little extra money and without any subscription, you can probably get an additional receiver on your dish to pick up programmes from other satellites, e.g. Astra and Eutelsat in the UK. Programme guides are published in most newspapers, satellite TV magazines and online.

Foreign language DVDs and videos can be purchased abroad or online through Internet retailers. Different standards have been adopted around the world, both for DVD and for video, so before you purchase anything, make sure the DVD or video you are buying is compatible with your equipment. Multi-standard players are available but may be more expensive than ordinary machines.

Task 7.4 Foreign TV stations

Find out which TV stations you can access in the language you are learning.

Comment
Your cable or satellite provider should be able to advise if you are already a subscriber, or consult a local retailer/installer.

Video recorders and read/write DVD players offer language learners a number of advantages. First of all, you can record a TV programme and watch it as often as you like. Programmes are professionally made to be interesting and entertaining in their own right. They provide an unending variety of speakers, young and old, male and female, and, in many cases, from different regions around the world where the language is spoken. Subtitles are used increasingly, and seeing the speakers' lips move can help you recognize individual sounds and words. You also see speakers moving and gesturing, and the situation in which the conversation is taking place. With images supporting the content of the speech, it is much easier to deduce the meaning than on radio, for instance.

Types of TV broadcast

Newscasts are perhaps the easiest to find and one of the most obvious programme types to use, although they can present particular challenges for language learners. The newsreader is, by definition, reading a script rather than speaking spontaneously, so the language does not have all the little hesitations, pauses and repetitions which slow down natural speech and sometimes make it easier to understand. Newsreaders speak rapidly, and the use of film clips from different locations means there are lots of voice-overs where you cannot see the speaker, and inevitable background noises can make understanding difficult. News items can often take local knowledge for granted, such as which government post an interviewee holds, or which new piece of proposed legislation has brought workers out on strike. Unless you live in the country, you may not have such back-ground information, although this can be a good way to acquire it. On the other hand, international stories which you are already aware of will be much easier to follow.

One way of making sense of news bulletins is to construct a factual grid to aid your understanding, as shown in Task 7.5.

Task 7.5 Working with television news

Check your understanding of a television news item using the following grid. Try it with an item in your own language first, then one in your target language.

What?	Why?	When?	How?	Where?	Who?

Comment
Both the content of the news and the way it is presented (the choice of items, relative importance given to local, regional and national stories, treatment of politicians, impartiality or bias, etc.) give you an insight into the cultures whose language you are studying.

Adverts provide some of the best television. They have to, given how expensive each second is to make and transmit. Usually the visuals and the words have to convey the same message, which helps comprehension, although sometimes they move too fast or have music or sound effects which can be an obstacle. Since adverts are designed to sell products or services, they may give an insight into the lifestyles of some target language speakers. You can also compare and contrast the use of publicity, the approaches adopted by advertisers, or how the same product is sold in your own country and in the country where your target language is spoken. Once again, a comprehension grid as in Task 7.6 can help.

Task 7.6 Using a comprehension grid with adverts

Record some TV adverts. Use the grid below to check that you understand what they are about.

Product name
Product type
Features or qualities highlighted
Target buyer or user (not necessarily the same!)
Appeal (to science/greed/laziness/fantasy/ sexuality/snobbery, etc.)
Presentation (humorous, factual, mini-soap, sexist stereotypes, etc.)
Language (key words, slogans, etc.)

Comment

Adverts can provide useful models for pronunciation, intonation and fluency. Listen to the slogan and imitate the speaker as closely as possible. With several attempts, you should get close to the sounds and speed of the original. TV adverts can also help you get used to which adjectives are used to complement which nouns. Try scripting your own advert if you enjoy being creative.

Feature films also lend themselves to a file-card or grid approach. For example, you could record the title, genre, date, period set, summary of story as well as more interpretative comments on actors, costumes, music, camera work, what you did or did not like.

Soaps are an excellent source of the language of everyday life. How do people say *hello* and *goodbye*, *sorry* or *thank you*? How do they answer the phone, start or finish a phone call? How do they invite, accept, refuse, argue, express their love, their friendship or their hatred? Soaps offer you some insight into the everyday lives of people in the countries whose language you are learning. Foreign language soaps can become addictive, which is great for your language learning!

Task 7.7 Working with feature films

Devise your own grid or file-card system for recording information about the feature films you watch. Test it first with a film in your own language, then use it for target language films.

Comment
You can use your summary as a prompt when you tell others about the film.

WORKING WITH VIDEO CLIPS OF ALL KINDS

There are many fun activities you can do with recorded video clips, whatever the type of programme. Some of them involve prediction (see Chapter 5, 'Active reading and listening'). As well as providing quite a few laughs, prediction can help you read non-linguistic clues which aid understanding or focus on language forms by comparing your predicted expressions with those of the video characters.

Predicting with and without sound

Choose a short piece of recorded video, maybe a news item or a dialogue scene from a film, and watch it a few times with the *sound off*. Try to work out what is probably being said, and work up your own target language script, checking structures and vocabulary as necessary. Then watch the scene with the *sound on*. Compare your version with the real soundtrack, noting any differences in the words and phrases used.

Predicting with a partner

A variation on the previous suggestion involves working with a partner. Without listening to the soundtrack, both of you choose a short video extract and prepare an imaginary script based on the pictures alone. Listen on your own to the soundtrack of your partner's extract, turning your back on the television and imagining what is happening on the screen. Then switch off the video and bring your partner back into the room. Use the target language to try to put together what you have heard (but not seen) and what your partner has seen (but not heard) in order to reconstruct the whole piece, before comparing it with the real broadcast. Reverse the roles and do the same with the other extract.

Predicting headlines and what happens next

Another variation of this activity is simply to watch the headlines of a recorded newscast, and, either alone or with a friend, script what you expect the item to be about. You can also use this as a starting point for vocabulary work. If the headline is 'rail chaos' or 'new ideas at the local school', what words would you expect to hear? Do you know them all in the language you are learning? Look up any you may not know before watching the piece. Or you could watch the first exchanges of an interview and ask each other what happens next. Invent some questions and answers and compare them with the reality. You can also try this with recordings of films, soaps, sporting events, etc. Simply stop the recording after a short extract and discuss what happens next. This is a valuable exercise. In real-life conversations, without being conscious of it, listeners are constantly trying to infer what is coming next. This helps them to understand and to respond quickly and spontaneously.

Using video for speaking practice

Other speakers of your target language are an excellent model for your pronunciation and intonation. But be aware that, as noted in Chapter 6, 'Improving your pronunciation and intonation', they may speak one of a number of different varieties of the language. Listen several times to a short speech or dialogue, then use the pause button to repeat after the character on screen. Practise with a friend and then, with the sound turned off, imagine you are providing a new soundtrack to the great love scene or the confrontation between the baddies!

Other active ways of using video

As you can see, using foreign language video is not necessarily a passive activity. There are other ways of making sure you are really concentrating on how people communicate in the language. Try writing a summary of a news item or documentary. Again you can compare the results with a friend. This can become more sophisticated if you watch an extract several times, concentrating on the essentials (gist comprehension) the first time through, and adding detail at each viewing. You could ask yourself the following questions:

- What is the theme?
- What is the presenter's argument?
- How does s/he support the argument?
- What are the examples s/he mentions?

You can also look at the language:

- How does s/he introduce an example . . .
- . . . or a contrast?
- How does s/he link one point to the next?

More advanced students can learn a lot about style and register (see Chapter 6) from this kind of linguistic analysis. How formal is the situation? Why do they use *tu*, *tú* or *du*, for example? Often the conventions for how to behave, such as giving thanks, accepting an invitation or greeting a friend or colleague, differ from one country to another, and appreciating these distinctions moves you closer to the people of the country concerned.

Any broadcast can be a basis for discussion with a partner, both of the content, and of many other aspects. Stretch your vocabulary by trying to describe the background music, or the mood of a particular scene. After watching a film together, describe one of the characters (appearance, dress, habits, personality) and invite your partner to guess who it is. If you are feeling more ambitious, act out the scene or script a similar one of your own. Alternatively, you might want to write a short critique of the film like those you find in a newspaper or magazine.

Longer, cumulative tasks can really pay off. For example, an interest in environmental issues could lead you to monitoring daily newscasts for items on this topic, and scanning the programme schedules for any documentaries or discussions. By taking notes, and compiling a dossier over a few months, you can become an expert not just on the topic but also on how people talk about it in your target language. This way, you are gaining both improved language and insight into how speakers of the language think about an issue. But, as was stressed earlier, concentrate on what you enjoy doing, focus primarily on the meaning and enjoy the whole visual experience.

Task 7.8 Working with video

Find a partner and try out two of the activities suggested in the working with video section. What worked well? What didn't work? What will you try differently next time? If you cannot find a partner, choose two activities you can do on your own.

Comment
Chapter 4 explains the importance of reviewing what you do in order to get the most out of your learning activity.

The following sections examine ways of using radio/audio and printed materials respectively. Although they are in separate sections, you can create some interesting tasks by comparing one medium with another. For instance, find the same story in a TV newscast or a radio bulletin and a national newspaper, then compare the information, the treatment and the language used. Which has more detail? Which uses more formal language? How does the TV item use images compared with the newspaper?

RADIO AND OTHER AUDIO

Radio

Getting started
Listening to the radio in your target language can help to improve your listening comprehension once you have got your ear 'tuned' to the language. Some radio stations can be received on short wave at various times of the day. The Internet not only provides information about radio station frequencies, but increasingly allows you to listen live. (See Chapter 8, 'Finding materials and resources on the Web', for advice on using search engines to locate resources.) You can also access digital radio stations through satellite television. Some stations are specifically aimed at international audiences and broadcast in a variety of languages. Many of the techniques and approaches to get the most out of watching TV or videos can be used with radio programmes.

Sample radio station websites:

http://www.dw-world.de (German)

http://oe1.orf.at/service/international (Austrian)

http://www.rfi.fr/ (French)

http://www.rtve.es/rne/ree/ (Spanish)

http://www.101.ru (Russian)

http://radio.rai.it (Italian)

http://www.latinworld.com/radio/ (lists radio stations from different Latin American countries).

http://windowsmedia.msn.com/radiotuner/Findstations.asp/ (lets you find new stations by genre or language).

As with film and television, choosing the right programme to listen to depends very much on your personal interests and your level of proficiency. As a language learner, the radio gives you a lot of choice. Radio programmes are relatively easy to access, available at almost any time and offer you a certain amount of flexibility. You can listen to the radio in front of your computer, on your home stereo, or, with a portable set or personal stereo, almost anywhere. You will hear authentic language, a wide variety of types of language (depending on your choice of programme) and possibly different regional accents.

On the other hand, the language you hear is totally natural, and there is little to help you understand it. It is often spoken at high speed and sometimes quite colloquial. You have no second chance. Either you understand what is being said immediately, or not at all. This can be quite daunting for a language learner. In addition, some programmes may require a high level of knowledge of the country in order to make sense of what is being discussed, and many topics may not be of immediate interest. One solution is to record potentially interesting or favourite types of programmes and then listen to them several times.

Types of radio broadcast

News bulletins have the advantage of being short and covering a variety of news items but they can be quite hard to understand because of the fast pace. If you are interested in news and listen to it in your own language, the news from abroad may be easier to follow because some of the stories will be the same and cover international events. Some of the words and expressions you hear may be familiar to you because they are international or the same as in your own language. Bulletins tend to be frequent and often repetitive so you can hear them again without having to record them. You could set yourself a task to see how many items in the news bulletin you understand. Try again an hour/a day/a week later to see how much you have improved.

News magazine and feature programmes are generally longer and offer a more in-depth treatment of issues, with a slower pace, more interviews and more repetition. If you are a less advanced learner, such programmes may be easier to follow.

Radio plays or drama offer an opportunity to listen to different types of language, sometimes with regional accents. Radio drama can range from adaptations of classic plays to crime stories and humorous and satirical sketches, and offers you an insight into the cultures of the communities who speak your target language.

Music programmes, whatever your personal taste, provide the chance to listen to music which is popular in other countries, be it rock, pop, jazz or classical. When you tune into a pop/rock station, in many countries most of the songs you hear are in English, but you will also hear how the DJ talks about or links the items played. On the other hand, such programmes demand less attention and concentration when your main purpose is to listen to the music.

Discussions and phone-ins give you an opportunity to hear a range of people expressing opinions on the same topic, or to hear the same kinds of question put to different people.

Adverts during the breaks on commercial radio stations are short, often supported by sound effects to set the scene. You can employ a similar approach with these as with TV adverts.

Task 7.9 Finding the right radio programmes for you

Locate a radio station broadcasting in the language you are learning.

Listen to at least three different types of programme.

Which do you find most interesting or easiest to follow? Why do you think this is?

Comment

When you look for radio stations and programmes, try out a whole range of programmes and choose according to your interests. Programmes on topics which you have already heard or read about in your own language or in the language you are studying are likely to be easier to follow. A familiar programme format, such as the weather forecast, quizzes or phone-ins can also be a great help.

When you have found a programme you like, you could record an edition and listen to it later, for gist first, then for more detail. You might like to use a grid or checklist such as the ones for use with TV broadcasts in the previous section.

Audio books

These have become popular and widely available in many countries. They can be purchased in good bookshops or from an Internet bookseller. Your local library may have some in foreign languages. Cultural institutes which have libraries (see 'Embassies and institutes') may offer audio books and recorded radio drama on loan when you join their library. Like radio, audio books are very flexible and you can listen to them wherever you have access to a cassette recorder or CD player. You might also be able to use the original book as a transcript and to refer to sections of it while you are listening.

Obviously, the language of audio books is not the same as the language of live discussion. Audio books are readings of written texts, both fiction and non-fiction, and follow the conventions of such texts in terms of the vocabulary, grammar, structures and registers used. So you need to be aware that what you hear in audio books is not necessarily the same kind of language that you will hear when talking to speakers of the language or even on some radio programmes.

NEWSPAPERS AND MAGAZINES

Reading or browsing through newspapers and magazines written in your target language can not only improve your reading skills but also increase your understanding of the cultures of communities where the language is spoken and the issues that preoccupy them. A range of newspapers and magazines in a variety of languages may be available from newsagents in major towns and cities in the country where you live. Most newspapers and magazines also have Internet editions although some are only accessible by subscription. (See Chapter 8 on searching for resources.) It goes without saying that there are considerable differences between the various types of newspapers in most countries. It can be interesting to compare the headlines of a tabloid in your target language with those of a quality paper from the same day to see what the main differences are. If you are a more advanced learner you could examine the content and compare some of the articles in terms of format and language used.

Sample websites for non-subscription newspapers:

Süddeutsche Zeitung	http://www.sueddeutsche.de (German)
Der Standard	http://derstandard.at/ (Austrian)
Le Monde	http://www.lemonde.fr/ (French)
Corriere della Sera	http://www.corriere.it/ (Italian)
El Mundo	http://elmundo.es (Spanish)
Asahi Shimbun	http://www.asahi.com/home.html (Japanese)
Pravda	http://www.pravda.ru/ (Russian)

http://www.onlinenewspapers.com offers a comprehensive list of newspapers from all over the world which are available online.

To read and hear news presented in a wide variety of languages look at http://www.bbc.co.uk/worldservice/us/languages.shtml

continued

If you live near a university library, you may have access to Lexis-Nexis, an online gateway to the press of the whole world, with a sophisticated search facility which helps you focus on people and themes you are interested in.

Once you find an Internet edition of a useful newspaper or magazine, set it up as your Internet home page. Even if you don't have time to read much as often as you would like, you will see the headlines every time you use the Internet.

For lighter reading, you could consider magazines written for particular audiences (e.g. fashion, men's health, fishing, cookery) or look at the celebrity or gossip press. Although these magazines do not interest everyone, they have certain advantages for the language learner over other newspapers and magazines. The articles tend to be shorter, there are lots of photographs, and the topics are similar to what you would read in equivalent magazines in your own language. These features make this type of real-life reading material accessible to learners at all levels.

Magazines specifically produced for language learners are also available for some languages. They offer edited texts with additional support, such as vocabulary or extra exercises and sometimes come with a CD or an audio cassette. For example, *Authentik* (http://www.authentik.com) publishes magazines of articles and activities with cassette or CD for learners in German, Spanish, French or Italian. *Champs Elysées* (http://www.champs-elysees.com/) produces audio magazines with transcripts in French, Spanish (*Puerta del Sol*), Italian (*Acquerello italiano*) and German (*Schau ins Land*).

BOOKS

Reading for pleasure, becoming engrossed in a good plot or story line, is an excellent way to unconsciously absorb the language you are learning. This kind of reading has also been shown by research to be a very good way to build up your vocabulary.

The type of book you may choose to read for pleasure obviously depends on your personal interests and your proficiency in the target language. Cartoons, comics or short stories are often more accessible than longer or more serious fiction or non-fiction. Alternatively, as suggested earlier, you could find a dual-language text which has the original and the translation in your own language side by side. Such books are available in many languages through bookshops or Internet booksellers. Another possibility is to buy a target language version of a book which you are already familiar with in your own language. Reading it in the foreign language will be much easier because you know the story line already.

If you are concerned about tackling a 'real' book, you could look for graded readers. These are simplified versions of well-known works of fiction or non-fiction produced especially for language learners at different levels. They sometimes include questions or activities to guide you through the text.

Task 7.10 Finding reading material

Search your home/workplace/neighbourhood/district/the Internet to locate appropriate reading material written for speakers of your target language.

Comment
To remind yourself how to make the most of any reading material you find, refer to Chapter 5.

THE INTERNET

Chapter 8 examines ways in which a language learner can make use of the Internet and the Web. As you have already seen, most newspapers, magazines (including programme listings), television and radio stations have websites. In addition to information or articles, they often offer streamed audio and video broadcasts, games and discussion boards where you can read different opinions, get a real understanding of the range of viewpoints in any country and even make your own contribution. Using the target language like this can be extremely motivating. But, as Chapter 8 makes clear, the Web is largely unregulated and you can find many rather obscure sites. If you browse in your mother tongue, you will easily and almost immediately recognize different types of website. This might be a little harder to do in the target language. Use your common sense and stick to well-known websites from providers that you recognize and trust.

Task 7.11 Using a website

Go to the website of a TV station broadcasting in the language you are learning.
What current issues are being discussed on the site?
How do they compare with what you have heard or read about current issues in your own country?

If you feel confident in using the target language and inspired by a topic, you might want to add a comment yourself.

Comment

There are many other activities you can do using websites. Try to use them in the way the designers intended, even if you are only pretending. For example, look at travel and hotel sites to plan a real or imaginary visit. Shop at store websites for clothes or electrical equipment (but remember it is just language practice and don't place an order at the end!). Use tourist information sites to schedule a week-long tour. Many tourist websites have versions in several languages, so after having organized a virtual tour in your target language, you could check your understanding by reading the version in your mother tongue.

PEOPLE ARE RESOURCES TOO!

Competent speakers of the target language can be very useful to you as a learner. When you are abroad, set yourself tasks which will force you to talk to the locals. Ask the way to the station. Say you are a foreigner and looking for the best bakery. If you are staying for a while, in a French gîte for example, try to get to know the owners or the neighbours. Invite them for an *apéritif* or a game of tennis. You will probably need to overcome your own reluctance, but being bold can pay off linguistically (see Chapter 3, 'Taking risks and learning from mistakes'). If you find that people almost immediately start speaking to you in your own language, try to explain to them that you are serious about learning their language. It might be a good idea to work out how to say this in advance. It is likely to have a positive effect on them and they may adopt a more patient attitude towards your attempts in their language.

Even at home, you may find there are competent speakers of the target language in your area. Do not neglect personal security, but perhaps you might post a notice in the post office or the local college saying you want to exchange English for Japanese or Italian conversation, for example. This could lead to regular meetings at a mutually convenient time and place when you agree to speak for one hour in each language. Sympathetic speakers of the language will provide support by repeating, speaking slowly and clearly and explaining when you don't understand, so this kind of exchange can be very productive indeed. (See Chapter 10 for more on 'Making the most of support from other speakers of the language').

Embassies and institutes

Most embassies offer not only visa and consular services but are active in promoting their country in many different ways. Very often embassies have departments devoted to national culture which offer a lot of information, sponsor events and organize a variety of cultural activities.

The cultural institutes of foreign countries are also a good resource for language learners. These organizations may offer language courses (either in your home country or in the countries where the target language is spoken), and can provide information about these countries, organize events and exhibitions, sometimes have libraries which you can use and normally have fairly comprehensive websites with lots of information and links.

For a list of foreign embassies around the world, go to http://www. embassyworld.com

To find information about cultural institutes in the UK, go to http:// www.visitingarts.org.uk/uk_cultural_institutes.html

Clubs and associations

Many clubs, especially charitable associations, such as the Lions and Rotary in the UK, have links with their equivalents in other countries. There are also town twinning associations. Check whether your city, town or village has a twinning arrangement with the country whose language you are interested in. You can then take part in (or even set up) visits, cultural or language exchanges. Furthermore, many towns and cities, especially those with universities, have foreign language associations which run varied programmes of cultural and social events. They may also have arts centres which sometimes show foreign language films.

Libraries

Libraries are another potential resource for you as a language learner. If you have a library in your area it may have a collection of materials in foreign languages which you can use. Many libraries welcome suggestions for books and other materials to be ordered. All libraries offer an inter-library loan service, i.e. you can request a book that your library doesn't hold and they will get it for you from another library (there may be a fee for this service). Libraries in the UK also offer access to the Internet so that you can browse for relevant target language websites or read parts of a newspaper online if you do not have the facilities at home.

Task 7.12 Using the world as classroom

Now that you are aware of the variety of real-life resources at your disposal and how you might use them, think again about your priorities for your language learning.

Make a note of three real-life language resources which you can use to help you work on a priority area:

- Decide how you will use them.
- Remember to set yourself a deadline for completing each activity.
- When you have finished, review the results.

Comment
You may find it helpful to review what you did for Task 7.3 and refine the plans you made at that point.

Summary of key points

- There are many real-life resources available to support your language learning.

- TV, radio, printed media, the Internet and other speakers of the language offer valuable insights into the cultures of your target language and resources for language learning.

- There are activities you can do on your own or with a partner using real-life resources to improve your reading and listening, as well as your writing and speaking.

- For successful learning and high motivation, choose real-life resources that are right for you, and which match your interests and level of proficiency.

- Real-life resources are available for learners at all levels.

- Most adult learners benefit from concentrating more on the meaning when using real-life resources, while looking out for examples of language forms or vocabulary they have studied.

- As a learner, you are very likely to be more successful if you take an active approach to using real-life resources in your target language.

8

Using ICT to support your language learning

Lesley Shield, Klaus-Dieter Rossade,
Fernando Rosell-Aguilar and Tita Beaven

Information and Communications Technology (ICT) is increasingly used in language courses and to support language learning. It offers a wide range of different language learning opportunities, from CD-ROMs and electronic dictionaries to word-processing, email and the World Wide Web (Web). This chapter is about the role ICT can play in supporting and enhancing your language learning and how you can use these opportunities to best advantage.

Because ICT is a rapidly changing area, the chapter does not provide information about individual tools and applications; rather, it offers ideas about some of the ways in which you may use these in your language learning. While it contains advice and ideas for very experienced ICT users, it is mainly for people who have some experience of using ICT but wish to extend their skills to support their language learning. It also offers information for people with some ICT skills but with little or no experience of using ICT in their studies and who wish to explore further the possibilities it offers. If you have no knowledge of ICT, you may wish to leave this chapter until you have learned basic technical skills.

TYPES OF ICT TO SUPPORT LANGUAGE LEARNING

This chapter is divided into three major sections which explore:

- *Electronic resources* These include materials specially developed for language learning, like those you can find on CD/DVD-ROMs and the Web. They are grouped under the umbrella of **Computer Assisted Language Learning (CALL)**. You will also find out more about resources such as electronic books (**e-books**), electronic dictionaries and target language websites.

- *Productivity tools* These include **word-processors, spreadsheets, data-bases** and **referencing tools**. This section examines some of the ways productivity tools can benefit your language studies.
- *Communications tools* These allow you to communicate with other people through your computer, for example via **email** or **Instant Messaging (IM)**. They are classified as **Computer-Mediated Communication (CMC)**.

USING ELECTRONIC RESOURCES IN YOUR STUDIES

There are a large number of electronic resources to support you in your language learning. Depending on the type of learner you are (see Chapter 1) and your language learning priorities (see Chapter 4), you may find some more useful than others at different points in your studies. Base your decision about which type of electronic resources to use on the activity-types offered and what you intend to achieve, rather than on the medium alone.

Computer Assisted Language Learning (CALL) materials

CALL materials currently come in two main formats: CD/DVD-ROMs, and web-based. Some are designed for classroom use, whereas others can be used independently. They can provide support for language learning through a wide variety of exercises. They may be useful if you have limited access to traditional classes or like to work independently but they can also provide extra practice to supplement attendance at language classes. CALL materials allow you to work at your own pace and at your own convenience, providing language practice, as well as some cultural insights.

They may be available through libraries, some booksellers, in language centres or located by searching online (see 'Finding materials and resources on the Web').

CD/DVD-ROMs
These usually contain audio and/or video resources, as well as text, with a variety of tailor-made 'interactive' exercises suited to a specific language level.

Among the language learning resources you may find on CD/DVD-ROMs are:

- grammar explanations and quizzes;
- texts and reading comprehension exercises;
- dictionaries and vocabulary-building exercises;
- audio and video clips;
- speech recognition/recording facilities;

- word and sentence pronunciation activities;
- dictation activities;
- games and quizzes.

Examples of these activity types may include:

- reading a grammar explanation and then completing exercises that illustrate the grammar point explained (or vice versa);
- reading a text, listening to an audio or watching a video clip and answering questions about its content;
- repeating the sounds in an audio clip, recording yourself, listening to your recording and comparing it with the original.

As well as using multimedia materials such as CD/DVD-ROMs, you may find that language courses offer you the opportunity to take part in other computer-assisted activities, such as text-based gap-filling, multiple choice and text reconstruction activities (e.g. putting a text in the correct order). You may be introduced to game-like text mazes which lead you to different outcomes depending on the options you choose or answers you give at different points in the game. In some cases, you may even be asked to use specific software to create your own text-based language learning activities, because this will help you to understand more about the structure and content of the target language.

Language teachers often develop such text-based CALL activities to accompany a particular course. Therefore they are more closely tailored to the content of your course than more generic CD/DVD-ROM materials available from publishers. These resources share many of the advantages and disadvantages of commercially produced CD/DVD-ROMs for language learning considered below, but have the advantage that they can be regularly updated and are included in the price of your course.

Web-based CALL materials

CALL materials are also available online via the Web. While a large number can be accessed free of charge, some require a subscription. Many of these resources are similar to those on CD/DVD-ROMs, but others provide links (called hyperlinking) to resources outside the materials. For example, in order to complete an activity you may be asked to click on these links to obtain information from a daily online newspaper, or to search for meanings in an online dictionary.

Advantages and disadvantages of CALL materials

Style of activities/content

CALL materials often offer you the opportunity to compare your own spoken and written performance with spoken and written models using similar techniques to those suggested in Chapter 6 for pronunciation, for example. Because CALL learning activity types are usually designed from a template, they can sometimes lack variety or be repetitive. However, repetition can be a good way of reinforcing what you have learned. If you need more repetition to help you produce different structures or expressions automatically, then such exercises are ideal.

A major advantage of CALL materials is that they offer instant feedback on your performance. However, such feedback can be limited; for example, a good answer may be deemed wrong because of a capital letter or a missing accent. This is because the computer can usually do no more than provide a standard model answer to compare with your own version, rather than responding to different ways of expressing the same ideas. If you want to work on improving your accuracy, this feedback can be very helpful. If you are more interested in creating your own responses or elaborating on your ideas, you may find this type of feedback frustrating.

The types of activities and feedback available mean that many students find language learning CD/DVD-ROMs are best suited to beginner and intermediate levels. Web-based CALL materials can offer more variety through the use of hyperlinks, but feedback is still limited to automated responses or emails with results from completed exercises.

Just as representations of the cultures of the target language offered by courses using books, audio and video tapes can sometimes perpetuate stereotypes, this is something you should also be aware of when using CALL materials.

Access and use

Language learning CD/DVD-ROMs are widely available in a range of prices, although it is important to be aware that price does not necessarily reflect quality. Such resources can date quickly and may have limited use. Once you have completed the exercises you can redo them, but if you want new ones you may have to buy another CD/DVD-ROM, or gain access to a dedicated website with updates and additional resources. Navigating through the materials can also be complicated. Some packages include features such as sound effects (e.g. signalling a right or wrong answer). These can be motivating or become distracting depending on your personal preference. Find out as much as you can about a particular CD/DVD-ROM before purchasing it.

The quality of web-based materials also varies enormously. Try to find out as much as possible about the site you want to use. Self-made sites can be interesting, but be aware that most have not gone through a strict editing or quality assurance process. Normally, materials created by universities or reputable providers are a good starting point, so look closely at the web page address to check who hosts the site. Web-based materials can be updated more easily than those on CD/DVD-ROMs. Navigating web-based CALL materials may be easy, as long as you are familiar with web browsers (for more on these, see the next section), although this is not always the case.

Web-based CALL materials have the advantage that, unlike CD/DVD-ROMs, access to a particular operating system (e.g. Windows or MacOS) is not necessary. Problems with non-functioning web pages or busy networks can still occur. Accessing and using these materials also requires you to stay online. As with all online materials, speed of access depends on the bandwidth (Internet connection) you are using. Users with faster connections experience significantly better performance from sites incorporating audio and video clips. However, activities that rely on video files in particular are usually best accommodated on CD/DVD-ROM. These also allow you to locate specific points in video and sound clips both quickly and easily.

The Web

Many people use the terms **Internet** (or **Net**) and the **World Wide Web** (or **Web**) as if they were the same thing. In fact, the Internet refers to a network of connected computers, the 'physical' side. The World Wide Web is one of the facilities the Internet offers for obtaining information from other computers that are also linked to the Internet. This information is held in the form of web pages, which may be linked to one another. A web browser enables you to locate the information, save it, bookmark it and so on. A web page has an 'address' which is what the web browser looks for when connecting different pages. These addresses are called **URLs** (**Universal Resource Locators**).

The Web is not a structured database and no one keeps an eye on what is there or what is missing from the information available. Its content in many ways depends on its users. As anyone can do their own 'publishing' online, the subjects covered vary widely in terms of content and quality.

Despite this, the Web offers access to many resources and activities: it can be used to access web-based CALL materials (described above), locate real-life materials in the target language, access electronic libraries, find information on an infinite range of topics, use grammars and dictionaries, translate texts, and more. In order to access some resources, particularly audio and video files, you may need to download additional programs (usually available free and known as **plug-ins**) from the Web.

What sorts of resources are available on the Web for language learners?

There are two main categories of online resources: those designed specifically for language learners, and those primarily aimed at speakers of the target language for a multitude of purposes unconnected with language learning. Some resources designed for language learning have already been mentioned (web-based CALL material), others are considered in the later parts of this section on electronic resources.

Web resources intended for speakers of the target language

Chapter 7 suggests a variety of ways in which you can make use of these real-life resources for language learning. You can also make use of web pages that have been written primarily for speakers of your target language in the same way as you might use 'traditional' sources of information such as books, newspapers and brochures. Web pages usually provide up-to-date information (though check when they were last updated) which you can use when preparing essays or projects, for example, in the same way as you would use materials from a library.

Your use of the Web for language learning does not have to be restricted to language practice, essay or project preparation. You can also find information about the weather, local traditions or music, for example, or follow your own interests by searching for information about your favourite hobby, celebrity, film and so on, all in the target language. You can find bilingual websites and read about a particular topic, first in the target language and then in your mother tongue to check your understanding. You can access different varieties of your target language and obtain information about the geography, history, government and so on of the different places where it is spoken. These resources are available as texts as well as audio and video clips, ranging from songs to news reports, cartoons or films.

Advantages and disadvantages

Web-based audio and video files can give you access to materials that might otherwise be difficult or expensive to find outside the area where the target language is spoken. They can provide an opportunity to experience other cultures without having to travel. This material may be difficult to understand if it assumes knowledge of the politics or history of a country, for example. Chapter 7 also explains the importance of selecting material appropriate to your level of language and gives guidance on what may make some video, TV broadcasts or text-based materials easier to use than others.

As in the case of web-based CALL materials, web pages do not require access to a particular operating system, but they can present similar problems in relation to speed of access. Some web page providers offer the option to vary sound or picture quality, thus making the material available to people with slower connections.

Finding materials and resources on the Web

The Web offers two main ways to find material: **browsing** (or **surfing**) and **searching**. Browsing involves following links from page to page. You may start in a directory of useful addresses (such as those offered by many language centres). This acts as an index to different, previously selected pages. Directories of this sort are usually divided into content sections, and permit you to follow links related to topics that interest you. For example, if you go to the website of a cultural institute (see Chapter 7) you will find links which you can follow to a variety of other sites on the arts, media and society in the country concerned.

Searching involves using **search engines**, tools for finding information Based on the **keywords** you enter, a search engine finds matches and shows all the links to web pages related to these keywords. The 'search' facility on your computer employs one of the many search engines available. The search systems of individual search engines are different, so if you cannot find something by using one search engine, try searching with another. Some search engines also offer directories so you can both browse and search.

If you are studying a language course through a college, university or other educational institution, you are likely to be given access to electronic library resources. Make the most of this opportunity and make sure you obtain information about how to use the library effectively. Some electronic libraries provide language resources identified by specialist librarians and language teachers who have already carried out searches for relevant materials for learners of different target languages. These may include links to target language websites, to e-books that may be of interest or to electronic dictionaries, with advice on how to use them. They may also include advice on how to insert special characters into your word-processed documents or how to set up your computer to read and produce non-Roman character sets. (See also the section 'Using productivity tools in your studies' later in this chapter).

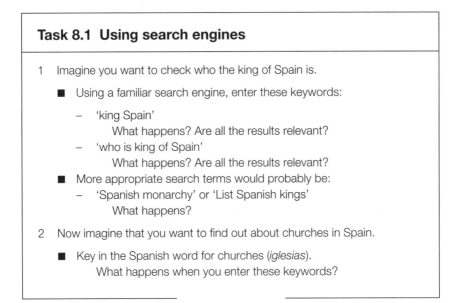

Task 8.1 Using search engines

1 Imagine you want to check who the king of Spain is.

■ Using a familiar search engine, enter these keywords:

  – 'king Spain'
    What happens? Are all the results relevant?
  – 'who is king of Spain'
    What happens? Are all the results relevant?
■ More appropriate search terms would probably be:
  – 'Spanish monarchy' or 'List Spanish kings'
    What happens?

2 Now imagine that you want to find out about churches in Spain.

■ Key in the Spanish word for churches (*iglesias*).
  What happens when you enter these keywords?

Comment

The different results from these searches show the importance of choosing keywords carefully and being as precise as possible. Otherwise you may end up with links to hundreds of irrelevant web pages. Your search for information about churches in Spain for example may have led to web pages about a pop-singer with that name. If you want to improve these results, you need to qualify the type of church, e.g. 'Romanic churches' or 'iglesias románicas'.

Using search engines

- Use a search term in your target language. If you want to find out about types of house in Spain, for example, type *casa* rather than *house*.

- Limit your search results to pages either in the target language or from areas where it is spoken. Many search engines allow you to set this option by going to 'preferences' or 'language tools'.

- Use either a search engine from the area where the target language is spoken or an international search engine in your target language.

- Most search engines have an 'advanced search' option or will give you tips on how to use symbols to limit your search. For example use inverted commas ("") to make sure that the search terms you key in appear together in the results, or use symbols such as +, −, AND, OR to specify whether your search terms must all appear in the results, terms you do not wish to appear, etc.

Task 8.2 Using target language search engines

Go to the home page of a familiar search engine. Is there a link to versions from different countries (and in different languages)? Follow one of these links to try using a search engine in your target language.

Try changing the '.com' or '.co.uk' ending from your usual search engine for that of the country where the target language is spoken (such as '.es', '.fr', or '.de'). In some cases this will give you that country's version of the search engine.

Try using search terms in the target language. Imagine, for example, that you are interested in finding out about London from a Spanish point of view. Go to the Spanish version of your usual search engine and type *Londres* rather than *London*. Limit the results to those only in Spanish to see what difference this makes.

Comment

With practice and time to experiment, it becomes easier to locate relevant web pages and information. However, once you have found them, you will need to evaluate them, as explained in the section 'Evaluating Web materials and resources'.

It is useful to make a note of relevant URLs located by browsing or searching, as well as the addresses of web pages you use frequently. Organize them in the appropriate folder in your web browser so you can find them quickly at a later date or use them as references in your written work. The content of the Web changes constantly which makes it an excellent source for up-to-date materials. Yet, at the same time, some of the resources you use or like may disappear without warning. You can, however, store information you find online in a number of ways. You can print pages, save them in their original format, or cut and paste what you need into a document, making sure that you are not violating copyright declarations. You need to acknowledge all online material you use in your work and ensure you are not inadvertently plagiarizing information (see Chapter 6 on incorporating language from other sources and Chapter 9, 'Completing your assignment'). Rules to acknowledge online material vary, but usually you will need to provide the URL and the date when you accessed the material, as most pages are updated and the content may change at a later date.

Evaluating Web materials and resources

The fact that anyone can publish material on the Web without any sort of editorial 'quality control' means that the information you find may not be accurate, the use of language may be incorrect or the author may be biased. It may even be a hoax.

Examine online sources carefully using the following questions:

- What is the URL? Is it from a reputable source?
- Who is the author? What are the author's sources?
- What is the purpose of this site? Might it be biased in favour of a particular point of view? Who is the intended audience?
- Who has links to this site? What other sites does this site link to?
- When was this site last updated?

Task 8.3 Evaluating websites

Go to a familiar search engine and type (between inverted commas) 'feline reactions to bearded men'.

   Among the results you should find a page with a research paper on the topic of cats and bearded men by Catherine Maloney and others. Click on it. Read the paper and the references and then answer the questions listed above.

   What do you conclude about this web page?

Comment

As you will have probably found, the site is a satire on academic writing. The URL will have given you a clue, as well as the content, the authors and titles in the references provided. Although at first glance it may look like an academic paper, it is only by reading it that you notice the humorous tone. Going back to the sites that link to this web page, do you think that everyone that links to it has noticed its real purpose?

Publishing your own material on the Web

Although web publishing is outside the scope of this chapter, your language course may require you to use the Web to present information to your peers, either by yourself or in collaboration with others. If so, it is likely that you will either provide your tutor with material for publishing or be given clear instructions on how to publish it yourself.

E-books

An e-book is an electronic version of a paper book. You may wonder why you would want to use an e-book as opposed to a paper one. Paper books are usually more portable than a computer, but e-books do not have to be kept on a desktop computer. You can download an e-book to a laptop computer or Personal Digital Assistant (PDA) and take it with you. Individual paper books may be portable, but it is much easier to transport large numbers of e-books on a single computer or PDA than it is to carry several paper books with you.

   Like paper books, you can bookmark and annotate e-books although not all e-books have the same features or functionality. However, unlike paper books, they can be searched quickly for specific items and may include multimedia content such as sound and video clips as well as providing built-in dictionaries that allow you to find the meaning of any word simply by clicking on it.

To examine one of the oldest and largest selections of free e-books, type 'Project Gutenberg' in your preferred search engine. Otherwise, for a variety of websites where you can download e-books, simply search starting with the keyword 'e-books'.

Electronic dictionaries and grammars

Electronic dictionaries and grammars are available in a variety of formats which are described in this section. Some people like to use paper dictionaries and grammars, others prefer to use electronic devices. See Chapter 3 for ways of using a dictionary and the features which a good dictionary should have. Look at both types of dictionary carefully to find out what they offer and what you would find most useful.

CD/DVD-ROMs

A range of electronic dictionaries is available on CD/DVD-ROM. Some of the features of these dictionaries are not available in paper-based dictionaries. For example, some offer a 'pop-up' facility. If you are working on a document on your computer, you can click on a word, and a window with a definition or translation instantly opens, a useful feature when reading or writing electronic documents in a foreign language.

Some CD/DVD-ROM dictionaries provide a pronunciation guide; you can listen to the pronunciation of a word, and sometimes even select the regional accent you want to listen to, recording yourself in order to compare your pronunciation with the original. Other features may include maps, pictures and video clips to clarify meanings, and activities and games such as crosswords to test and practise your vocabulary.

The major publishers of dictionaries also produce CD/DVD-ROM versions. You may find details through a bookshop or Internet bookseller, or through an online search.

Handheld electronic dictionaries and translators

These devices can store vast amounts of data, and are very portable. You can key in a word, or part of a word, and immediately access its meaning or translation. Sometimes you can also listen to its pronunciation, either alone or in context. Some handheld electronic dictionaries even contain banks of commonly used phrases, similar to traditional phrase books.

Scanning pens

A number of monolingual or bilingual dictionaries produced by reputable publishers are available to use with scanning pens. These tools can be used like a highlighter to scan and save text from a book or other printed document, and then transfer it to a computer or PDA. When using one with these dictionaries, you slide the pen over a word or phrase to obtain an instant definition or translation. For accurate scanning, you may need to practise with the angle and speed of the pen.

Concordancers

A concordancer is a software tool that allows analysis of very large amounts of language. These are kept in collections of texts or transcriptions of spoken utterances known as **corpora**. Used appropriately, concordancers can demonstrate how a language is used in different contexts. This can assist language learners by providing examples of real use to supplement the model examples found in textbooks.

Corpora and concordancing tools are best accessed through university libraries and may require a subscription. Learning to use a concordancer can be both technically and conceptually challenging. However, examining a corpus with a concordancer can rapidly reveal information about the target language such as:

- frequently occurring words;
- rarely used words;
- differences between spoken and written usage.

Concordancing can also show:

- any patterns, known as collocations (see Chapters 5 and 6) that occur in the use of certain words or phrases;
- the context in which words occur.

USING PRODUCTIVITY TOOLS IN YOUR STUDIES

The productivity tools covered in this section can help you with all aspects of text production (**word-processing**), presenting your work (**presentation tools**), processing and calculating data within tables (**spreadsheets**), and organizing and finding stored information (**databases**). Often also referred to as 'office' applications because of the everyday office tasks they support, these are now used widely in education.

Each office component application is optimized for specific tasks. If you are learning a language for general purposes, word-processing and presentation tools may offer you the best return for the time you need to familiarize yourself with the application. If, however, your needs are more specific, you may find that understanding how to work with databases and spreadsheets, for example, is well worth the effort.

As with all modern technology, the excitement about what is technically possible needs to be balanced against your learning needs and how much time you require to familiarize yourself with the software. If all your needs can be met by word-processing, for example, you might not need more than this and could use the remainder of the time for your language studies!

Word-processing

Language learning often involves producing written work (dialogues, notes, plans, essays, etc.), and word-processing can assist you at any stage of the production process (see Chapter 6, 'Preparing what you want to say and write', and 'Strategies to help with composition').

Gathering ideas, planning and organizing your work
You may welcome the opportunity just to write what comes to mind and put your thoughts in order later. This could lead to a plan for an essay where you detail how you will present the information you gathered and the structure of your argument. Different **headings** and font sizes, indentation, *italics* and **boldface** font can help you structure your plan. At the same time, these features of word-processing mean that you can choose the font, font-size, colour and background colour which you find clear and easy to read, whether composing your own text, or reading material from other sources.

Each time you add or change content this will be incorporated into the existing document. You can work on any section at any time or simultaneously on several sections. A word-count facility allows you to monitor your progress. This is particularly important if you have a strict word limit.

It is possible to enter all your notes into one document and save useful quotations there too, perhaps using different heading styles and paragraph numbering to keep track of what you have entered. Later, you will be able to find any section instantly by looking for key words with the 'find' function. If you are working with electronic sources, you can copy and paste useful sections straight from the source to your 'notes' document for a particular topic, which can then be used for assignments. This can save time, prevent spelling errors and, over time, help you build an impressive personal resource base, a kind of electronic index card system which you can draw on whenever necessary.

Earlier in this chapter, you were advised to keep details of sources of information you find on the Web. In the same way, make sure you reference such material appropriately, both in your 'notes' files and when you include quotations in any work you present as part of your language studies.

Many word-processing applications include a **thesaurus**. A thesaurus can 'teach' you new words with either similar or opposite meaning (synonyms and antonyms) as and when you need them. This can help you to convey ideas in your own words or may help you understand and remember new words or expressions in future. Other functions supported by many word-processing applications include automatic footnotes or endnotes and contents pages, which may be of use if your course requires you to write a more academic essay.

Word-processing applications can perform a number of sorting actions, by lines or paragraphs, alphabetically or numerically. These can be used in building your personal glossary or encyclopedia on any aspect of the target language and culture. Just enter new information or vocabulary as you find it and sort it alphabetically or by topic at your convenience.

Checking your work

All but the most basic word-processing applications have a spellchecker which may even correct common spellings automatically as you type. Some also have a grammar-checker which you can use to help you with your language production. You will need to select the appropriate language, and in some cases the language variety you prefer (e.g. Colombian Spanish, Swiss German or Canadian French).

Target language grammar-checkers available in word-processing programmes as standard are sometimes difficult to use as a language learner. They require an advanced understanding of the target language grammar in order to use them effectively. However, grammar-checkers specifically designed for language learners are being developed. Some of these offer explanations of specific points of grammar based upon analysis of frequently occurring errors.

Producing your documents

For some, word-processors are invaluable as they allow users to write quickly without worrying about legibility. If you type regularly, even the 'two-finger-touch-type-method' will lead to considerable speeds. However, if your course or your preferred mode of study requires a lot of writing, you should perhaps consider taking an inexpensive or even free touch-typing course. A few sessions will give you the basics of ten-finger typing, while speed and accuracy will develop when you apply your typing skills during your language learning. Whichever method you use to type, however, your finished product will be easy to read.

You can type language specific characters like the German *ß* or the French *ç* in a number of ways. For computers using Windows, one way is to press Number Lock, hold the ALT-key on your keyboard and enter, for example, 225 for the *ß* character to appear. For Macintosh computers, enter Option + s. Character key charts for Windows and Macs are widely available on the Web. Alternatively, use the 'Insert' menu or its equivalent, select 'Symbol' and look for the character you need.

If you type a lot in the target language, it may be worth changing your keyboard setting to that language. Each time you press a specific combination of keys, your keyboard settings will switch from one language to another. Consult the manual for your computer's operating system to find out how to do this or search the Web, as a number of sites explain the procedure in great detail.

Task 8.4 Using target language characters

Connect to the Internet and search the Web for general information about specific characters in your target language. In your preferred search engine, type 'foreign language character charts'. Search also for information on keyboard layouts for your target language.

Comment
When you find the information, print it out and keep it to hand for future use.

Presentation tools

Presentation tools allow you to combine text, drawings, images, charts, artwork, audio and video files. The resulting document can be projected via a computer and a data-projector (beamer) onto a large screen.

Presentation tools may appear to offer possibilities far beyond your needs as a language learner, but even the short presentations you may be required to make will be more accessible if presented attractively, perhaps supported by a few well-chosen visual aids. We learn languages most effectively in realistic contexts and if you are asked to give a brief presentation to fellow learners, you will benefit most if you try to engage your 'audience', in the same way as any public speaker would do.

One of the most valuable features of presentation tools is that they offer a number of preformatted slides and attractive backgrounds. You don't have to be a designer to design slides, A4-size transparencies or handouts that present text and images in exciting ways help take your audience just about wherever you want them to be. Some presentation tools also allow you to time your presentation, which is helpful if you have to keep within a time limit.

Another useful function is the overview mode, which can be either a linear list or several small-sized slides (thumbnails) spread over the screen. This function can help you to organize slides of information, opinions and arguments in such a way that they support the natural delivery of your presentation in the target language. Once the stages and sequence of your presentation are finalized, you can print off a concise aide-memoire to guide you through the delivery of your presentation. The handout-printing facility which lets you print off several slides on one A4 sheet of paper is of particular benefit to language learners. Your audience can focus on the content of your presentation rather than trying to take notes using words that may be unfamiliar to them. Chapter 6 gives further advice on preparing for and delivering a presentation.

Remember to check what facilities are available at the place where you will be making your presentation. Make sure you have a 'plan B', perhaps a set of transparencies and printed copies of your slides, in case arrangements do not work out as expected.

Spreadsheets, databases and referencing tools

Spreadsheets organize numerical data in cells, columns and rows and facilitate a wide range of calculations. If you are studying business together with a foreign language, or if your language course contains a vocational element, you may need to calculate or present information in tables or charts. A spreadsheet can save you valuable time here.

You can also use the table structure in spreadsheets for your own bilingual glossary, especially if you anticipate a large number of entries, as the management of cells, rows and columns is generally easier than in word-processing applications. You can add new vocabulary, sort it later and, depending on your requirements at the time, regroup sections of your glossary without much effort. Remember, however, that spreadsheets are not suitable if you want to enter large amounts of text into one cell (for example, a lengthy definition).

Databases, like spreadsheets, organize data in cells, columns and rows. They are most suitable for large volumes of data, for example the resources held in a library. Here, databases have effectively replaced card index systems, because the latter cannot match the search facilities of the former.

Database tools may provide more functionality than most language learners need. However, if your course requires you to handle large numbers of references and citations, or you intend to continue studying the target language to higher levels in an academic context, you may want to investigate reference and citations managing software. Such applications allow you to store references and citations and integrate this data into essays and presentations. All the hard work of designing a database is done for you. Time spent on formatting footnotes and writing bibliographies is greatly reduced, especially if you use individual references in different contexts.

It takes time, patience and diligence to build up your own database of references and quotations, so, if you need one, it is advisable to start 'collecting' data right from the start of your studies even though it may seem like extra work with the benefits still a long way off.

USING CMC IN YOUR STUDIES

Computer-Mediated Communication (CMC) allows you to communicate with others by using the computer to *mediate* your communication rather like a telephone.

Types of CMC

Most CMC tools permit you to communicate both with individuals and with groups. However, some only allow one-to-one communication, similar to a telephone conversation (e.g. some sorts of Internet telephony). Others only allow communication to and within groups as though you were in a meeting or lecture, (e.g. some types of chat tool where you can only send a message to an entire group, not an individual).

You can use CMC to communicate **synchronously** (in real time, e.g. text chat) or **asynchronously** (in deferred time, e.g. email). Some CMC tools allow synchronous and asynchronous communication within the same environment, for example Instant Messaging described below. In other words, you can 'chat' in real time with friends and colleagues who are online at the same time as you and you can leave a message for others to collect the next time they log in.

Finally, some CMC tools may allow you to communicate only in text or in sound and/or in pictures (video). Others, such as audiographic conferencing, may let you draw on a whiteboard or edit documents with other learners, or share websites and use text chat, for example, at the same time as talking to them. Table 8.1 describes a range of types of CMC in more detail.

A particular language course will probably use only some of these tools.

If your language learning provider does not already support some form of CMC, you might consider organizing your own online learning group. An Internet connection, a messaging application with audio support, a web browser and a shared web space are all you need. The software is available free of charge, and once you have made the necessary arrangements with other learners, you can communicate with them whenever you wish. Chapter 3 explains the benefits of 'Learning with others'. CMC is also important because it can enable contact with speakers of your target language, thus offering you the opportunity to use your language skills in a meaningful way, as well as allowing you to find out more about their culture(s).

Mobile technologies

You may already have a mobile phone or Personal Digital Assistant (PDA) and use these to communicate with other learners. Your language course may also use forms of communication like SMS (short messaging service) that employ technologies like mobile telephones or PDAs to send text messages. For example, you may be sent vocabulary items via SMS, while

Table 8.1 Types of Computer-Mediated Communication (CMC)

	Description
Email	Send a message or reply to one or more recipients. You can usually also attach audio, video and graphics files as well as text-based documents to your messages.
Bulletin boards and discussion lists	Send messages that can be read by anyone who subscribes to that **forum**. Messages may be *threaded*, i.e. grouped according to topic, or *unthreaded*, i.e. you have to search through all postings to find related messages. **Note**: if you send a message to a public forum, make sure that you have read its policy about what constitutes an acceptable posting.
Text, audio and audiographic conferencing	Membership is usually restricted and uses special conferencing software. In **text** conferencing, messages are posted into topic areas and then presented in *threads*. You can send messages to the entire readership or to specific individuals. **Audio** conferencing can be synchronous or asynchronous; either you talk in real time with others or you can leave voice messages in the same way as you leave text messages in a text conference. As well as supporting real-time audio and text conferencing, **audiographic** conferencing introduces *shared* tools such as a whiteboard, shared documents or shared web browser.
Blogs (weblogs)	A type of diary that you can publish on the Web. You can publish text, graphics, audio and video clips and links to other websites. Your blog may be public or private and may be on any topic that interests you. You can write a blog by yourself or allow others to post entries to it.
Chat and Instant Messaging (IM)	Among the most popular forms of web-based communication. Initially, they were text-based, and the term **chat** is used in this chapter to refer to synchronous communication in text, but now you can use them to communicate in real-time audio and video as well. **Chat** may use **chatrooms** or **channels** which can be public or private. **IM** permits you to make lists of your friends and tells you when they come online. As well as chatting, IM usually allows you to send audio, video or text files, for example, in real time to others online and permits you to leave messages for people if they are offline.
Virtual worlds	Often mistakenly considered to be another form of chat. While virtual worlds *do* allow you to chat, they were developed from multiplayer role-playing games in the 1970s and permit users to 'build' their own areas, in text or graphics, which are viewable by others. Chat only

Table 8.1 continued

Virtual worlds (continued)	exists while users are online; if nobody else is in a chatroom, there is nothing for a user to do. Virtual worlds exist whether or not anyone is logged in. Language learning worlds often contain puzzles, quizzes and language learning activities that you can interact with while exploring the 'surroundings'.
Video conferencing	**Point-to-point**: one group is gathered in a specific real-world location to talk to others in another real-world location. This sort of video conferencing is particularly useful for lectures and presentations. **Desktop**: connect to a video conference with other individuals from your own computer. Unlike point-to-point video conferencing, which is usually supported by technicians, you are in charge of your desktop video conference and have to manage it by yourself.

you can use your PDA to read e-books as described earlier. If you have a mobile phone, you could choose your target language as the setting for your telephone. So, for example, if you are learning Swedish, you could set your phone up so that it only shows the menus and commands in Swedish. That way you quickly become familiar with these words. Although it is also possible to send text messages from a computer to a mobile phone and to divert email to your telephone or PDA, communication via mobile technologies is not the focus of this section.

Communicating in text

You can use audio, audiographic and video conferencing tools to keep in touch with other learners or your tutor, but text is still an important means of communication, using either asynchronous or synchronous CMC. The choice will depend on your reasons for communicating in text as explained below.

Asynchronous text-based CMC
Asynchronous text-based CMC takes many forms, ranging from email to text-conferencing systems, mailing lists and bulletin boards. Because contact is deferred rather than immediate, these tools may be particularly helpful if you are worried about contacting someone at an inconvenient time or making a mistake in public. You can read or record each message at your own convenience, using a dictionary to help you if necessary. Once you have received, considered and understood a message, you can edit and re-edit your own response, sending it only when you are happy with it.

This type of CMC is probably most useful if you want to produce a carefully crafted contribution or take part in in-depth discussions which require you to explore and research topics and issues that are of relevance to your course and to the reasons you have for learning another language.

Synchronous text-based CMC

Like asynchronous text-based CMC, there are many different types of synchronous text-based CMC, such as chat. Despite differences in how they operate, what these tools all have in common is that they allow real-time communication with others in your target language. Although you may worry about picking up bad habits by using chat because other users make typing, spelling or grammatical errors that remain on the screen, this usually does not happen; typing errors are generally noticed and corrected. If you notice that you or someone else is having difficulty with a grammatical point, for example, this can also be a good opportunity to talk about the language and find out more about how it can be used.

When you use chat tools, you can often use a nickname and even adopt a different personality from your 'real-life' persona. This may make you feel more confident when you use the target language, since nobody knows who you really are, and so you may feel less embarrassed when you communicate in the target language.

You may notice that when you use synchronous, text-based CMC, your contributions to the discussion are shorter than when you use an asynchronous tool like email. Nevertheless, text-based conversations of this sort offer you an opportunity to practise using the target language in real time in an environment that allows you to edit your contribution before you make it. As nobody can see what you are 'saying' before you send it, you can edit your message until you are happy with it.

While you are likely to find asynchronous CMC most appropriate when you want to reflect and edit before you 'go public' with your thoughts, synchronous CMC is useful for quick-fire exchanges of ideas and comments, or if you simply want to respond briefly to a question or request for information.

Audiographic conferencing

In audiographic conferencing, several technologies combine into a kind of communication 'one-stop' shop.

- You can actually hear and speak to other language learners and simultaneously share visual, or 'graphic', tools such as online whiteboards, word-processing and image editors.
- A text chat tool may allow you to have conversations 'on the side' or make announcements, for example, *I'll be back in 2 minutes*, while the main discussion continues.

- You can talk to an individual or to a group. The person speaking may be indicated in some way. You usually meet in a virtual 'room', but learner groups may also split up into separate rooms for group work.
- You can either work and learn together or settle for casual social interaction.
- Any participant of a learning group may be able to manipulate the content of any of the shared graphical tools.
- You may be able to alter text documents, make notes of discussions and perhaps represent results visually in diagrams or flow charts.
- You may be able to insert images for controlled language work, e.g. a map, for practising giving directions, cartoons or pictures to stimulate open discussion.

Some audiographic CMC tools offer visual clues:

- a button indicating that someone wishes to speak can help groups with turn taking;
- yes–no vote buttons allow you to give quick, non-verbal feedback, similar to nodding or shaking your head in a face-to-face situation;
- small icons, or **emoticons**, like a smiley ☺ or sad ☹ face can provide rudimentary feedback in place of the non-verbal interaction features (smiling, frowning) that characterize face-to-face encounters.

Any of these will make communicating online easier, but they are not essential. If your language course requires you to use audiographic CMC, you should be offered some form of technical support, such as a telephone helpline.

Audiographic conferencing can overcome the restrictions of time and space. You can meet with or without your tutor, organize self-help study groups or work together on projects at times that are convenient, irrespective of where people live. Since language learning benefits from regular and frequent practice, it is easy to see how audiographic conferencing can assist the process by enabling learners to meet and practise easily outside scheduled classes. When you meet online, remember to establish basic communication rules, e.g. Will anybody 'chair' the chat? How long will it last? What is expected of you?

People bring their personal character traits with them when they meet online, just as when they meet in other contexts. Learners from other cultures may adhere to different communication conventions. Online communication also has its own etiquette, or **netiquette**, which needs to be considered. Lists of such virtual 'rulebooks' are widely available on the Web.

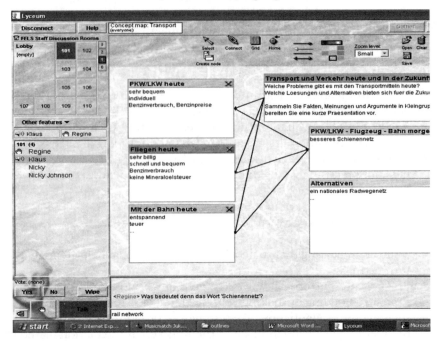

Figure 8.1 Four learners share access to an online discussion worksheet. Klaus is speaking and Regine is waiting for her turn. She had typed a vocabulary question in the text chat window earlier which another learner is about to answer.

Task 8.5 Finding out about netiquette

Applying the techniques outlined in 'Finding materials and resources on the Web', use a familiar search engine to find information about netiquette.

Comment
As suggested in Task 8.2, try replacing the endings '.com' or '.co.uk' in the URL for your search engine with the address for a country where the target language is spoken (such as '.es', '.fr' or '.de'). Now search for netiquette, limiting your search to pages in the target language. Are there any differences?

Websites offering advice on netiquette vary depending on the nature of the site, but also according to national conventions. Some deal with the use of formal and informal language (*tu* or *vous*?). Some focus on the human perspective of online communication, reminding you to keep it brief and not to post messages in haste (you may later regret what you said). Others emphasize technical aspects such as avoiding capitals (which is the equivalent of shouting) or unusual characters which may not be universal or may be 'translated' into different characters.

Instant Messaging

While email is the preferred communication channel for many, Instant Messaging (IM) is also hugely popular, with millions of users around the world. Anyone can message and the software is generally free. Although IM primarily uses a written channel, in some applications it is possible to communicate in speech, too. It offers another way of keeping in contact with other learners, your tutor or other speakers of your target language.

Check whether your Internet Service Provider (ISP) also provides access to IM. If so, download the software. You then need to define one or several lists of people you want to communicate with regularly. An example is shown in Figure 8.2. If you click on a name in a 'buddy list', a window opens into which you can type your message. If your buddy is online at the same time as you, your message is delivered immediately and not, as in the case of email, to a server from which it is forwarded to your inbox. Instant Messaging 'feels' more immediate than email and tends to lead to more spontaneous and shorter online conversations. If your buddy is offline when you send a message, it will be stored until they are online again. Whether delivered at once, or stored, your message or some kind of alert will pop up on your buddy's screen as soon as they log in.

Each time your buddies go online and log in you will be notified, for example by a symbol changing colour next to their names. The same will happen on their screens when you log in. This awareness of each other's presence can lead to an increased sense of a language learning community, fellow learners who may be able to support you when necessary. Instant Messaging with buddies from countries where your target language is spoken can support a formal or informal TANDEM language learning arrangement of the type described in more detail in Chapter 10.

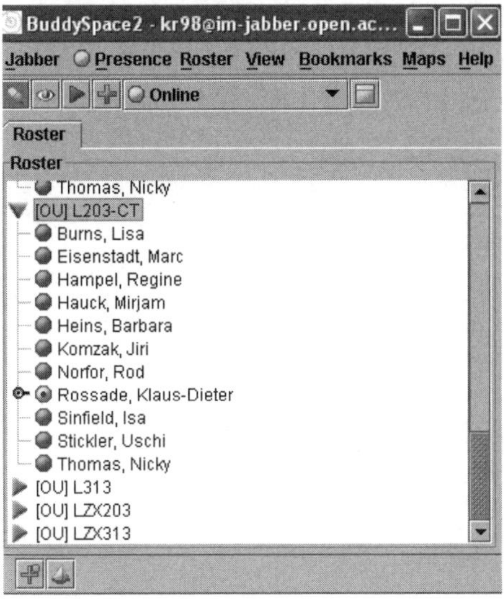

Figure 8.2 A typical Instant Messaging window showing all the members, or buddies, of a messaging group.

However, because contact is not convenient at all times, most IM applications permit you to signal to your messaging community whether you are ready to engage in conversations. Status messages such as 'free for chat', 'busy', 'online, but away' give you and your friends a richer picture of each other's presence, not just when they are online, but also whether they want to talk. Compare this to telephoning a friend, only to find that the line is busy or nobody is answering! You can even go a step further and refine your status message by saying that you are working on an assignment and don't want to be disturbed unless it is about that assignment. Language learners in need of opportunities to practise real-time communication in the target language stand to gain considerably from regular contact via IM.

Summary of key points

- ICT can be used for language practice, organizing and storing language items, researching, preparing and producing written work or presentations.

- ICT can enable you to establish and maintain regular contact with your tutor, other language learners and other speakers of your target language.

- Examine the different features offered by ICT tools and choose according to how they can help you achieve your learning goals.

- Balance the time you spend familiarizing yourself with specific ICT applications against the total time available for your studies.

- Using ICT for language learning also increases your general ICT skills and potentially your employment prospects in the information age.

9

Assessment

Concha Furnborough, Annette Duensing and Mike Truman

Assessment is as much about learning as about getting marks and a qualification. This chapter aims to give an overview of the different types of assessment that may be included in a language course, and to explain some of the terminology you may encounter. It provides general advice and specific tips on how to plan, complete and benefit from doing assignments as well as how to prepare for exams.

As language courses vary widely in their approaches to assessment, you will find some parts of this chapter more relevant to your needs than others. Start by taking a general look at the aims and content of your course, and then select sections of this chapter to read in more detail.

THE PURPOSE OF ASSESSMENT

There are many different views of assessment. Some people find assessment motivates them by providing them with a goal. Some need the grade to obtain a specific qualification. For others it is something of an ordeal or an obstacle to their learning. Nevertheless, assessment can help you become a better learner if you consider it more as a diagnostic process than simply a statement of your weaknesses.

Task 9.1 What assessment means for you

Before you read on, take some time to reflect on assessment and what you personally might gain from it. What are the benefits and drawbacks of assessment for you? Why do you feel like this?

Comment

Assessment can serve as:

1 a basis for accreditation, obtaining a qualification;
2 a progress check for you on your learning;
3 a progress check for your tutor;
4 a source of feedback;
5 an opportunity to check on strengths and areas for revision;
6 an opportunity for further learning.

Whether or not point 1 is important to you depends on your personal aims. However, points 2–6 can be valuable in helping you to make progress on your course. Each will be explained in more detail in the following sections.

Assessment for accreditation, to gain a qualification

Accreditation is an obvious reason for making assessment part of a language course. In order to obtain your qualification, you will need to provide evidence to the awarding institution that you have reached a certain standard in your learning.

The assessment for your course could be **internal** or **external**, or even a mixture of both, depending on who sets the assessment tasks, who decides on the criteria by which students will be assessed, and who awards the qualification.

- Internal assessments are set, graded and awarded entirely by the institution providing the course, for example, in an institution-wide language programme at a university, or on Open University language courses.
- Courses may prepare you for an externally set exam, such as the RSA Certificate in Business Language Competence. In this case, your teaching institution will help you prepare for the assessment but will have no influence on the content of the examination.
- In other cases, an external body sets the syllabus, but the teaching institution sets the assessments, for example, if your language study is part of a National Vocational Qualification (NVQ), or the Open College Network (OCN).

This distinction between internally or externally set assessments may not matter to you. However, depending on your reasons for learning a language, you may want to consider different options and their benefits. For example, if having a qualification as proof of your language level is important to you, a nationally or internationally recognized award could be beneficial, whereas if your aim is to learn a language for holiday purposes, the form of accreditation may not be crucial.

- Consider how important accreditation is for you.

- Consider whether you need a nationally or internationally recognized qualification.

- Find out what sort of accreditation your course offers.

- Ask your tutor for advice if you are not sure that the accreditation your course offers is right for you.

However, accreditation is not the only reason for assessment, and this chapter is largely about showing you how much more assessment can offer you.

Assessment to help you with your learning

Everyone needs some sort of benchmark against which to judge progress in learning a language. For some, it could be the extent to which they can follow a television news bulletin, or understand a business letter. If you are able to use the language in everyday life (through work or frequent visits to the country), this can provide opportunities for informal progress checks. Many people feel the need for a more formal measurement of their progress. This is where assessment comes in, providing a 'third-party' verdict to reassure you of your progress in a more structured way, linked to the aims of your course.

Assessment provides regular progress checks for both tutor and learner. Your tutor will want to find out what you can do well and what you still find difficult. This kind of knowledge helps tutors to adapt their teaching, providing you with help where you need it. Similarly, you gain an awareness of your own strengths and weaknesses, both through the mark and the feedback you receive on a particular piece of assessed work. You can then adapt your study accordingly, and spend time on what is necessary, as suggested in Chapter 4.

Formative and summative assessment

Connected to the two main purposes of assessment are two terms that you may well come across in your course documentation (i.e. the written information about your course), formative and summative assessment.

Formative assessment

The main aim is to help you learn by informing you and your tutor of how well you are doing. Formative assessment can simply consist of activities or tests designed to show you whether you have successfully learned a certain language point. It may also be intended as a 'dry run' for an assignment or examination. In all cases, the emphasis is not so much on passing judgement on your performance, but on identifying your strengths and weaknesses, and suggesting strategies to overcome the latter. Where marks are awarded, their prime function is to provide you with feedback and guidance.

Summative assessment

This form of assessment 'sums up' your learning. It usually takes place at the end of a course of study, or of a particular unit or module within your course. Once again, you will usually receive feedback on your performance, but a major aim is to provide a grade for the completed section, in order to give proof of the overall level you have achieved.

HOW ARE YOU GOING TO BE ASSESSED?

You will need to find out what form of assessment is used in your language course, because this has implications for the way in which you plan your study. You should consider the following issues:

When will you be assessed?

Throughout your course you may be set exercises, tasks or projects that you submit to your tutor by a certain deadline. This is called **continuous assessment**. There may also be a **final assessment**, i.e. an overarching task, project or exam. Marks from both types of assessed tasks are likely to count towards the final mark for the course. To avoid creating too much stress or anxiety for students, institutions that award qualifications are placing more and more emphasis on continuous assessment. Final assessment is used to check what students have achieved, taking into account everything they have learned on a course.

Who will assess you?

Tutor, assessor or examiner?

You may have to hand in tasks at regular intervals during the course or send them to your tutor by post or email. In other cases, e.g. assessment for National Vocational Qualifications or for the Open College Network, you may be required to perform tasks under observation as part of the lessons

Name of Tutor: *******	Unit No. FK12QQ006
Centre Name: *******	Unit Title: Exchange Opinions and Ideas (Speaking)
Run Number: 1	Level: Two/Intermediate

Learning Outcomes	Student Names					
	Jim	Niko	Sue	Tej	Ana	Amir
1. Exchange ideas on a chosen topical matter, in the target language.	✓	✓		✓	✓	✓
2. Exchange opinions on a topic of current public or social interest.	✓			✓	✓	✓

Figure 9.1 Tutor checklist: exchanging opinions and ideas.

Source: adapted from Chiltern Region Open College Network, Modern Languages Framework, Tutor Checklist.

or in the workplace. Here you may not be given a grade, but so-called 'can do' statements are used to describe your performance (see Figure 9.1).

Self-assessment
Self-assessment is also being used more and more. It can take different forms but they all aim to help you evaluate your own progress and give you responsibility for and influence over your own learning. One form of self-assessment is the self-marked progress check which often tests grammar or comprehension. You usually score these tests yourself with the help of an answer key. The key may include explanations or references to course material if you are unsure about a particular answer (see Figure 9.2). The scores give you an understanding of which language points or skills you need to study further and which you understand well.

Computer-marked assessment
This is similar in form to the self-marked progress check described above. Tasks are done online and then submitted electronically for scoring (see Figure 9.3). In addition to the score, you may receive automatically generated feedback as described in Chapter 8, 'Advantages and disadvantages of CALL materials'.

Learning log
Another, more personal, method of self-assessment is the learning log or diary, described in Chapter 4, in which you reflect on your own progress and record your observations. You can also measure your progress by setting short-term and longer-term goals and deciding what evidence you will need in order to show that you have achieved them.

In the text below, each gap has been assigned a question number (in brackets). For each gap, three options are given, each identified by letter. Decide which option is correct.

Jeannine a un métier passionnant: elle **(1)** _____ journaliste pour un hebdomadaire national. Cette profession, elle l'exerce **(2)** _____ bientôt vingt ans. . . .

Q1 **A** est employée comme une
      B travaille comme
      C fait du
Q2 **A** depuis
      B pendant
      C il y a

Answer Key

Check your results and read the explanations carefully. The letter enclosed in a box indicates the correct answer. In some cases we have explained why certain answers may not be possible or appropriate in the context of a particular sentence or phrase.

Q1
B   *Travaille comme journaliste* means 'works as a journalist'.

A   *Est employée comme journaliste* (i.e. without the indefinite article *une*) would have been correct. In French, the article is not used when stating someone's profession, except when an adjective is used with the noun (e.g. *c'est   une journaliste remarquable*).

C   *Fait du journalisme* would be correct: *faire du/de la* introduces mention of an activity, but cannot be used with a person (e.g. *journaliste*).

Q2
A   *Depuis*, used with a verb in the present tense, gives a meaning equivalent to 'has been …ing for/since' in English, so is correct here: *exerce (ce métier) depuis bientôt vingt ans* means 'has been doing (this job) for almost twenty years'.

B   Means 'during (a period of)'. *Pendant* is not used with an activity which began in the past and is still continuing at the time of speaking/writing.

C   *Il y a*, the equivalent of 'ago', does not make sense with *exerce* in the present tense (but note that *il y a … que* is the equivalent of *depuis*; therefore it would have been correct to say *Cette profession, **il y a** bientôt vingt ans **qu'elle** l'exerce*).

Figure 9.2 Example of self-marked assessment: multiple choice.

Source: the Open University, Student Marked Assessment Book, *Nouvel envol*, 2003, pp. 3 and 29.

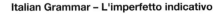

Italian Grammar – L'imperfetto indicativo

1. Una volta l'Italia non [▾] una squadra di rugby, ma ora sì. (avere)

2. Una volta gli abiti di Benetton [vendeva] bene, ma ora vanno meglio quelli di Diesel. (vendere)

3. La polizia fascista [catturavano] i mafiosi con metodi duri. (catturare)

4. Quando ero piccolo non mi [▾] gli spinaci. (piacere)

5. Mia mamma da giovane mi [▾] i capelli neri, ma ora sono grigi. (avere)

[submit test]

Figure 9.3 Example of computer-marked assessment: gapped text.

Source: http://www.well.ac.uk/languageExercises/Student/showTest.asp?testName=Italian+Grammar&testID=1000129

Peer assessment

Other students may play a part in assessing you, and vice versa. Assessment may take the form of a presentation or role-play presented to the whole class, or a piece of written work that students edit for each other. Fellow students may be asked to check, for example, on elements of the language as well as on the content or structure of the work. They may also be involved in deciding on (part of) the grade. This may seem daunting, but it is usually a beneficial learning process for both sides, as peers are likely to be sympathetic and comment on things the original writer or speaker has done well, but might not have been aware of otherwise. In return, fellow students see an example, good or bad, which they can learn from.

It is possible that your course employs a mixture of the assessment types listed above. For example, continuous assessment may consist of tutor-marked assessments of your writing and speaking skills, and computer-marked tests checking grammatical knowledge. This could be rounded off by an end-of-course oral presentation, where one part of the grade is given by fellow students and the other by an assessor.

What tasks constitute the assessment?

As part of your assessment you will usually be asked to perform different tasks. These may be written or spoken, either in the target language or in your mother tongue, or both. Table 9.1, together with the examples in Figures 9.2–9.5, gives you an overview of the more common assessment

Table 9.1 Assessment tasks with written and spoken outcomes or answers

	What is tested?	Possible test formats
Tasks with written outcomes or answers		
Test of vocabulary or structures	your knowledge of vocabulary or structures in the target language	■ gapped text (see the example in Figure 9.3) ■ matching exercise (you match target language words with their mother tongue translation) ■ multiple choice
Comprehension test	your understanding of a reading or listening passage in the target language	After reading a text or listening to a recording you: ■ put in order/select from a list the topics discussed (see the example in Figure 9.4) ■ answer questions about them in the target language or your mother tongue (see part of the example in Figure 9.5) ■ select multiple choice answers (see the example in Figure 9.2)
Pieces of writing in the target language	your ability to write in the target language	■ at lower levels: short note, letter, email, telephone message ■ at more advanced levels: newspaper article, essay, project, dissertation
Translation	your ability to translate from the target language into your mother tongue and vice versa	This is mainly used as part of degree-level study, or more advanced vocational qualifications

Tasks with spoken outcomes or answers

Monologue	your ability to speak for a specified amount of time on a set topic	You record your answer (for distance education) or speak in front of the examiner or your class: ■ answerphone message (see part of example in Figure 9.5) ■ as if for a radio programme ■ short talk/speech (simpler topics, e.g. 'you and your family' for beginners, more complex ones, e.g. politics or the environment, for more advanced students)
Dialogue	your ability to talk to and interact with an assessor in the target language	■ interview, conversation ■ role-play (e.g. booking a hotel room, business negotiations) ■ discussion ■ short talk/speech (by you on a prepared topic, see above) followed by questions from the assessor
Group conversation	your ability to interact with fellow students in a group situation in the target language	■ discussion ■ role-play
Interpreting	your ability to provide a spoken ad hoc translation	■ orally translating a monologue, e.g. speech in mother tongue into the target language or vice versa ■ orally translating a conversation between a speaker of your mother tongue and a speaker of the target language This is usually only used in assessment of degree-level study or more advanced vocational qualifications

You are having lunch in a restaurant with a colleague. You overhear bits of conversation from the other tables, where people are commenting on the food and other things. Listen to Track 9 on your CD and note down the order in which you hear the following topics mentioned.

Escuche y anote.

el tráfico • la comida • el restaurante • el tiempo • planes para más tarde

Transcription of CD Track 9
Listen to these customers in the restaurant and decide what topics they are talking about. Escuche a los clientes del restaurante. ¿De qué temas hablan?

a) – ¡Qué calor !, ¿verdad?
    – ¡Uy!, sí, horrible. . . ¡Un calor insoportable!

b) – ¡Qué restaurante tan grande!
    – Sí, sí, es enorme. ¡Qué barbaridad!

c) – ¡Qué tráfico!, ¿no?
    – Sí, bueno, es que hay un partido de fútbol y. . .

d) – La paella está riquísima, ¿no te parece?
    – Mm, sí, muy rica.

e) – Oye, ¿vamos al cine después? ¿Qué te parece?
    – Sí, no es mala idea. ¿Qué ponen?
    – Pues mira, una película de miedo. . . .

Answer key
The correct order is: *el tiempo, el restaurante, el tráfico, la comida, planes para más tarde.*

Figure 9.4 Example of assessment task: putting a list of topics in order.

Source: adapted from the Open University, *Portales* 5, 2003, pp. 16, 52, 119.

task types, but this list is not exhaustive. Some assessments combine a number of tasks as part of an overall scenario or context for the assessment (see Figure 9.5). These tasks are carried out in sequence.

Portfolio assessment
In portfolio assessment students are asked to present evidence of their achievements in language learning. The portfolio can be summative or formative, and it consists of a collection of tasks done at home, in class, during a formal assessment or even elsewhere, e.g. a letter you wrote at work. Portfolios are very different from other forms of assessment because they allow you to select for yourself the material that will be used to assess your performance, rather than completing a specific task set by your tutor or an external body. The main advantage of a portfolio is that it encourages you to examine critically what you have learned and achieved in the target language. It gives you a much greater input into the assessment process, but also gives you increased responsibility, since you have to take decisions

In this assignment you will read a brochure from a language school in Munich (Part A), fill in a course enrolment form (Part B), listen to fellow students talking to the school's receptionists (Part C) and leave a message on the school's answerphone (Part D).

Part A (Reading)
Read the brochure [not shown here] from one of Munich's numerous private language schools and answer the questions on your answer sheet.

Part B (Writing)
You have decided to enrol for a one-week intensive course for beginners at *Spracheninstitut Dehmel*. Look at the enrolment form on your answer sheet and complete the form by filling in your own details.

Part C (Listening)
While waiting in the queue to confirm your enrolment at *Spracheninstitut Dehmel*, you hear other students enrolling for language courses talking to the school's receptionists. Listen to your Assessment Cassette and answer the questions on your answer sheet.

Part D (Speaking)
Now leave a message on the answerphone of *Spracheninstitut Dehmel* announcing your arrival in Munich. You should include the information listed below. Record your message **in German** on a blank Speaking Assignment Cassette. It should last no less than 30 seconds and no more than a minute.

In your message, make sure you say:

• hello;
• your name;
• the country you are from;
• that you are coming to Munich tomorrow;
• that you will stay at the Park Hotel Schwabing;
• the telephone number at the Park Hotel Schwabing is 089 36 00 10;
• good-bye.

Figure 9.5 Example of a series of assessment tasks as part of an overall scenario.

Source: abridged from the Open University, Assessment Book 1, 2003–4, *Rundblick*, 2003, pp. 10–11.

about what you will select for assessment. Portfolios can also be used as a way of recording your progress (see Chapter 4, 'Personal development planning').

If your course uses portfolio assessment, there will be guidelines that specify what kinds of material and how many examples you should present in your portfolio. These usually include language work, independent learning activities (such as learning logs or diaries), self-assessment and reflective activities, e.g. evidence of reflection on differences and similarities between cultures, or evidence of critical understanding of your own and other cultures.

- Consider what you know about the assessment on your course:
    - When will you be assessed?
    - Who will assess you?
    - What tasks constitute the assessment?

- Ask your tutor or course organizer as soon as possible if you are not sure about any of these points.

DOING AN ASSIGNMENT

The word assignment usually describes a particular task or connected group of tasks which you have to prepare for your continuous assessment.

Preparing an assignment

Start by reading the task carefully, so you understand clearly what is required. It is very important that you do exactly this, i.e. not too little, or too much, or the wrong thing. If you are unsure at any point about what you have to do, seek advice either from your tutor or a fellow student. Leave yourself plenty of time to do this, especially for the first assignment, when you are still becoming familiar with the course and its requirements.

Looking at the **task**, consider what exactly is required:

- *Content* Which items of information do you have to include?
- *Language* What vocabulary and structures do you need for the topic as it is set out? Is it a formal or an informal context? Is it a speaking or a writing task? Sometimes grammar points or structures may be asked for explicitly, e.g. a certain tense. If nothing specific is prescribed you can assume that a good spread of the different vocabulary and structures covered by the course will be expected.
- *Intercultural skills* What critical understanding and abilities do you need to demonstrate with respect to the language and cultures you are studying? You may be required to show, for instance, interest and appreciation of differences between cultures, or willingness to understand and engage with other views of the world.
- *Source materials* Are you asked to refer to certain sources as a basis for your writing or speaking, e.g. a text or an audio recording provided as part of the task, a particular reference book, or a website?
- *Length* Is there a prescribed length, i.e. a particular word limit for a written task or a specified time limit for a spoken task? Make sure you keep to it, because there could be penalties.
- *Format* You may be required to produce your assignment with a certain layout, e.g. word-processed with a margin on one side to allow for tutor

comments. You may also receive advice on writing the script of the language you are learning (e.g. Cyrillic or Arabic) or characters that only occur in the foreign language (e.g. ü, ß, ê, ñ, å). On some courses the presentation of your assignment may be graded as well as the language and content.

It is also important to be aware of the following points. Depending on your course, some of this information may not be found in the task itself, but in the accompanying course documentation.

- *Assessment criteria* Most language courses provide you with the assessment criteria for your assignments (see the example in Figure 9.6). These specify what is assessed, for example, language only, or also

---

Marks for role-play performances are awarded positively on a scale of 1–10 using the following assessment grid. The mark awarded reflects the extent to which the task as a whole has been successfully communicated and completed. To determine if a candidate should gain the upper or lower number of marks in the box which best describes the performance, it is important to refer to the boxes above and below. If the candidate's performance borders more on the performance of the box below than the box above, then the lower mark is allocated. On certain occasions, a candidate performance may require a 'best fit' mark.

Role-play A	Communication and content
9–10	Conveys all information required Interacts extremely well No prompting necessary
7–8	Conveys most information required (At least three prescribed tasks) Little or no prompting necessary
5–6	Conveys half the required information (At least two prescribed tasks) Little prompting necessary
3–4	Conveys less than half the required information (At least one prescribed task) Some prompting necessary
1–2	One prescribed task completed satisfactorily Extremely hesitant, reliant on prompting
0	No effective communication

Figure 9.6 Example of assessment criteria for a spoken task.

Source: specification, Edexcel GCSE in Urdu, issue 1, January 2001, p. 25,
http://www.edexcel.org.uk/VirtualContent/18108.pdf

content, presentation and awareness of social and cultural customs (often called Intercultural Competence), and what standard you have to reach in order to receive a certain grade. Ask your tutor if you are unsure what is being assessed or what is expected of you.

- *Pass mark* What is the minimum grade you need to pass an assignment? Being aware of this can often help to set your mind at rest. Do you have to pass all assignments, or only a certain number, in order to pass the course?

- *Weighting* How much do individual assignments contribute to the overall grade of the course? Are oral and written assignments equally important? Do you have to pass all of them, or is it enough for your average grade to be above a certain level?

- *Submitting the work* How do you have to submit your assignment? If you are attending a regular class this may be easy for you, because you just take the assignment along in the specified week. However, what should you do if you cannot attend in that week? Can you take it to your tutor's office, or send it to your tutor or course organizer? For other courses you may be expected to take it to an office or send it to a particular address. Make sure you know how to do this (precise address, name, proof of posting). If you clarify the necessary procedures you can avoid misunderstandings, such as your tutor thinking you have submitted late, when in fact your assignment was on time, but went to the wrong person.

- *Late submission/extension* How strict are the deadlines for individual assignments? Is it possible to ask for more time to finish an assignment? If so, what do you have to do to be granted this? Please note that some institutions have a policy of deducting marks for late submission.

- *Resubmission* Do you only have one go at each assignment, or is there a chance to revise it and resubmit?

- *Additional requirements* What provision is there to take care of any additional requirements you may have due to your personal situation, e.g. if you are hearing-impaired and have difficulty listening to a CD, or if you have difficulty writing? Teaching institutions have a duty to support learners with additional requirements and are happy to help. Get in touch with your course organizer or tutor to discuss such issues as early as possible in your course.

- Read all the assessment-related documentation for your course as soon as it is available to get an overview of the number and type of assignments, as well as related rules and regulations.

- Always ask for clarification from your tutor or course organizer if you are unsure about anything in relation to assessment.

Task 9.2 Assessment rules and regulations for your course

Look at your course documentation and check these details about the way your learning is assessed:

1 what is assessed – content, language, intercultural awareness, presentation?
2 resources and materials required or allowed;
3 word length or time limits;
4 format required;
5 pass mark;
6 weighting of individual parts of an assignment;
7 procedures for submission;
8 procedures for obtaining an extension;
9 possibility of resubmission;
10 arrangements for meeting additional requirements.

Comment
If you cannot find the information for points 1–4 and 7, you should definitely ask your tutor before you start on your first/next assignment. The same applies to point 10 if you have additional requirements. The remainder are less urgent and you should decide whether you want to find out more about them depending on your personal circumstances.

Completing your assignment

The following advice will help you to produce a good written or spoken assignment.

- *Get together all the information you need* Before you start preparing for a written or spoken assignment, gather all the information you need. For example, in addition to the task description, you may have vocabulary lists for a particular topic area or source texts to refer to (see Chapter 6).
- *Get down to it* It is often hard to get started. This may be because you feel insufficiently prepared. There are always more texts you could read or points in the textbook you could go over, and you could go on preparing forever. Usually it is a matter of forcing yourself to start and seeing how you get on. If you then get to a particular point where you feel you need more information, you can check it specifically, e.g. in your textbook or dictionary.

- *Check content and language* Once you have prepared your assignment, check carefully that the content is relevant and the language is accurate. If you already have feedback from your tutor on previous work, refer to it (see the following section, 'Getting your assignment back').
- *Practise a spoken task* If you are giving a talk, have one or two practice runs before the event. If you are preparing for a dialogue or discussion, you might like to practise it with a fellow student or talk to yourself about the topics required.
- *Use your own words and acknowledge sources* In a language assignment naturally you want your contribution to sound as good as possible. By all means use some words or expressions from your course or assessment materials or other sources, but make sure you do not copy large chunks from them. It is important that you show your own ability to use the language, rather than someone else's, as explained in Chapter 6, 'Incorporating language from other sources into your speech or writing'. Too much copying could be considered as plagiarism or cheating, which is a serious matter subject to severe penalties.

  If you are working at a higher academic level (for example, preparing a report or an essay) you will probably be required to draw on a variety of sources. In these cases make sure you reference both direct and indirect quotations appropriately. If this is required, you will be given guidance on the format to use.
- *Consider asking for more time if you really need it* If extensions to deadlines are permitted, they are intended to help you out in an emergency. There is no need to feel embarrassed to ask for one if you are experiencing difficulties. However, make use of them only if you really need to.
- *Always try to hand in SOMETHING* It is usually better to hand in something to your tutor than not to submit anything. Often it will be sufficient to pass, even if the mark is lower than you would have liked. Even if you should fail, you will benefit from the feedback you receive. In some courses it may be possible to drop one of several assignments; others require you to complete them all, and non-submission could cause problems for continuing the course. Always seek advice from your tutor or course organizer about the implications, and whether there are any other options.
- *Review your own goals* Spend some time on thinking about how you feel the work on the assignment went for you. Which parts did you feel went well or badly, which were easy or difficult? How did work for the assignment contribute to the achievement of your language learning goals? It is often useful if you communicate these thoughts to your tutor before they mark an assignment, as they can respond in their feedback (see Chapter 4).

This may well seem like a very long list to consider. These issues are likely to take quite a lot of time to sort out for the first assignment. However, many of them will become second nature to you once you have been studying your particular course for a while.

GETTING YOUR ASSIGNMENT BACK

Making the most of marked assignments

Regardless of the grade it receives, every marked assignment provides valuable opportunities for further learning, so you should review each one carefully as soon as possible after it is returned to you. Do not spend too much time on this, 20 to 30 minutes should be sufficient. For suggestions on how to do this see the section 'How to work with corrected assignments'. Keep the results of your review for future reference.

In addition to the grade, feedback on language assignments provides detailed comments on specific points, plus more general observations. It usually covers three aspects of your work:

- your control over the target language (verb endings, adjective agreements, pronunciation of vowels, and so on);
- your ability to express your ideas coherently and succinctly;
- the extent to which you have completed the task.

Together, these give you a rounded picture of your performance, as well as useful pointers for the future.

Corrections and what they can tell you

Chapter 4 suggests ways to monitor your progress and to assess your strengths and weaknesses in relation to the specific tasks, skills or knowledge needed to complete a forthcoming assignment. The following sections consider how you can adapt this approach to maximize your learning from marked assignments.

Tutors give feedback on your use of the target language in different ways. Some write out corrections in full, but others may prefer to use a marking code (a series of symbols or abbreviations used to identify the most common problems), for example: **VT** (Verb tense error), **A** (Article error) or [ ] (Omit unnecessary word/phrase). Your tutor may also comment on other aspects of your work using a marking code, for example: **Rel** (Relevance of content), or **Str** (Structure of content). Keep any explanatory notes from your tutor to hand as you check through your assignments.

On some courses you may be able to submit assignments electronically. Instead of writing corrections on your script, tutors make electronic annotations. Typically, this involves the use of tools in word processors (e.g. the comment and tracking facilities available in Word). If these tools are needed, your tutor or course documentation will explain how to use them.

Oral assignments may be submitted on audio tape or, perhaps, emailed as sound file attachments. In addition to written feedback, tutors may provide recorded comments (e.g. on pronunciation or intonation). You may be invited to repeat words or phrases that have caused you difficulties. Although this may seem a little strange or embarrassing at first, it is well worth the effort to act on such highly focused, individualized feedback that will help you overcome your own specific problems.

Most important of all, remember that tutors do not only look for what is wrong with your work: they are also interested in what you have done well, and will give praise where it is due. Ticks and encouraging comments are important indicators of your progress, so it is a good idea to take careful note of them and think about how you can reuse the things you have learned and the skills you have acquired in future assignments.

How to work with corrected assignments

Whatever the form of the corrections, they can help you to identify and eliminate recurrent language mistakes. A corrected assignment can also give you advice and guidance on non-linguistic aspects of your work, e.g. unclear arguments or incorrect referencing. For written assignments, as a first step, go through and try to group corrections of the same type in lists under headings such as:

• verbs
• adjectives
• pronouns
• prepositions
• spelling
• choice of vocabulary

or any other categories related to target language use or to the content or structure of your assignment.

You can do the same for oral assignments. Using your tutor's taped or written comments, add categories such as pronunciation, intonation, etc. to your lists, as appropriate. Note all the favourable comments, too, including the points your tutor has simply ticked. Remember that it is important to build on your successes as well as learning from your mistakes. Make a note of any alternative words or expressions suggested by your tutor.

More advanced students may want to subdivide broad categories of corrections, e.g.

- Verbs
  - form
  - tense
  - subject–verb agreement, etc.

The categories you identify will vary according to specific features of your target language, for instance, case (German), personal *a* (Spanish), or tone (Mandarin). Keep these categories and lists of corrections to hand when you prepare for your next assignment as a reminder of things to watch out for. Tasks 9.3 and 9.4 help you to put these suggestions into practice.

Producing multiple lists in this way may seem like a chore, but it is a good way of identifying gaps in your knowledge, or skills that need to be developed, helping you to learn more effectively. In the longer term, categorizing your tutor's corrections and comments can help you to chart your progress and adopt a more strategic approach. Why waste time working on things you can already do well when it makes much more sense to concentrate on things you do not know or have not yet assimilated? Categorizing things you did well, mistakes and corrections can help you to identify your strengths and weaknesses and make a realistic assessment of your progress. Lastly, as you eliminate the types of mistake corrected by your tutor, you can cross them off the lists, and this can be a great boost to your morale!

Task 9.3 Categorizing comments and corrections

Take a previously marked assignment and categorize the favourable comments and corrections made by your tutor, as described in the text. Note the number in each category. Now list them in order, putting the category with the greatest number first.

Comment
Does anything surprise you about the result? Keep this list to hand for the next task.

Using feedback to become a better language learner

Tutors may not necessarily provide full corrections for all mistakes, but simply underline them, or indicate the sentence or paragraph in which they occur. This does not mean that tutors are not doing their job properly, but is simply recognition that you, as a learner, have a role to play in the correction process too. Making you look for certain mistakes and then rectify them does mean more work and more responsibility for you, but at the same time it gives you a chance to think through the rules again and learn them.

Apart from correcting individual mistakes, tutors may make more extensive comments on your script dealing with recurring problems, or points that do not lend themselves to brief corrections. They may also provide a general commentary, usually on the cover sheet of the assignment. In the most helpful commentaries, tutors explain how they arrived at the grade they awarded, relating your performance to the assessment criteria (see the example in Figure 9.6). Tutor commentaries give you an overview of your progress in your language studies. They can include general advice, such as:

- clarification of any elements of the task, instructions or assessment material that you may have misinterpreted or misunderstood;
- advice on how to present and structure your answer more effectively;
- suggestions for further practice or references to sources of help (e.g. sections of the coursebooks, grammars, etc.);
- general tips about developing your language skills.

Remember, however, that tutors are often working to tight deadlines, so they do not always have time to comment on every aspect of your work in great detail. You may occasionally find their comments unclear, or that you need specific examples to help you grasp a more general point. In such cases, do not hesitate to get in touch. Tutors would much rather spend time helping students to overcome difficulties than leave them struggling unaided.

Sometimes your tutor will ask you to make contact to discuss your work. Students are sometimes too embarrassed to do so, but if you receive such an invitation, do take it up, as it will be a golden opportunity for you to obtain personal advice and guidance.

- When you receive marked assignments, categorize the corrections made by your tutor, grouping them under headings (e.g. verbs, adjectives, etc.). Listen to any comments on oral assignments, and do the same.
- Note all favourable comments too, and think about how you can reuse the things you have done well in future assignments.
- Use these lists to identify your strengths and weaknesses.
- Summarize your tutor's general comments, paying particular attention to:

- explanations of how the grade was arrived at;
- clarification of the instructions or other aspects of the task;
- advice on presenting and structuring your answer;
- suggestions on further practice and sources of help;
- study tips.

- Compare specific comments and corrections with your tutor's general commentary, noting items requiring attention before you start your next assignment.

- Give yourself credit for the progress you have made, take the opportunity to check on whether you have achieved your goals and set new ones (see Chapter 4).

- Contact your tutor if invited to do so, or if you have any queries.

Task 9.4 Drawing up an action plan

Draw up an action plan for the assignment you worked on in Task 9.3. Look carefully at your tutor's remarks on the script itself and in any general written or recorded commentary. Summarize the points made, both positive and negative, together with any suggestions for revision. Look again at the lists you drew up in Task 9.3 as well. Use all of this information to produce a plan of things to do before submitting the next assignment. You may find it helpful to group them under these headings:

■ Completing the task (complying with instructions, presentation and structure of work).
■ Improving my language.

Comment
Remember that the aim is to establish priorities, so concentrate on a few essential points (two or three per heading at the most, e.g. the largest categories identified in Task 9.3) to make your action plan focused and its aims achievable. If you are unsure about anything, discuss it with your tutor.

Another effective review technique is to redo the assignment, taking all the tutor's feedback into consideration and targeting areas where there is room for improvement. If possible, exchange revised assignments with another student and give each other feedback. Redoing the assignment provides opportunities for active learning and for measuring your progress.

Assignments, feedback and corrections all have the potential to help you to learn, but you have to unlock it by asking the right questions, concentrating not so much on *What did I get wrong?*, but on *How can I use my strengths and weaknesses to learn more efficiently and effectively?* Learning from assessments should be a key part of your short-term action plan as well as a step towards your longer-term goals (see Chapter 4, 'Assessing your strengths and weaknesses: setting goals').

MAINTAINING A POSITIVE ATTITUDE: COPING WITH SETBACKS

Most people experience highs and lows during their studies. Chapter 3, 'Maintaining your confidence', suggests ways of managing low points. Maintaining a positive attitude in the face of setbacks is important for your progress and your morale at all times, especially when approaching assignments and exams.

You may be finding a particular aspect of your course hard to grasp or you may be experiencing difficulties in areas unrelated to your studies. Even a relatively minor family or work issue may seem more acute at these times. Recognizing that these are common experiences and tackling them as early as possible, will help you to maintain your momentum.

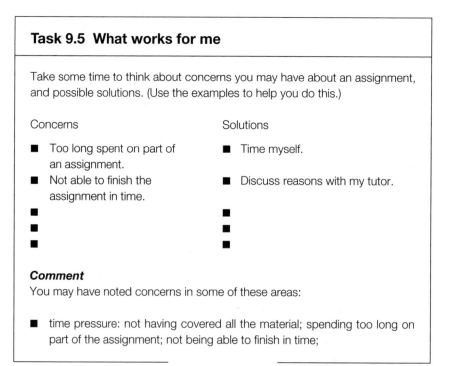

Task 9.5 What works for me

Take some time to think about concerns you may have about an assignment, and possible solutions. (Use the examples to help you do this.)

Concerns

- Too long spent on part of an assignment.
- Not able to finish the assignment in time.
-
-
-

Solutions

- Time myself.
- Discuss reasons with my tutor.
-
-
-

Comment
You may have noted concerns in some of these areas:

- time pressure: not having covered all the material; spending too long on part of the assignment; not being able to finish in time;

■ anxiety or panic: not quite understanding the task; concern about not having the skill or knowledge required; handing in something you are not totally satisfied with;

■ feelings of disappointment, frustration or anger: a lower mark than expected; a mark that doesn't seem to reflect the effort you have made.

Some practical solutions are given in the next section. Whatever your concerns, devote some time to working out the best solution. Then put it into practice and stick to it.

Keeping positive: some solutions

If you are facing real **time pressure**, try to assess honestly how this has arisen, so that you can take the appropriate action. See also Chapter 2, 'Managing your time'. The same strategies can be applied to assessment tasks. Ask yourself how you could avoid falling behind in the future. Be honest with yourself. Are you under time pressure primarily because you are a perfectionist? If so, be tough on yourself. If you are tackling an assignment, give yourself a deadline for starting (even if you feel you are not quite ready), as well as for finishing. In future you could time yourself when doing course activities; this may help you when you come to the next assignment.

If, on the other hand, your lack of time is due to unforeseen circumstances, then it is reasonable to get in touch with your tutor or course organizer. You may be able to negotiate more time or drop an assignment (see the advice on extensions and non-submission in 'Completing your assignment'). Check the rules which apply on your course. Don't be tempted to ask for extra time to avoid forcing yourself to get started. Remember that any delay increases the danger of falling behind with subsequent work.

If your study plan has not quite worked out and you feel there is just too much material to get through in the time available, review and select what is most relevant for this assignment. Be pragmatic and focus on what is needed now. You can go back to other material later by allowing time for it in a revised study plan.

If you are feeling anxiety or panic about how well you can do, it is useful to take stock of the strengths you already have. Focusing on your strengths will help you feel better about your achievements and maintain a positive attitude in tackling your assignments. Think about what you *can* now do that you couldn't do before (see Figure 9.7).

Having managed to complete the assignment, the first thing you will probably do when you get it back is look at the mark or grade. If it is what you expected, or even higher, you will feel elated and ready to carry on

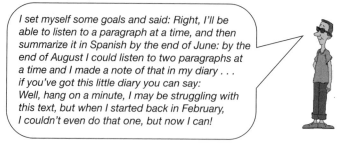

I set myself some goals and said: Right, I'll be able to listen to a paragraph at a time, and then summarize it in Spanish by the end of June: by the end of August I could listen to two paragraphs at a time and I made a note of that in my diary . . .
if you've got this little diary you can say:
Well, hang on a minute, I may be struggling with this text, but when I started back in February, I couldn't even do that one, but now I can!

Figure 9.7 A student view: keeping positive.

with renewed energy and increased motivation. If it is lower, you may feel disappointment, or even anger or frustration if you feel your tutor has misunderstood or misjudged your work. Talk to your tutor if you do not understand what is wrong. No matter how you feel, it is always worth considering the feedback carefully, as suggested above, and making an effort to learn as much as you can from it. You might like to do this straight away, or wait a while until you can view it dispassionately.

Sometimes it is helpful to talk with others. Chapter 10 considers how to make the most of support from others, but in relation to assignments in particular, you could talk to:

- other students: you may well discover that you are not the only one who found part of an assignment difficult. It may be a relief to realize that you are not alone, but more importantly, through discussion you can also pick up new tips and approaches;
- friends or to your family: they may, for example, help you make more time available for your studies;
- your tutor or a language adviser (see Chapter 10) if one is available: this may help you arrive at a viable solution. Try to come out of the meeting with a realistic plan for how to progress (see Figure 9.8).

. . . I had a really good tutor last year. Instead of saying: 'I don't know how to do this, I can't do Spanish'; I could say: 'Look, I'm ever so sorry, but can you give me some tips, because I am struggling with X'; and I found that my tutor was absolutely brilliant at giving me help. . . .

Figure 9.8 A student view: talking about a problem.

Whatever you choose to do, don't keep the problem to yourself. Learning is a process, and assessment is part of it. Share the good times. Successfully completing an assignment is very motivating, but recognize that setbacks may occur at some stage. You need to find out what solutions work best for you and be prepared to give them a go. It is all part of becoming an effective learner.

- Assess time pressures honestly to find the best solution for you.

- Look at what you can already do; don't give in to negative self-talk.

- Share your good experiences and your concerns. Talk to others (students, family or friends, tutor).

EXAMINATIONS: HOW CAN I MAKE SURE I DO MY BEST IN AN EXAM?

What makes an exam different from assignments?

For assignments you have probably been working without time restrictions, although you may have been advised how long to spend on them. In a language exam you will be working within time limits. If you have practised doing this beforehand you will feel under less pressure in the exam itself.

For your assignments you can normally use as many reference materials as you like; for an exam there will be regulations as to what you can take into the examination room. Check in advance what types of dictionary, grammar book or textbook are allowed, if any. In an exam you may need to refer to specific material (for example a reading passage, a listening text or a picture) that you have either studied beforehand or are given on the spot. In contrast to assignments that you do during the rest of the year, you are likely to receive no feedback on your exam or final assessment.

Work throughout the year

The nature of language learning makes regular work throughout the year of paramount importance. A language is less of an 'information' subject than many others. It is more about developing your listening, speaking, reading and writing skills, and using them in context, by giving a presentation in the language, for example. You develop language awareness and improve your use of the language, building on vocabulary and grammar related to the topics studied in your course. You transfer the language you learn from one situation to another. You also develop cultural and intercultural awareness and understanding. These skills are built up gradually through regular practice of the language; they cannot be acquired through last minute cramming.

However, revision is important!

Revision

Task 9.6 Effective exam preparation

Think about the following question and note down your responses:
What do I need to consider when planning my revision in order to prepare effectively for my exam?

Comment
You may have considered the following:

- timing (a revision schedule);
- content of revision (what to revise and how to revise it);
- exam technique (self-testing and trial run of exam-type tasks).

Revision schedule
When planning your revision schedule, allow enough time before the exam to be able to revise what you identify as crucial, taking into account any other commitments. Do not leave revision to the last few days in case there are unanticipated demands on your time. Managing your time effectively will also help you to feel more relaxed.

What and how to revise
Make sure you know what will be examined, and how. Then start by concentrating on these specific skills and topic areas.

Task   Depending on your language level and the nature of the exam, you will need to prepare for different types of tasks (see Table 9.1).

Strategies   By now you will have built up a set of strategies for approaching different reading, listening, speaking and writing tasks and you should know what works best for you. You will have noted what you found easy and what worked for you, and what you found difficult and how you dealt with that. Go through potential problem areas again and discuss them with your tutor, a language adviser or fellow students.

Vocabulary   Revise specific vocabulary or expressions for the type of task you are expecting, for example, essay writing. Work on vocabulary related to topics on your course; use mind maps, or any other topic-related revision system that you find helpful. Test yourself.

Grammar Make a list of points to be checked during a written exam, based on a review of your previous performance throughout the course. Work on those points you are still having problems with.

Topics Some language exams also assess factual knowledge. Check whether this is the case and revise accordingly. Even if it is not assessed you need to be sufficiently conversant with the topics in your course to be at ease with new situations or perspectives on these topics presented in an exam.

Essays If you have to write essays make sure you recognize, understand and know how to respond to the various process words like *analyse*, *compare and contrast*, *illustrate*, etc. in your target language. Practise drafting plans before you write or speak (see Chapter 6, 'Preparing what you want to say or write', and 'Speaking and writing from notes').

Presentation If you have to give a timed presentation, make sure you know how much you can say at your normal speed within a given time. Practise adjusting your main points to the time available.

Handouts If you have to use specific material made available beforehand for either a written or an oral exam, make sure that you have done your preparation thoroughly.

Trial run

In your preparation, include a trial run of the type of tasks required for the exam, either with a fellow student or with another speaker of the target language. This could include working through a specimen paper or a past paper if available. Working through a written paper will give you the chance to discuss content, approach and linguistic features. A trial run of an oral will give you a feel for the interaction, what works, and why. In both cases it will give you a sense of the timing. Practise under exam conditions so that you can judge better where any possible problems may lie.

Checklist for monitoring your performance

- Did I understand clearly what the task entailed, what I needed to do?
- Did I spend too long deciding what to write/say?
- Did I write/say a lot about some points and nothing/not enough about some others?
- Was this because of lack of time . . .
- . . . or because I did not have enough to say?
- Did I not have enough time to finish? Why?

The person with whom you are doing the trial run could also use this checklist; you could then discuss and compare ideas together. This will help you identify what you do well, and any areas where you may need further practice and revision, perhaps returning to other relevant sections of this book.

On the day

On the day, all this practice and tactical planning will help you to deal much more easily and comfortably with the exam. You will be in a better position to:

- judge your strengths and weaknesses and choose the task(s) most suited to you, if there is a choice;
- manage the time available for the task(s);
- check automatically for possible pitfalls;
- interact comfortably and contribute in a focused way in orals.

Also don't overlook these general points which apply to any exam:

- Put together in advance any resources you are allowed to take into the exam, e.g. dictionary, pen, your examination number and proof of identity if required.
- If you have any special requirements do make sure that you have discussed them well in advance of your exam, so that the necessary arrangements are in place for the day.
- Check the time and place of the exam.
- If you are travelling by public transport make sure you have got the right timetable and allow enough time to get to the examination centre in plenty of time.
- If you are travelling by car make sure you know in advance how long it will take you and allow for any eventualities. Find out about parking facilities.
- Try to keep calm under pressure – try some breathing exercises before going into the exam, and during the exam if necessary.

You are now set for the day. Once you are there, sit comfortably and do your best.

Summary of key points

- Find out what sort of accreditation your course offers and ask your tutor for advice if you are unsure.

- Find out when you will be assessed, who will assess you and what tasks the assessment will consist of.

- When doing an assignment make sure you have all the information you need; complete it following the guidelines; check it thoroughly for content and language and hand it in on time.

- When you get your marked assignment back read your tutor's comments carefully and draw up an action plan.

- Maintain a positive attitude; share good experiences and any concerns.

- Prepare systematically and in good time for an exam.

10

Making the most of support

Annie Eardley and Cecilia Garrido

Whether you are learning independently or attending a language class, there are plenty of sources of support you can draw on. Earlier chapters have highlighted the importance of friends and family, fellow students, work colleagues and interaction with other speakers of your target language in particular. This chapter examines the types of support you can expect from your tutor or from a language adviser, if you are studying through an educational institution, before considering in more detail how you can make the most of these other sources of support. It concludes by looking at your ultimate goal: putting your newly acquired language skills into practice.

MAKING THE MOST OF SUPPORT FROM YOUR TUTOR OR LANGUAGE ADVISER

The role of tutors and language advisers

Tutors provide tuition and academic support for learners enrolled on courses in traditional classroom settings or in distance education. They have overall responsibility for monitoring your progress in the target language. Note that the best tutor is not simply a fluent target language speaker. Most important is the tutor's ability to explain concepts clearly and devise activities which will help you practise and consolidate what you have learned.

Language advisers usually provide support in self-access or 'drop-in' centres or language centres. Their role is to complement the work of tutors by helping you to locate appropriate resources in these centres and to give you advice on how to study effectively.

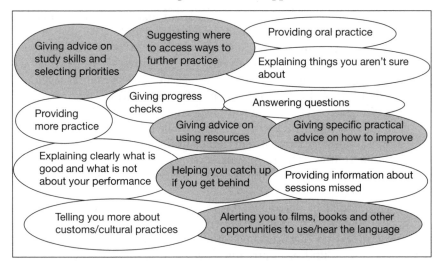

Figure 10.1 The role of tutors and language advisers.

Task 10.1 Support from a language adviser or your tutor

Look at the types of support shown in Figure 10.1.
   Which could be provided by a language adviser?

Comment:
The shaded items would normally be where a language adviser could offer help.
In institutions where there is no self-access or language centre, these roles are
also fulfilled by the tutor.

Seeking and using support

Figure 10.1 shows the various types of support your tutor or language adviser
can provide. Although, in some cases, you could get this support from other
people, in the following situations the most appropriate person to contact
is your tutor:

- *When you have questions about your course or need explanations and
  examples for specific language points, or advice about assignments* There
  may be times when you find the explanation of a new language point
  difficult to follow or you are uncertain how to tackle a particular
  assignment. It is much better to seek advice straight away if you have
  a problem. You are likely to make more progress and obtain better grades
  in your assessed work if you understand these points fully and know
  exactly what is expected of you.

Before you contact your tutor, work out exactly what you need to know or would like to have explained. It may help to write out your questions if you are making contact by phone. Check that you have understood your tutor's explanations by repeating them in your own words, e.g. *Can I just check that? The adjective ending changes when. . . .* Another way of checking is to create a few examples of your own in the target language and ask your tutor how they sound or if they are written correctly. You may want to do this in a subsequent call or an email. Your tutor also knows your course materials well and may suggest you repeat certain activities or revise certain sections. Note the explanations and advice carefully and put them into practice as soon as you can afterwards.

- *When you feel that you are not progressing fast enough*   Do not expect to make progress at the same pace throughout your course. Sometimes learners feel they have reached a plateau and that they are not covering much new ground or improving their performance. This can be frustrating and demotivating. Contact your tutor and explain how you feel. Your tutor can give you clear, objective advice on what you are capable of and may suggest concrete ways in which you can measure the progress you have made (such as suggestions in Chapter 4, 'Monitoring your progress' and Chapter 9, 'Making the most of marked assignments'). Talking to your tutor and sharing his/her enthusiasm for the target language and culture can re-inspire you and revive your motivation to continue.

- *When you need to clarify feedback on your performance in assessments* Chapter 9 explains how to make the most of feedback on assessed work and advises you to contact your tutor if you have any questions. As with other questions, try to be as clear as possible. Your tutor will not necessarily remember the detail of your work. It will help if you provide the context or a copy either by email/post or when you meet. Check your understanding of any explanations as suggested above and note them for future reference. Use the information in the same way as the rest of your tutor's feedback (as suggested in Chapter 9, 'Making the most of marked assignments').

In the following situations it is appropriate to contact a language adviser if available, or your tutor.

- *When you need further language practice*   Before you look for additional practice, make sure you get the most out of any classes by being as active and involved as possible, even if some activities are unfamiliar to you at first. (See Chapter 3, 'Learning with others in a language classroom', for some examples of typical language class activities.) Try to be open-minded and not to dismiss any outright. If you do not understand their aims, ask. Make every effort to attend, even if the classes are optional for your course. If you still feel you need additional practice or if attending language classes is a problem, ask your tutor or a language adviser to suggest other sources of practice activities or an alternative to classes. Chapter 7 contains suggestions for further practice using real-life target language resources and Chapter 8 explains how to access electronic resources. Language advisers can usually put you in touch with speakers of the target language through the TANDEM network (see 'Making the most of support from other speakers of the language'.)

- *When you want to use the self-access facilities provided by your educational establishment*   Your institution may have self-access or 'drop-in' facilities where you can work on specific skills. Resources usually include reading and audio material with accompanying notes, exercises and answer keys; access to target language TV channels by satellite or recorded programmes; selected CALL programmes (see Chapter 8) for grammar or writing practice. In order to make the most of support, make sure you think through the sort of practice you need. You may do this by assessing your strengths and weaknesses as suggested in Chapter 4, as well as by reviewing your performance in assignments (Chapter 9). The language adviser will then be able to suggest appropriate material and the sort of activities that would be most helpful to enable you to achieve your goals.

Contacting your tutor

Keep your tutor's contact details to hand, i.e. email addresses, telephone numbers and contact times. It is also a good idea to check the best way to make contact. Tutors will be only too happy to offer help when they are free to respond. Remember, however, that they have many students and cannot be expected to provide extensive one-to-one language practice.

Chapters 1 and 2 encourage you to define your long- and short-term language learning objectives. Make contact with your tutor early in your course to talk through your objectives and expectations. In return, your tutor will explain what help you can expect, and offer advice as appropriate. Establishing a good relationship makes it easier to seek help when you need it and ensure that you take advantage of support. Remember, however, that although your tutor is there to guide you, it is you who do the learning.

MAKING THE MOST OF SUPPORT FROM YOUR FELLOW STUDENTS

The major benefit of attending language classes is that they will give you the opportunity to meet fellow students and feel part of a learning community, which can provide mutual help and support.

Task 10.2 Support from other students

Jot down five ways in which your fellow students can help you in your language learning.

Comment

It is a popular misconception among many language learners that they cannot learn from other learners, but there are many advantages in establishing close links with your fellow students. You may have thought of the following:

■ practising the language together;
■ sharing study tips, e.g. for remembering vocabulary;
■ sharing useful information, e.g. helpful websites or target language films showing locally;
■ pooling resources or effort, e.g. joint purchase of magazines or sharing the reading of course material and explaining it to each other;
■ mutual encouragement.

Some of these ideas are discussed in more detail in this chapter.

Practising your oral skills

Practising your oral skills with other students can provide you with instant feedback on your performance and give you informal indications of your progress. One frequent concern is that this can reinforce bad habits and mistakes and may generate new ones. In fact it can help you in many ways. If other students are less proficient or confident than yourself, you may need to rephrase what you are saying in order to be understood. This is a useful skill. Many language learners tend to reuse familiar expressions and structures making little attempt to extend their range. Having to explain something to someone who has not understood you can extend your range as well as helping to clarify it in your own mind.

Working with students who appear to be more able than you also has advantages. It can give you a dry run in situations similar to those you will encounter when you interact with fluent speakers of the language. This can make you more confident in your ability to cope. Working with students who are at a similar level to you can also bring benefits. Each learner has different strengths and weaknesses so you will always find that you can learn from others.

Remember that other students may appear more proficient, but this may reflect higher levels of confidence rather than real levels of competence in the language. It is natural to make mistakes when learning a language. Furthermore, it is neither practical, nor desirable to expect every single mistake you make to be corrected. This can make you self-conscious and less fluent. Mistakes are not a problem in many real-life situations, as long as they do not impede communication. In many cases you will realize you have made a mistake and self-correct it, just as you would in your first language.

Mutual support and encouragement

Working with your fellow students will give you the opportunity to share enthusiasm and interests with like-minded people. You can exchange information about local resources such as films, twinning associations or conversation groups. Other students can act as an additional source of help and advice outside scheduled sessions, creating a sense of solidarity. They can also give you information about classes you have missed if you cannot contact your tutor. This mutual support can take the form of occasional contacts or more regular study group sessions.

Study buddies and groups

As already explained, studying together provides an opportunity to share skills, generate new ideas and learn from one another. Chapter 3, 'Studying independently', outlined the ways in which working with a study buddy can enhance your language learning, particularly when you are learning independently or feel that you are not able to interact easily with other speakers of the language. Speaking a language is a social activity so it makes sense to create practice opportunities in a social environment. The following advice focuses on self-help study groups, but applies equally to work with an individual partner.

The success of a study group session depends on its content. Just as you would hope to come out of a class feeling enlightened, stimulated and motivated, you should leave your study session with a feeling of achievement which does not, of course, prevent you from enjoying yourself as well. It is worth spending some time discussing the content of your meetings and the activities you will include.

What can you do in a study group session?

- Work on activities that extend what you did in your class or new exercises that practise what you are currently studying. Your tutor should be able to help with ideas.
- Repeat activities from the course material, particularly those which are open-ended and do not have a set answer, for example activities which ask you to describe your locality or give your opinion about an issue. If the original activity was to be done in writing, take the opportunity to discuss it instead.

- Discuss the topic of your next assignment. There is nothing wrong with sharing ideas, before you prepare your own work. You can gain a lot from this process. It can help you to consider other points of view, to debate and argue your own case in the target language. Of course, unless the assignment is specifically intended to be a collaborative project, your actual submission must be your own individual effort. There are usually heavy penalties for presenting work which is not entirely your own.
- Watch a video of the news in a country where your target language is spoken. See Chapter 7 for ideas on how to work with recorded material.
- Organize a book club which would meet on a regular basis to discuss a book you have read. You could ask your tutor to recommend suitable books.
- Invite guest speakers of the language to talk to your group. You may know of students from other countries, for instance, who would welcome the chance to meet more local people.

Setting up a study group
Setting up a study group requires organization, and the most successful groups often have one person who takes responsibility for making the arrangements. Consider the following points:

- Find a place convenient for all those involved. If you cannot find a room in your college or university, you could meet in a café, community centre or group member's home. Hotel foyers often have quiet places open to non-residents. Your local library may be able to help. Look for a venue which is accessible to all group members, e.g. has wheelchair access.
- Keep to the same time and day for each session; people are less likely to forget the arrangement.
- Consider telephone or online conferences if travel is a problem. These are fairly easy to organize. Three-way telephone conferences are available to private telephone users. Telephone companies and some community organizations can facilitate larger conferences. You can find examples of types of CMC (Computer-Mediated Communication) in Chapter 8.
- Agree ways of keeping in touch with each other.

The more care taken over the initial arrangements, the easier it will be to maintain the group's momentum.

Setting up a study group

- Agree on content and activities. Ask your tutor for help if necessary.

- Find a suitable venue or convenient way to meet.

- Agree on a particular time and day and how often to meet.

- Ensure that all members are easily contactable.

MAKING THE MOST OF SUPPORT FROM FRIENDS AND FAMILY

Chapter 2 points out the potential impact of your studies on your friends and family. You need to plan frequent study sessions and maximize opportunities to hear and practise the language. This is much easier with the support of your friends and family. They may be able to help in a variety of ways.

Task 10.3 Support from friends and family

Think of the friends and family members who could help your language learning and list the kind of support they could give you.

Comment

There are plenty of possibilities. For example, they may:

- help you to clarify and extend your ideas by discussing a particular topic with you in your mother tongue;
- offer you encouragement when you need it;
- be happy to join you at a cinema to see a target language film (providing there are subtitles for them) or record programmes on video for you;
- be able to offer tips and/or practice if you have friends who are also studying the language or have done so in the past;
- look out for opportunities for you to practise or hear the language.

MAKING THE MOST OF SUPPORT IN THE WORKPLACE

Benefits of languages in the workplace

Benefits to the company
Companies who have contacts with suppliers, partners or clients abroad benefit from having employees with skills in the language spoken in the countries where these are based. First of all, foreign companies appreciate it when some effort is made to speak their language. Furthermore, awareness of the culture of the country enhances communication between the various partners. By offering you help and support in your language learning, your company will be able to interact more efficiently with their overseas associates.

Benefits to yourself
If you are an employee, learning a relevant language may improve your career prospects. You may be promoted to a post where you are in daily contact with the language you are learning. The first time you are asked to take a telephone call in the language may be daunting and may make you feel exposed. However, if you prepare what you want to say to obtain the information you need, it should be much easier and become more natural. You will have opportunities to learn new expressions and to make informal checks on your linguistic performance. Moreover, many of the new skills you acquire will be transferable to other areas of your work.

Support from employer

How can your employer support you in your language studies?

- By funding your study if you can demonstrate benefit to the company. If you cannot obtain full funding, you may be able to negotiate part-funding. In some cases, loans may be available.
- By providing a quiet place for you to study at lunchtime, especially if the company has training rooms which may be fitted with VCRs, CD/DVD players or computers. This can help you keep to your study plan.
- By allowing you to take some time off to study for exams. It will be much easier to do so away from the distractions of work.
- By providing opportunities for work-based assessment and accreditation.

Most companies value employees who want to develop their skills and will be happy to offer help and support. It is worth discussing this with your employer.

Support from work colleagues

You may want to encourage some of your colleagues to join you. They may decide to study with you or simply practise their existing language skills with you. You can also try to maximize opportunities to use the language with your opposite numbers in companies overseas. Your work colleagues may also provide help and encouragement.

Task 10.4 Support from your employer

If you are an employee, what opportunities are there for you to use your target language in the workplace?

What support is your employer able to offer?

Support from careers advice services

If no opportunities to use your language skills exist within your company, you may want to consider other career paths. Services such as Learndirect provide advice on jobs and careers as well as courses and information on possible funding for learning:
http://www.learndirect-advice.co.uk
    If you have a high level of competence in your target language,
http://www. prospects.ac.uk provides information on a wide range of jobs available to people fluent in another language.

MAKING THE MOST OF SUPPORT FROM OTHER SPEAKERS OF THE LANGUAGE

Reasons for wanting to learn a language are varied, but being able to interact with people who speak this language will probably feature high on your list. You might like to try the following suggestions.

TANDEM learning

Chapter 1, 'Opportunities and providers', introduces the TANDEM network and this approach is also referred to in other chapters. Some language learning institutions organize TANDEM learning schemes for their students. These schemes pair you with a speaker of your target language who is studying your first language and living in your country. You are likely to be provided with guidelines to help you establish a good learning relationship, but here are some points to consider:

- Agree which language to use and when. This depends on the level and ability of each language learner. One approach is to use both languages equally but this may be impractical if the levels are very different. If there is no clear agreement, one language may dominate, defeating the purpose of the scheme.
- Think about how you want to deal with error correction. Review the comments in the section 'Practising your oral skills' in this chapter and the likely negative effects of constant correction. You may find it more helpful to ask your partner to summarize some key points for you at the end of your conversation, starting with your successes. What you talk about in the sessions is up to you. Chapter 3, Task 3.3, gives some suggestions. Working with a speaker of your target language in this way can give you real insight into their culture and vice versa.

Penfriends or email TANDEM partners
Other organizations can put you in touch with a TANDEM partner or penfriend abroad. Your institution or language adviser may be able to give you details of such organizations. Alternatively, you can find information about the International TANDEM Network at http://www.slf.rub.de (see Chapter 1, 'Opportunities and providers').

Communicating by letter or using CMC, for example, email or text chat gives you the opportunity to practise your writing skills. If you use CMC, the language you produce is likely to be closer to the spoken form than to formal writing. Your messages are likely to be shorter and more spontaneous than a letter to a penfriend. If you communicate by letter, you can practise structuring your writing and decide on the content which puts you in control of what you write, as opposed to when you write assignments.

A penfriend or TANDEM partner allows you to have regular contact with people who use your target language daily, and who can provide you with more information about a country in which it is spoken. Your partner may also be willing to correct your mistakes and may ask you for clarification if what you say is not conveyed clearly – an opportunity for even more practice!

Local resident speakers of the language

Local resident speakers of your target language may be happy to help you practise your oral skills as an opportunity to speak their own language, especially if they are homesick. The advice in Chapter 6, 'Interacting with others', will help you get the most out of such conversations. Some speakers may offer to give you extra tuition. Remember that they are not necessarily teachers and cannot be expected to have the same sort of expertise as your tutor. What they can offer is the opportunity to hear other accents, to find out about certain areas of a country, 'local' customs or dialects, and to learn new words or expressions or try out structures and phrases learned. Some communities organize events to foster integration of new residents. Your library should have details of such events.

Visiting the country

Going to a country where the language is spoken is a wonderful way to increase your motivation and can renew your interest and enthusiasm in the language. You will have the opportunity to pick up resources such as magazines or advertisements and perhaps watch television or listen to the radio. Chapter 7 suggests many ways to use such real-life material and also points out that it is up to you to make a special effort to interact with local people when on holiday in a country where the language is spoken and not limit yourself to conversations in shops. To ensure total immersion in the language, you could consider staying with a family, enrolling on an intensive course at a language school or finding work there.

Staying with a family

Some organizations specialize in finding families willing to welcome foreign guests or exchange partners. You will be expected to write to your hosts before travelling. To benefit fully from your visit, be ready to adapt to a new routine. In most cases you will be expected to live as one of the family, rather than being entertained by them. Try to find out about the place you will be staying in before you plan any activities. Instead of using organizations, you may decide to ask friends or your tandem partner/penfriend to help you find suitable hosts.

Language schools

Many language schools offer intensive residential courses in countries where the target language is spoken. You will be able to concentrate on your language studies and benefit from total immersion as well. You will find your fluency improves and this will sustain your motivation when you get back home. Before choosing a course, check the credentials of the organization you have selected as well as the nature of the programme of studies they offer.

Working abroad

The idea of working abroad may be challenging, but it will provide you with some of the best opportunities to develop your language skills, particularly if the work involves plenty of contact with local people. Your work may involve staying in a country where the language is spoken with support from your employer. Otherwise, if you are learning a European language, you may find opportunities through one of the programmes within *Socrates*, a European education programme which offers grants in certain circumstances for study, teaching, work placements or training courses in another European country: http://www2britishcouncil.org/socrates

The British Council also provides information on opportunities for training and work experience in other countries: http://www.britcoun.org/learning-international-experience.htm

PUTTING YOUR LEARNING INTO PRACTICE

Learning a language opens a gateway to exciting opportunities to learn about others. The richness of that experience is not only dependent on your command of the language, but also on your knowledge and understanding of the other culture.

Differences between your own culture and that of the speakers of the language you are learning may seem obvious, but beware of rushing to conclusions, whether positive or negative, based on lack of knowledge or misinterpretation. Different customs are usually a reaction to local conditions. Understanding the cultural patterns represented by the language you are learning requires practice as well as a genuine interest in discovering what makes that particular culture what it is. You will find evidence of these patterns in the people, their history, their art, their food, their customs, their values, in every aspect of their lives. Intercultural understanding does not mean ignoring or giving up your own cultural values and beliefs, but it does require a conscious effort on your part to appreciate those of the other culture and be prepared to modify your original attitudes if appropriate.

The first encounter with another culture is often described as 'culture shock'. It is possible that after the initial excitement, you may feel disappointed because things are not as you imagined. However, taking the opportunity to discover and analyse what lies behind particular types of behaviour, and to reflect on your experience will gradually help you to understand the differences, respect them and feel comfortable with them. You will be in a better position to enjoy the new environment and all the opportunities it offers for practising your language skills.

Unlike many other subjects, language learning is more than an academic exercise, it is a social activity. The aim of language learning is to interact with other people whether in person, through books and other texts or through the Web. Although you need quiet time on your own to study and reflect on your progress, you can benefit from contact with others and the support they provide for your learning. Being able to communicate effectively with speakers of another language opens doors to new worlds in a journey of discovery.

Bon voyage!

Summary of key points

- Contact your tutor about questions or concerns.

- Make your questions as precise as possible, check your understanding of explanations and put the points into practice as soon as you can.

- Contact a language adviser for guidance on appropriate resources in a self-access centre.

- Working with a study buddy or a self-help study group is a very effective way of increasing practice opportunities and maintaining motivation.

- Friends and family can support your language learning in a variety of ways.

- Employers and work colleagues can provide practical support and encouragement.

- You can make contact with speakers of your target language both locally, e.g. through TANDEM learning schemes, and by visiting a country where the language is spoken, e.g. staying with a family, taking a course or working.

- Interacting with speakers of your target language allows you to explore a whole new world and gain fresh perspectives on your own.

Glossary

Talking about language learning involves, as it does with most subjects, the use of some technical terms. This glossary provides a list of terms which appear in the book. There is no need to read them first, but you may find it useful to refer to the glossary from time to time as you read individual chapters.

Active and passive vocabulary A distinction is made between:

- your **passive vocabulary**: the words and expressions that you may recognize but do not actually use, and
- your **active vocabulary**: words and expressions which you as a learner produce regularly.

Language learners usually find that their passive vocabulary is far larger than their active vocabulary.

Alliteration Words beginning with the same sound to produce a particular effect, e.g. *sizzling sausages* or *busy bees buzzing*.

Cloze texts or exercises Texts or exercises where certain words or phrases have been blanked out. Learners fill in the blanks by reading the surrounding text in order to work out what is missing. The gaps may be a particular type of word, for example all the verbs in the text or words related to a specific topic such as the weather, or they may be random, for example where every tenth word has been blanked out.

Cognates Words that are the same or similar in your language and the language you are learning and have the same or similar meaning. For example, *begin* (English) and *beginnen* (German) or *respond/reply* (English) and *responder* (Spanish) or *répondre* (French).

Collocations Words that often occur together in a particular order, such as *chalk and cheese; an almighty crash; pitch black; a deep breath*.

Compensation strategies Strategies which you can use in advance or on the spot in order to avoid potential difficulties in communication. They are particularly useful in unpredictable situations. Examples include:

preparing for a situation by checking the vocabulary for topics which are likely to come up in conversation; paraphrasing what you want to say if you can't think of a specific word or asking the name of a particular item or how to describe an activity in the target language.

Connotations Cultural and social associations conjured up by particular words and phrases, for example the images that come to mind for English speakers if they hear the word *school* or *high street*. Connotations differ between languages and between groups of language speakers as they reflect the cultural and social life of the countries and communities where the target language is spoken.

Corpora Large collections of texts or transcriptions of spoken material in a specific language. These illustrate how target language speakers actually use the language in a variety of situations. They can be analysed using a software tool known as a **concordancer** in order to identify regular patterns of language use, for example how people greet each other on formal occasions or the language used by members of particular professions in their work.

Discourse markers Words or phrases used to structure language, e.g. sequences: *first of, all, then, next, finally*. You will find further examples in Chapters 5 and 6.

Emoticons During online communication, icons called emoticons, like a smiley ☺ or sad ☹ face, are sometimes used. These provide some indication of the contributor's feelings in place of the non-verbal signals (e.g. smiling, frowning) that characterize face-to-face communication.

Fillers The term used for the exclamations, words or phrases used in any language to plug gaps, indicate hesitation or gain thinking time. Examples in English include: *erm . . .; well . . .; like . . .; that's an interesting question . . .; y'know . . .; absolutely . . .; I'm not sure, but . . .; to be honest . . .; I don't know . . .; yes, I think so; really? surely not!*

Grammar Grammar classifies words into categories (e.g. nouns, verbs, adjectives). Grammar is also the name given to the patterns followed by the smaller units of language (e.g. words) as they combine to form larger units (e.g. sentences). It distinguishes between the role they play, in relation to one another, within a sentence (e.g. subject, verb, object). Grammar also describes the systematic ways in which words change their form when combined with other words to form larger units. The way in which grammar structures the language also has an impact on meaning. If you are unsure of the meaning of grammatical terms used in your language course, dictionary or in this book, consult one of the books available which explain grammatical terms, for example the series *English Grammar for Students of . . .* published by Hodder Education.

Intonation The term used to describe the way a speaker's voice rises and falls, in other words, the 'music' of the language. Intonation patterns vary between languages so it is important to listen out for and copy the patterns in the language you are learning rather than simply transferring the patterns from your own language, so that you can be easily under-stood. Intonation patterns can indicate emotions and attitudes such as anger, interest or impatience. They can provide information on the grammatical structure of speech, e.g. differentiating a statement *You're coming* from a question *You're coming?* They can also be used to give prominence to specific points by stressing certain words, e.g. *I didn't say it was <u>wrong</u>* (I think it might be right) and *<u>I</u> didn't say it was wrong* (someone else did).

Metaphors   Figures of speech where a word or phrase is applied to a person, object or action which it could not literally apply to, e.g. *You are my sunshine.*

Netiquette   Online communication has its own conventions or etiquette, known as netiquette. The conventions vary between cultures, for example they may cover the use of formal and informal language (in French: *tu* or *vous?*) as well as more technical aspects such as avoiding capitals (which is the equivalent of shouting).

Onomatopoeia   Words used to convey sounds or other specific effects, e.g. *Bang! Woosh! Cockadoodledoo!*

Productive skills   Speaking and writing are often called productive skills because they involve producing language in the spoken or written form.

Receptive skills   Reading and listening are often referred to as receptive skills because they involve receiving written or spoken messages from others, rather than producing spoken or written language.

Register   This refers to different styles of language which are used according to the circumstances in which people find themselves. The differences depend on a number of factors:

- the mode of language use, i.e. whether written or spoken. The conventions used in these two modes vary. For example, the ending of a telephone call differs from that of a letter.
- the relationship between the participants, which may be formal or informal. For example, the language used in an email to a friend would be informal and personal compared with the more formal language found in a letter of application for a job, or an essay written for an exam.
- the subject matter. For example, the language used in scientific papers is different from that used in a tabloid newspaper or a recipe book.

Features of style and register differ across languages and cultures and it may not be appropriate to adopt conventions from your own language when communicating in your target language.

Reported speech   This is used to report or relate what someone has said, e.g. *He said he was cold.* This reports his actual words (direct speech): '*I'm cold*'.

Rhetorical devices   These are used to make language more persuasive or to engage the audience by making the communication more lively or interesting. Examples of some of the most common devices include:

- using evocative vocabulary and sound patterns;
- repetition;
- rhetorical questions, e.g. to end a presentation or an article in order to leave the audience with a question in their mind, such as: *But at what cost? When will we know for sure? Is this really what we want for our children's children?*

You will find further explanations and examples in Chapter 6, 'Style and register'.

Self-access centres Many institutions have self-access or 'drop-in' facilities where language learners can work on specific skills. Resources usually include reading and audio material with accompanying notes, exercises and answer keys, access to target language TV channels by satellite or to recorded programmes and computer-based or online learning resources. Self-access centres offer learners flexibility in terms of time and learning content. Some employ a learning adviser to give support and advice on learning methods and strategies.

Similes Figures of speech comparing one thing with something else, used to make descriptions more vivid, e.g. *as pretty as a picture*.

Stress The emphasis placed on different parts of words or phrases in spoken language is referred to as stress, and the patterns of stress give a language its rhythm. For example, in English, the following underlined parts of these words are stressed: *emphasis*, *different*, *patterns*, *altered*, *distorted*, *understanding*. In English, the stress tends to be placed on the first syllable of nouns or compound nouns and English speakers may be tempted to transfer this pattern to their target language. However, patterns differ from one language to another and if they are distorted or altered by using the patterns from another language, it can make understanding difficult.

Syllable A unit of pronunciation which has one vowel sound and forms the whole or part of a word, e.g. there are two syllables in *water* and three in *umbrella*, but only one in *house*.

Thesaurus A book or online resource that lists words with similar meanings (synonyms) in groups, together with related concepts.

Index

Note: References in **bold** refer to the Glossary.